# The Anchor Anthology
## of French Poetry

W9-BKW-945

# The Anchor Anthology
## of French Poetry
## From Nerval to Valéry
## in English Translation

EDITED BY ANGEL FLORES

INTRODUCTION BY PATTI SMITH

NEW HANOVER COUNTY
PUBLIC LIBRARY
201 CHESTNUT STREET
WILMINGTON, NC 28401

ANCHOR BOOKS
*A Division of Random House, Inc.*
*New York*

ANCHOR BOOKS EDITIONS, 1958, 2000

*Copyright © 1958, copyright renewed 1986 by Angel Flores*
*Introduction copyright © 2000 by Patti Smith*

All rights reserved under International and Pan-American
Copyright Conventions. Published in the United States by
Anchor Books, a division of Random House, Inc., New York,
and simultaneously in Canada by Random House of Canada
Limited, Toronto. Originally published in paperback in the
United States by Anchor Books in 1958, under the title *An*
*Anthology of French Poetry from Nerval to Valéry in English*
*Translation.*

Anchor Books and colophon are registered trademarks of
Random House, Inc.

Library of Congress Catalog Card Number 58-5937

**ANCHOR ISBN: 0-385-49888-8**

www.anchorbooks.com

Printed in the United States of America
10  9  8  7  6  5  4  3  2

# Contents

## STÉPHANE MALLARMÉ (1842–1898)

## PAUL VALÉRY (1871–1945)

## FRENCH ORIGINALS

# *Preface*

The poets who appear in this volume form a varied tradition which has been responsible for much of the vitality of modern poetry, not only in France, but throughout the countries of the West. The revolution, or series of revolutions, in European poetry which took place between Baudelaire and Valéry is a revolution which still continues, and has been the greatest force in giving poetry its effective modern voice.

Some of the poets—Baudelaire in part of his work, Mallarmé, Rimbaud, Valéry—can be loosely grouped together as "Symbolists." Though Symbolism is not susceptible of clear definition and never established a definite program, these poets have in common a sense of the function of poetry which is adumbrated in Baudelaire's *Correspondances* (pp. 21, 22). United in their protest against positivistic philosophy, sentimentalism, and didacticism, they conceive poetry as a search for the mystery of reality which underlies and interpenetrates the world of phenomena. The main instruments in the quest are the music of poetry and the poetic symbol, in which, by intuitive "correspondence," the emotional experience finds its truth and being in an image drawn from the external world. Suggestiveness and reverberation of meaning replace direct statement; analogy and insight replace logic.

Others among the poets—above all Apollinaire and Laforgue—are involved in an even more radical quest and rebellion, which turns them in fact against the transcendent element in Symbolist poetry itself in an effort to find an immediate voice for the arduous and complex realities of contemporary life.

The reader who wishes to pursue the questions raised by Symbolism and modern French poetry is referred to the brief biographical notes preceding the selections from each poet, and to the list of critical works in the bibliography at the end of the volume.

A substantial selection from the work of nine major poets, in translations by contemporary English and American poets, is presented in this volume in order to introduce the English reader to their most significant work. The translations have been chosen to stand as independent poems in their own right, and not merely as aids to the reading of the French. The original French texts in each case, except for the prose translations and for Mallarmé's typographically difficult poem, *Coup de dés,* can be found at the back of the volume.

# Introduction

BY PATTI SMITH

When I was sixteen, working in a non-union factory in a small South Jersey town, my salvation and respite from my dismal surroundings was a battered copy of Arthur Rimbaud's *Illuminations*, which I kept in my back pocket. Though I did not comprehend all that I read, it drew me into a world of heightened poetical language where I was more at home than with the crude argot that spewed from my fellow workers.

In the fall of 1964 I entered Glasboro State Teachers College in New Jersey. As an aspiring young artist, I felt estranged in the conventional setting of a teachers' college. I sought kinship by attempting to sign up as a volunteer worker for the college literary journal, *The Avant*. I remember the excitement of opening the door to its office, only to find the room empty. But on an old wood table I spied a humble paperback, pink and gray in color, with a sketch of a dreamy young poet gazing into the distance: *An Anthology of French Poetry from Nerval to Valéry*. I opened randomly to the poem "Shame," a poem by my sole inspiration Arthur Rimbaud, that I had never read.

The joy I felt in finding new poems by Rimbaud, as well as those written by poets he had so admired—Baudelaire, Verlaine, and Gérard de Nerval—was incalculable. I must admit that I pocketed this book as my own and it became the bible in my life. Edited by the aptly named Angel Flores, this anthology introduced me to some of the greatest poets in French literature, translated by the likes of Louise Varèse, Daisy Aldan, Richmond Lattimore, W. S. Merwin, Vernon Watkins, and Muriel Kittel.

I discovered Mallarmé, whose title alone "A Throw of the Dice Never Will Abolish Chance," charged my hungry mind. Through "Moon Solo" by Jules Laforgue I was made privy to the roots of "The Love Song of J. Alfred Prufrock" by T. S. Eliot. I was introduced to the dark beauty of Nerval and Verlaine and the lyric charm of Guillaume Apollinaire.

Through the mid-sixties only the work of John Coltrane and Bob Dylan matched the importance of this anthology in my growth as an artist and my appreciation of the work of others. It is my pleasure now to reintroduce this humble yet significant volume, so long out of print, to you now. And may I use this as an opportunity to salute and thank that unidentified soul who left this book upon a table in 1964.

Patti Smith
December 1999

# The Anchor Anthology
# of French Poetry

# Gérard de Nerval

## 1808—1855

# GÉRARD DE NERVAL

## 1808–1855

Obscured among the minor Romantic poets of the younger generation until late in the century when some of the Symbolists claimed him as a precursor—as the Surrealists were to do later with equally good reason—Gérard remains among the most perfect and the most pathetic of poets.

This amiable eccentric was a poet of dream, of a reality just beyond the edges of experience, of the fusions of dream with reality, and of nostalgia. His separation from the Romantics is to be measured in terms of imagination and of art, of his "method." Where the Romantics tend to be banal and explicit, Gérard is visionary and obscure, in poetry which, he said, would lose its charm if it were explicated —if it could be. This is not to say that his verse, or his prose, is merely atmospheric, for it deals boldly and precisely with its materials. It is the latter ultimately which refuse to lend themselves to explanation. Nerval is thus among the first to present a poetry dealing purposefully and nearly exclusively with what has always been the material of poetry *qua* poetry: those things to which prose is not adapted.

In this sense at least, modern poetry begins with this Bohemian with his background of German Romanticism, oriental mysticism, medieval recollections to be found in the folklore of his own country, this exquisite poet who, when reality finally became more real than—or indistinguishable from—the invisible world behind the gates of horn and ivory, hanged his humble and gentle self in a cellar in the rue de la Vieille-Lanterne on a freezing January morning.

# THE BEWITCHED HAND

*La Main enchantée*

EXCERPT

. . . On the morning of his execution Eustache Bouteron, who had been kept locked up in a dark cell, was visited by a father confessor who mumbled some spiritual consolations which, however, had little effect on him.

The confessor belonged to one of those families who, for the greater glory of their name, always make an abbot of one of their sons. His collar was embroidered, and he wore a smooth, tapering, perfumed beard, and a pair of mustachios elegantly trimmed. His hair was curly, and he strove to talk in a mellow voice which would sound affectionate.

Seeing him so dandified and superficial, Eustache found himself unable to drum up enough courage to confess. Instead he resolved to obtain God's pardon by means of his own prayers.

The priest gave him absolution, and then, to while away the two hours he would have to spend with the condemned man, he brought out a book entitled *The Tears of the Penitent Soul; or The Sinner's Return to God*. Eustache opened to the chapter on royal prerogatives and read remorsefully from the beginning: "Henry, King of France and Navarre, to my beloved, loyal subjects . . ." etc., down to the phrase "In these trials and wishing to treat favorably the said petitioner . . ." At this point he could not contain his tears and returned the book to the priest, saying how extremely touching it was and that he feared he would weaken if he read any more. Then the confessor drew from his pocket a very smart-looking deck of cards and proposed that his penitent play a few games. Thus the good priest took the liberty of winning from Eustache some money which Javotte had sent him to alleviate his wants. Eustache paid little attention to the game and seemed indifferent to his loss.

At two o'clock Eustache was taken from the Châtelet and led to the Place des Augustins, located between the two arches that form the entrance to the Rue Dauphine

and the Rue du Pont-Neuf, where he was honored with a scaffold made of stone. Since so many people were watching him—the Place des Augustins was the most popular spot for executions—he showed considerable firmness in climbing the stairs. However, since one delays as much as possible before his "leap into nothingness," just as the executioner was about to throw the rope around his neck, as ceremoniously as if he were about to decorate him with the Golden Fleece—for such men, when performing before a large public do their work very ably and with no little grace—Eustache begged him to tarry a bit so that he would have time to say a couple of prayers to St. Ignatius and St. Louis de Gonzaga whom he had kept for last since they had not been canonized until 1609; but the executioner replied that the folks stationed there had their chores to do and that it would not be proper to keep them waiting, especially for such a paltry spectacle: a single hanging. Meanwhile, he tightened the rope, shoved him off the ladder, and drowned out Eustache's petition. . . .

We knew for a fact that when all was over and the executioner on his way home, Maître Gonin peered out of a window of the Château Gaillard overlooking the square.

Just then, although Eustache's body was perfectly rigid and inanimate, his arm lifted up and his hand waved gleefully, like a dog's tail in his master's presence. This drew from the crowd a shout of consternation, and those who were leaving turned back hurriedly, like theatergoers who think the play is over, only to discover that a few acts are still to come.

The executioner put back the ladder, climbed up, and touched the feet of the hanged man. He felt the pulse of the ankles. There was no throbbing. Just to make sure, he severed an artery, but no blood flowed and the arm continued to shake wildly.

The executioner was not the kind of fellow who frightens easily: he climbed up on the shoulders of his victim amid the public outcry.

The hand irreverently stroked the executioner's pimply face.

Indignantly he whipped out a big knife which he always

carried under his coat and cut off the bewitched hand with two clean-cut slashes.

The hand gave an amazing leap and fell, bloodstained, in the middle of the crowd, which dispersed, terrified. Then, sauntering along, thanks to the elasticity of the fingers and to the path opened for it by everyone, it soon found itself at the foot of the little tower of the Château Gaillard. Next, the hand climbed up by its fingers, like a crab, along the rough, cracked walls and reached the window sill where Maître Gonin was waiting for it.

ANGEL FLORES

## FANTASY

*Fantaisie*

There is an air for which I'd gladly give
All Mozart, all Rossini, all Von Weber,
A languid, ancient, solemn-sounding air
That yields its secret charm to me alone.

Each time it happens that I hear it played
My heart grows younger by two hundred years:
I live in former times . . . and see portrayed
A green slope gilded by the setting sun,

And then a feudal castle flanked with stone,
Its windows tinted to a glowing rose,
Bounded by spacious parks and with its feet
Bathed by a stream that through a garden flows.

And then a lady in a window high,
Fair-haired, dark-eyed, and dressed in ancient style . . .
Whom, in another life, perhaps I've seen,
And whom I now remember with a sigh.

ANTHONY BOWER

## THE CYDALISES

### Les Cydalises

Where are our sweethearts?
They are in the grave:
They are more fortunate
In a better place!

They dwell near angels,
In the depth of the blue sky,
And they sing praises
Of the Mother of God!

O pure betrothed!
O young maid in flower!
Forsaken loved one,
Blighted by grief!

Profound eternity
Smiled in your eyes . . .
Lights smothered by the world,
Be rekindled in heaven!

DAISY ALDAN

## THE DARK BLOT

### Le Point noir

He who has gazed against the sun sees everywhere
he looks thereafter, palpitating on the air
before his eyes, a smudge that will not go away.

So in my days of still-youth, my audacity,
I dared look on the splendor momentarily.
The dark blot on my greedy eyes has come to stay.

Since when, worn like a badge of mourning in the sight
of all around me where my eye may chance to light,
I see the dark smudge settle upon everyone.

Forever thus between my happiness and me?
Alas for us, the eagle only, only he
can look, and not be hurt, on splendor and the sun.

RICHMOND LATTIMORE

## EL DESDICHADO

### El Desdichado

I am the dark, the widowed, the disconsolate.
I am the prince of Aquitaine whose tower is down.
My only star is dead, and star-configurate
my lute wears Melancholy's mark, a blackened sun.
Here in the midnight of the grave, give back, of late
my consolation, Pausilippe, the Italian
sea, with that flower so sweet once to my desolate
heart, and the trellis where the vine and rose are one.
Am I Love? Am I Phoebus, Biron, Lusignan?
Crimson the queen's kiss blazes still upon my face.
The siren's naked cave has been my dreaming place.
Twice have I forced the crossing of the Acheron
and played on Orpheus' lyre in alternate complaint
Mélusine's cries against the moaning of the Saint.

RICHMOND LATTIMORE

## MYRTHO

*Myrtho*

I think of you, Myrtho, divine enchantress,
On lofty Posilipo with its thousand fires,
Of your forehead reflecting the radiance of the East,
And black grapes entangled with your golden tress.

In your cup I discovered the rapture of drunkenness,
And in the secret glint of your smiling eye,
When I knelt in prayer before the shrine of Bacchus,
For the Muse has made me one of the sons of Greece.

I know why that volcano is aflame . . .
Your light foot, passing, touched it yesterday,
And ashes fell like rain on the horizon.

A Norman duke once smashed your gods of clay;
Since then, beneath the boughs of Virgil's laurel,
Green myrtle and pale hydrangea intertwine.

BARBARA HOWES

## HORUS

*Horus*

The god Kneph, trembling, rocked the universe.
Isis, the mother, arose then from her couch,
Gestured in hatred at her savage spouse,
While an ancient ardor stirred in her green eyes.

"Look at him now," she cried, "the old pervert dies,
All the cold of the world has passed through his mouth;
Tie down his twisted foot, blind his squinty eye,
For he is the king of winter, volcano's god.

Already the eagle passes, a new spirit calls;
For him have I donned the garments of Cybele,
For this child, belovèd of Hermes and Osiris . . ."

So saying the goddess fled on her golden shell;
The sea brought back to us her divine likeness,
And the heavens streamed radiant from the scarf of Iris.

BARBARA HOWES

## ANTEROS
### *Antéros*

If you ask why my heart so swells with rage
And why, on its pliant neck, my head is unbowed;
It is that I boast of Antaeus' lineage,
And hurl back at the conqueror his thunderous arrows.

Yes, I am one the Avenger has possessed,
And he has stamped my brow with his fevered mouth,
Beneath the pallor of Abel, bloodstained alas,
Rises the relentless flush of Cain, my brother!

The last one, Jehovah, vanquished by your genius,
Who, from the depths of hell, cried "Tyranny!"
He is my father Dagon or forebear Belus . . .

In the waters of Cocytus three times they plunged me
    down;
Now, as sole protector of the Amalekite, my mother,
The ancient dragon's teeth I have sown again.

BARBARA HOWES

## DELPHICA

### Delfica

Do you remember, Daphne, that archaic strain
by the sycamore base, by pale laurels, below
the olive tree, the myrtle or disturbed willow,
that song of love forever rising once again?
Do you remember that huge court, the god's domain,
those bitter lemons where the marks your teeth made show,
the cave whose rash indwellers found death long ago
where sleeps the seed primeval of the dragon slain?
They will come back, those gods whom you forever mourn,
for time shall see the order of old days reborn.
The earth has shuddered to a breath of prophecy.
And yet the sybil with her Latin face serene
lies sleeping still beneath the arch of Constantine
where no break mars the cold gateway's austerity.

RICHMOND LATTIMORE

## ARTEMIS

### Artémis

The Thirteenth has come again . . . But is still the first,
And is always the only one—at the one moment.
But art thou, oh my Queen, the first or the last?
Art thou, King, the sole or the final lover?

Love her who loves you from the cradle to the grave;
She whom alone I love, loves me most tenderly:
Death she is, or the dead . . . Oh delight, oh torment!
The rose that she holds is the Mallow, the one in many.

Holy Neapolitan with your hands full of fire,
Rose with a violet heart, Saint Gudule's flower;
Have you discovered your cross in the desert of sky?

Wither, white roses, fall; you insult our gods!
Fall, white phantoms, out of your burning sky;
—The saint of the abyss is more saintly to my eye!

BARBARA HOWES


## GOLDEN VERSES

### Vers dorés


Man, free thinker! do you believe you alone can reason
In this world where life surges everywhere?
The forces that are yours are ordered by your freedom,
But the Universe is missing from all your deliberations.

Respect an active spirit in the beast:
Each flower is a soul open to Nature;
In metal dwells a mystery of love;
"All things are sentient!" And mold your being.

Beware of a spying gaze in the blind wall:
The Word is bound to matter . . .
Do not set it to profane usage!

Often in the meanest being a God is hidden;
And as the eyelid covers the nascent eye,
The Spirit grows under the surface of stones!

DAISY ALDAN

# Charles Baudelaire

## 1821–1867

# CHARLES BAUDELAIRE

## 1821–1867

The crucial figure at the beginning of modern art, the first
and perhaps the greatest of modern poets, as considerable
a critic—of art as well as letters—as he was a poet, Baude-
laire in an unparalleled fashion resumes the tendencies of
the past and introduces those which were to be the modern.

At times at least for the Romantic it is the passing of
beauty which is a source of anguish, and the poet recalls
youth and joy with nostalgia. Baudelaire, on the contrary,
tends to see experience as sordid, nature as inherently evil,
and it is in man's occasional transformations of experience
into art—or civilization—that he finds beauty. At the same
time Baudelaire is acutely conscious of the damage we con-
tinually do our better, our potential, selves. Man is a di-
vided being, drawn always toward both God and Satan.
The ideal and the sensual being equally potent for Baude-
laire, much of his poetry investigates the one or the other,
or attempts reconciliation of the two. Clear as the polarity
is, reconciliation becomes possible, and is a function of art,
because Baudelaire also believed in the unity of all exist-
ence, in the correspondence of all phenomena. Even oppo-
sites are functions, analogues, somehow, of each other, and
Baudelaire's vision of the world represents a contribution
to the understanding of its complexities which, given the
intensity of his creation of a view of modern man, has had
an incalculable effect, not only upon the arts, in the modern
world.

# TO THE READER

## *Au Lecteur*

Ignorance, error, cupidity, and sin
Possess our souls and exercise our flesh;
Habitually we cultivate remorse
As beggars entertain and nurse their lice.

Our sins are stubborn. Cowards when contrite
We overpay confession with our pains,
And when we're back again in human mire
Vile tears, we think, will wash away our stains.

Thrice-potent Satan in our cursèd bed
Lulls us to sleep, our spirit overkissed,
Until the precious metal of our will
Is vaporized—that cunning alchemist!

Who but the Devil pulls our waking-strings!
Abominations lure us to their side;
Each day we take another step to hell,
Descending through the stench, unhorrified.

Like an exhausted rake who mouths and chews
The martyrized breast of an old withered whore
We steal, in passing, whatever joys we can,
Squeezing the driest orange all the more.

Packed in our brains incestuous as worms
Our demons celebrate in drunken gangs,
And when we breathe, that hollow rasp is Death
Sliding invisibly down into our lungs.

If the dull canvas of our wretched life
Is unembellished with such pretty ware
As knives or poison, pyromania, rape,
It is because our soul's too weak to dare!

But in this den of jackals, monkeys, curs,
Scorpions, buzzards, snakes . . . this paradise
Of filthy beasts that screech, howl, grovel, grunt—
In this menagerie of mankind's vice

There's one supremely hideous and impure!
Soft-spoken, not the type to cause a scene,
He'd willingly make rubble of the earth
And swallow up creation in a yawn.

I mean *Ennui!* who in his hookah-dreams
Produces hangmen and real tears together.
How well you know this fastidious monster, reader,
—Hypocrite reader, you!—my double! my brother!

STANLEY KUNITZ

## BENEDICTION

### *Bénédiction*

When, by pronouncement of almighty powers,
The Poet appears among us in this tired world,
His outraged mother, racked by blasphemies,
Clenches her fists to God, who pities her:

—"Ah, I should have borne a string of vipers
Rather than suckle this foul mockery!
Damn that night of itching, short-lived pleasure
When my gaping womb conceived this misery!

Since, of all women, you have chosen me
To be my suffering husband's black disgust,
And since I cannot fling into the fire
This stunted monster, like a letter's lust,

I shall make your heavy hate rebound
Upon the damned instrument of your spite,
And I shall twist this miserable tree:
It will not bud forth, stinking, a green blight!"

She swallows, thus, the froth of her bilious hate,
And, unaware of what the sky designs,
Herself prepares in the lowest pit of hell
The fires reserved for cold, maternal crimes.

However, under unseen Angel care,
The poor Child raptures in a glorious sun,
And in all he drinks and eats he finds again
His home's red nectar and ambrosia.

He plays with the wind, converses with a cloud,
And joys in singing of the Cross and the road;
The Spirit that guards him on his pilgrimage
Weeps to see him gay, a bird in the wood.

Those he wants to love observe him through their fear
Or, emboldened by his rare tranquillity,
Goad him into wretched wails, complaints,
And use him as a test of their ferocity.

In the bread and wine intended for his mouth
They mix foul spittle, cinder, bitter ash;
Pretending fear of dirt, they throw away
The things he uses and avoid his path.

His wife goes shouting through the public squares:
"Since he finds beauty in me to adore,
I shall assume the pose of ancient idols
And, like them, ask to be redone in gold;

And I shall glut myself with nard, incense, and myrrh,
With genuflections, meat, and spicy wine,
To see if, even as I laugh at him,
I can usurp the homage of the divine!

And, when I tire of these impious farces,
I shall seize him in my delicate, strong hands;
And my nails, the nails of harpies, will then start
To dig a bloody pathway to his heart.

Like a young bird, trembling, fluttering in the hand,
I shall tear out that red heart from his breast,
And throw it with disdain upon the ground
To fill the belly of my favorite hound!"

Skyward, where he sees a splendid throne,
The Poet serenely lifts his pious arms,
And the vast illuminations of his lucid soul
Conceal men's pushing fury and alarms.

"Be praised, my God, who gives us suffering
Like a sovereign remedy for our impurities,
Which like the best and purest essence makes
Strong men fit for holy ecstasies!

I know that, for the Poet, you must keep
A joyous place among the holy Hosts,
And will invite him to the eternal feast
Of Virtues, Dominations, glorious Thrones.

I know that sorrow is nobility
Which neither earth nor hell can ever corrode,
And that the plaiting of my mystic crown
Enlists all space and all time's pain-filled roads.

Neither the lost jewels of old Palmyra,
Nor unknown metals, nor the pearls of the sea,
As mounted by your hand, could ever compare
With this bright diadem, so beautiful and clear;

For it will be composed of purest light,
Drawn from the holy spring of primal fire,
Compared to which the splendors of our mortal eyes,
At best, are but a tarnished mirror's lie!"

                                        STEPHEN STEPANCHEV

## THE ALBATROSS

*L'Albatros*

Ofttimes, for diversion, seafaring men
Capture albatross, those vast birds of the seas
That accompany, at languorous pace,
Boats plying their way through bitter straits.

Having scarce been taken aboard
These kings of the blue, awkward and shy,
Piteously their great white wings
Let droop like oars at their sides.

This wingèd voyager, how clumsy he is and weak!
He just now so lovely, how comic and ugly!
One with a stubby pipe teases his beak,
Another mimics, limping, the cripple who could fly!

The Poet resembles this prince of the clouds,
Who laughs at hunters and haunts the storms;
Exiled to the ground amid the jeering pack,
His giant wings will not let him walk.

                              KATE FLORES

## CORRESPONDENCES

*Correspondances*

Nature is a temple from whose living columns
Commingling voices emerge at times;
Here man wanders through forests of symbols
Which seem to observe him with familiar eyes.

Like long-drawn echoes afar converging
In harmonies darksome and profound,
Vast as the night and vast as light,
Colors, scents and sounds correspond.

There are fragrances fresh as the flesh of children,
Sweet as the oboe, green as the prairie,
—And others overpowering, rich and corrupt,

Possessing the pervasiveness of everlasting things,
Like benjamin, frankincense, amber, myrrh,
Which the raptures of the senses and the spirit sing.

KATE FLORES

## THE ENEMY

### L'Ennemi

My youth was no more than a dark, looming storm
Made bright here and there by transitory suns;
Thunder and rain have made such havoc of its form
That my garden scarcely shows what red fruits it had once.

So at last I have come to the Autumn of ideas,
And I must make use of the spade and the rakes
To restore the flooded ground till its form reappears
Where hollows great as tombs the delving water makes.

And who knows if the new flowers that dreaming I see
Will discover in this soil washed like sand on a bay
The mystic nutriment that would set their force free?

—O sorrow! O sorrow! Time eats life away
And the Enemy in hiding who gnaws at our side
On the blood we are losing grows and is fortified.

VERNON WATKINS

## THE FORMER LIFE

*La Vie antérieure*

Long years I lived under vast porticoes
That thousand fires of ocean suns stained bright.
Their huge, straight, stately columns, at twilight,
As if in grottoes of basalt uprose.

The coursing waves, where rolled the imaged skies,
Mingled in their mysterious, solemn modes
Reverberant music, surging strophic odes,
With sunset colors flashing on my eyes.

There dwelt I in the long voluptuous calms
Amid those splendors, azure skies, the waves,
And bodies heavy with perfumes, nude slaves

Who fanned my forehead with great leaves of palms
And knew one care alone: that secret anguish
To fathom that made all my being languish.

DWIGHT DURLING

## BEAUTY

*La Beauté*

Beautiful am I, oh, mortals, like a dream of stone!
And my breast, where each in his turn has been broken,
Is made to inspire a love in the poet
Eternal and mute as matter is lasting and still.

In the azure enthroned, an inscrutable sphinx,
I join a heart of snow and the whiteness of swans;
Movement I hate when it tampers with line,
And never do I weep and never do I laugh.

The poets, before my insolent poses,
Borrowed it seems from the proudest of statues,
Will consume all their days in rigorous trials;

For I, to fascinate these docile lovers—
Pure mirrors in which all things shine—
Have my eyes, my wide eyes, transparent forever.

BERT M-P. LEEFMANS

## POSTHUMOUS REMORSE

*Remords posthume*

When you shall sleep, my faithless one, under
A monument built all of gloomy marble,
And when for room and mansion you shall have
Only a false hollow, a rainy cave;

When the stone your timid chest oppressing,
And your flanks that nonchalance makes supple,
Shall keep your heart from beating and wishing,
Your feet from running their adventurous course,

The tomb, confidant of my infinite dream
(The tomb that always understands the poet),
Through the long nights when sleep is banished,

Will say to you: "Of what use, courtesan,
Not to have known what the dead were weeping?"
—And the worm will gnaw your flesh like a remorse.

BARBARA GIBBS

## I OFFER YOU THIS VERSE . . .

*Je te donne ces vers . . .*

I offer you this verse so that if once my name
Beaches with good fortune on epochs far away
And makes the minds of men dream at the close of day,
Vessel to whose assistance a great tempest came,

The memory of you, like fables indistinct,
May weary the reader like a tympanum's refrain,
And by a fraternal and most mystical chain
Still seem as though hanging, to my lofty rhymes linked;

Accurst being to whom, from the depth of the abyss
To the height of the sky, nothing but me responds!
—O you who like a shade whose trace none may retard,

Trample with a light foot and serene regard
The mortal dolts who judged you bringer of bitterness,
Statue with eyes of jet, great angel browed with bronze!

VERNON WATKINS

## THE VIAL

*Le Flacon*

There are potent perfumes to which nothing
Is impervious. They penetrate glass, it is said.
Opening a little coffer come from the East,
Its lock creaking and groaning reluctant,

Or some dark dusty cupboard in a derelict house
Suffused with the acrid aroma of time,
Sometimes one finds an old reminiscent vial
From which surges vibrant a spirit returned.

Darkling chrysalids, a thousand thoughts slumbered,
Soft in the dismal shadows throbbing,
Which loosen their wings now soaring aloft,
Azure-tinged, glazen rose, dappled with gold.

Intoxicating remembrances flutter
In that disquieted air; the eyes close; vertigo
Seizes the soul overcome and thrusts it with two hands
Toward a chasm dim with human miasma,

Pitching it to the brink of a centenary pit,
Where, scented Lazarus breaking through its shroud,
There stirs in its waking the spectral cadaver
Of an old moldering love, enticing and entombed.

Thus when I am lost to the memory of men,
When to the corner of some grim cupboard
I am tossed, old devastated vial,
Decrepit, dirty, dusty, abject, viscous, cracked,

I shall be your coffin, amiable pestilence!
Witness of your virulence and power,
Dear poison by the angels compounded, potion
Gnawing me away, O life and death of my heart!

KATE FLORES

## INVITATION TO THE VOYAGE

*L'Invitation au voyage*

My child, my sister, dream
How sweet all things would seem
Were we in that kind land to live together
And there love slow and long,
There love and die among
Those scenes that image you, that sumptuous weather.
Drowned suns that glimmer there
Through cloud-disheveled air

Move me with such a mystery as appears
    Within those other skies
    Of your treacherous eyes
When I behold them shining through their tears.

There, there is nothing else but grace and measure,
Richness, quietness, and pleasure.

    Furniture that wears
    The luster of the years
Softly would glow within our glowing chamber,
    Flowers of rarest bloom
    Proffering their perfume
Mixed with the vague fragrances of amber;
    Gold ceilings would there be,
    Mirrors deep as the sea,
The walls all in an Eastern splendor hung—
    Nothing but should address
    The soul's loneliness,
Speaking her sweet and secret native tongue.

There, there is nothing else but grace and measure,
Richness, quietness, and pleasure.

    See, sheltered from the swells
    There in the still canals
Those drowsy ships that dream of sailing forth;
    It is to satisfy
    Your least desire, they ply
Hither through all the waters of the earth.
    The sun at close of day
    Clothes the fields of hay,
Then the canals, at last the town entire
    In hyacinth and gold:
    Slowly the land is rolled
Sleepward under a sea of gentle fire.

There, there is nothing else but grace and measure,
Richness, quietness, and pleasure.

RICHARD WILBUR

## MUSIC

### *La Musique*

On music drawn away, a sea-borne mariner
    Star over bowsprit pale,
Beneath a roof of mist or depths of lucid air
    I put out under sail;

Breastbone my steady bow and lungs full, running free
    Before a following gale,
I ride the rolling back and mass of every sea
    By Night wrapt in her veil;

All passions and all joys that vessels undergo
    Tremble alike in me;
Fair wind or waves in havoc when the tempests blow

    On the enormous sea
Rock me, and level calms come silvering sea and air,
    A glass for my despair.

ROBERT FITZGERALD

## THE CRACKED BELL

### *La Cloche fêlée*

It is bitter and sweet, during the Winter nights,
To listen, by the quivering and smoking hearth-log,
To the memories withdrawn that ascend in slow flights
On the carillons whose music sings out through the fog.

Thrice fortunate the bell with a vigorous throat
That, in spite of old age, alert and still robust,
Flings faithfully the challenge of its religious note,
Like a veteran campaigner keeping watch at his post.

As for me, my soul's cracked, and when in gloom it longs
To people the chill air of the night with its songs,
It often befalls me that its enfeebled call

Seems a wounded man's rattle, forgotten by all
By a lake of blood under a vast heap of dead,
And who dies, without moving, in immense throes of dread!

VERNON WATKINS


## SPLEEN

*Spleen*

When the oppressive sky weighs like a cover
On the sick spirit, in the toils of ennui,
And embracing the horizon's curve
Pours on us, sadder than nights, a dark day;

When earth becomes a humid dungeon
Where Hope like a bat strikes her timid
Wing against the walls and beats on
The decaying ceiling with her head;

When the rain spreading its immense trails
Imitates a vast prison of bars,
And a mute crowd of infamous spiders
Comes to hang its threads at the back of our brains,

Bells suddenly leap furiously,
Launching a dreadful clamor to heaven,
Like wandering spirits without a country
Who start to complain stubbornly.

—And long hearses without drums or music drag
In slow file through my soul; Hope vanquished
Weeps, and atrocious, despotic Anguish
Plants on my bowed head her black flag.

BARBARA GIBBS

## HEAUTONTIMOROUMENOS

*L'Héautontimorouménos*

I shall strike you without anger
And without hate, as a butcher strikes,
As Moses struck the rock!
And from your opened eye,

To water my Sahara,
Shall flow the waters of our suffering.
My desire, swelled with hopefulness,
Upon your salt tears shall swim

Like a vessel which moves to sea,
And in my heart drugged by them
Your dear sobs will sound
Like a drum beating the advance!

Am I not a dissonance
In the divine symphony
Thanks to the hungry Irony
Which shakes me and which tears me?

It is in my voice, screeching!
It is my very blood, black poison!
I am the hateful mirror
Where the Fury scans herself!

I am the wound and the knife!
I am the blow and the cheek!
I am the limbs and the wheel,
And condemned and executioner!

I am the vampire of my heart:
One of the lost forever,
Condemned to eternal laughter
And who can never smile again.

BERT M-P. LEEFMANS

## LANDSCAPE

*Paysage*

I want, the more chastely to compose my verse,
To sleep close to the sky, like the astrologers,
And, neighbor of steeples, as I dream, to attend
To their grave anthems carried away by the wind.
Chin in hands, from the height of my garret I'll discern
The workshop that sings and that gossips in turn,
The pipe-stacks, the steeples, those masts of the city,
And the great skies that foster dreams of eternity.

It is sweet, through the mists, to see begin to glow
The star in azure dark, the lamp at the window,
The rivers of coal-smoke ascending to the height
And the moon with enchantment spending her pale light.
I shall witness the Springs, the Summers, the Falls;
And when Winter comes with monotonous snowfalls
I shall close all around me shutters and lattices
To build into the night my fairy palaces.

Then I'll dream of horizons the blue of heaven controls,
Of gardens, fountains weeping in alabaster bowls,
Of kisses, of birds singing morning and eve,
And of all that's most childlike the Idyll has to give.
The tumult at my window vainly raging grotesque
Shall not cause me to lift my forehead from my desk;
For I shall be absorbed in that exquisitely still
Delight of evoking the Spring with my will,
Of wresting a sun from my own heart and in calm
Drawing from my burning thoughts an atmosphere of balm.

VERNON WATKINS

# THE SWAN

## Le Cygne

*To Victor Hugo*

### I

Andromache, I think of you! —This little stream,
Poor wretched mirror resplendent once
With all the grandeur of your widow's grief,
This deceptive Simoïs, heightened with your tears,

Has suddenly, as I wandered through the new Carrousel,
Restored a fertile memory of mine.
—Old Paris is no more (the contours of a city
Change, alas! more quickly than a mortal heart);

Only in spirit do I see that regiment of booths,
That array of makeshift capitals and posts,
The turf, the rough stones greened by the puddle waters,
And, gleaming in the cases, the jumbled bric-a-brac.

There at one time a menagerie stood;
There I saw one morning, at the hour when, under cold
    clear skies,
The working world awakes, and the cleaners of the streets
Hurl into the quiet air a dismal hurricane,

A swan who had escaped his cage,
And, padding the dry pavement with his webbed feet,
Trailed his snowy plumage along the scraggly ground.
Beside a waterless gutter the creature opened his beak

And tremulously bathing his wings in the dust, cried,
His heart full of the lovely lake of his birth:
"Water, when the deluge? Tempests, when do you
    thunder?"
I can see that hapless one, strange and fatal myth,

Toward the heavens, sometimes, like Ovid's man,
Toward the heavens ironical and cruelly blue,
Bend his thirsting head upon his convulsive neck,
As though addressing reproaches unto God!


II


Paris changes! but my melancholy alters not a whit!
New palaces, scaffoldings, stocks,
Old neighborhoods to me are all allegory now,
And now my cherished remembrances are heavier than
  rocks!


Thus before this Louvre an image dejects me:
I think of my glorious swan, with his mad gestures,
Like the exiled, ridiculous and sublime,
And wrung by a truceless yearning! and then of you,


Andromache, fallen from a mighty husband's arms,
A lowly creature, beneath the hand of supernal Pyrrhus,
Bending down distraught beside an empty tomb;
Widow of Hector, alas! and wife to Helenus!


I think upon the Negress, tubercular and wasted,
Groveling in the mud, and seeking, with haggard eye,
Beyond the massive wall of mist,
Magnificent Africa's absent coconut palms;


Of all who have lost what cannot ever be regained,
Not ever! of those who drink their fill of tears
And suckle of Sorrow like a good she-wolf!
Of scrawny orphans desiccating like flowers!


Thus in the forest of my spirit's exile
An old Remembrance echoes full blast like a horn!
I think upon sailors forgotten on isles,
Of the captured, the defeated! . . . and of so many more!

KATE FLORES

## THE SEVEN OLD MEN
*Les Sept vieillards*

*To Victor Hugo*

Teeming city, full of dreams, where in broad
Daylight the specter grips the passer-by!
Mystery flows everywhere like sap
In the ducts of the mighty colossus.

One morning when mist in the gloomy street
Made the houses seem taller, like the two
Quays of a swollen river; when—décor
In harmony with the state of my soul—

A foul, yellow fog inundated space,
I went, steeling my nerves like a hero,
Disputing with my Soul, already weary,
Along the faubourg jarred by heavy carts.

Suddenly I saw an old man, in rags
Of the same yellow as the rainy sky,
Whose aspect would have made alms rain down
Except for the wicked gleam in his eye.

You might have thought the pupils of his eyes
Were soaked in bile; his gaze sharpened the sleet,
And his beard of long hairs, stiff as a sword,
Jutted forward like the beard of Judas.

He was not bowed, but broken, for his spine
Made a perfect right angle with his leg,
So that his staff, completing his presence,
Gave him the bearing and the clumsy gait

Of a crippled dog or three-legged Jew.
He stumbled over the snow and mud as though
He were grinding the dead under his shoes,
Hostile to life, more than indifferent.

His like followed him: beard, eye, back, staff, rags,
Nothing distinguished, come from the same hell,
This centenarian twin, and these specters
Walked with the same step towards an unknown goal.

Of what infamous scheme was I the butt
Or what ill chance humiliated me?
Full seven times, from minute to minute,
I saw this old man multiply himself!

Let him who laughs at my disquietude
And is not seized by a fraternal chill
Ponder that, for all their decrepitude,
These seven monsters appeared eternal!

Would I, and lived, have beheld the eighth
Counterpart, ironical and fatal,
Vile Phoenix, father and son of himself?
—I turned my back on the procession.

Enraged as a drunk man who sees double,
I went inside and closed my door, frightened,
Sick and chilled, my mind feverish and turbid,
Offended by the senseless mystery!

In vain my reason tried to take the helm;
The tempest rollicking led it astray,
And my soul danced, danced, like an old lighter
Without masts, on a monstrous, shoreless sea!

BARBARA GIBBS

## THE LITTLE OLD WOMEN

*Les Petites vieilles*

*To Victor Hugo*

I

In the winding folds of old capitals,
Where horror itself turns to enchantment,
Following my fatal moods, I spy on
Certain beings, decrepit and charming,

Misshapen creatures, these were once women,
Eponine or Lais! Broken or humped,
Or twisted, let us love them! they are souls.
Whipped by iniquitous north-winds they creep

In their tattered skirts and chilly fabrics,
Shaken by the din of omnibuses,
Clasping to their sides like relics tiny
Bags embroidered with flowers or rebuses;

They toddle like little marionettes,
Or drag their bodies like hurt animals,
Or dance without wishing to dance, poor bells
Swung by a pitiless demon! Broken

As they are, they have eyes that pierce like drills
And glimmer like the holes where water sleeps
At night; the divine eyes of little girls,
Who laugh with amazement at shiny things.

Have you noticed how the coffins of old
Women are often as small as a child's?
Canny Death in these like biers evinces
A bizarre and captivating taste,

And whenever I see one of these ghosts
Threading the teeming tableau of Paris,
It seems to me that the fragile creature
Is going softly towards a new cradle;

Unless, meditating on geometry,
I conjecture from the discordant limbs
How many times the workman must vary
The shape of the box that will hold these forms.

—Their eyes are ponds made of a million tears,
Crucibles spangled with a cooled metal . . .
Mysterious eyes, invincibly charming
To one suckled by austere misfortune!

II

Enamored vestal of the old Frascati;
Priestess of Thalia, alas! whose name
The dead prompter knows; famed butterfly
Whom Tivoli once sheltered in her prime,

All intoxicate me! but of these frail
Creatures some, making a honey of grief,
Have cried to the Devotion that lent them wings:
Great Hippogriff, carry me to heaven!

One educated to adversity,
One loaded with sorrow by her husband,
One a Madonna, transpierced for her child,
All might have made a river with their tears!

III

Ah how many of them I have followed!
And one, at the hour when the sinking sun
Bloodies the sky with vermillion wounds,
Sat thoughtfully by herself on a bench

To hear one of those concerts rich with brass
With which the soldiers sometimes flood our parks,
Pouring on golden evenings a kind of
Heroism in the hearts of burgesses.

She, still straight, proud, and feeling the rhythm,
Drank in avidly the bright, warlike song,
Her eye opening like an old eagle's,
And her brow as if made for the laurel!


IV


You go your way, stoic and uncomplaining,
Threading the chaos of living cities,
Mothers of the bleeding heart, courtesans
Or saints, whose names were once on every tongue.

You who were all of grace or all of glory,
None recognizes you! A rude drunkard
Mocks you in passing with a show of love;
A wretched child runs skipping at your heels.

Ashamed to be alive, shrunken shadows,
Fearful, with bent backs you hug the walls;
And no one speaks to you, strangely destined!
Human debris ripe for eternity!

But I, who watch tenderly, anxiously
At a distance your uncertain footsteps,
As if I were your father, what marvel!
Without your knowledge, taste clandestine pleasures:

I watch your novice passions unfolding;
Dark or bright, I summon up your lost days;
My heart, multiplied, revels in your vices!
My soul grows resplendent with your virtues!

O ruins! congeneric brains! each night I
Take solemn adieu of you! Where will you be
Tomorrow, octogenarian Eves,
On whom the dreadful claw of God lies heavy?

BARBARA  GIBBS

## THE LOVE OF DECEIT

*L'Amour du mensonge*

Whenever I see you pass, dear indolent one,
Amidst the surge of music in breaking waves,
Dangling your somnolent and slow allure,
Flaunting the ennui of your moody gaze,

When under the yellow gaslights I observe
Your pale forehead in a delicate artifice
Of torches that kindle an illusive dawn,
And your eyes like a portrait's cryptic glance entice,

I muse: How lovely she is, how fresh, bizarre!
The massive tower of memory looms above
And regally crowns her. Bruised as a fallen peach,
Her heart is ripe as her body for subtlest love.

I think of mellowed savors of autumn fruit,
A burial urn no rite of tears yet showers,
Scents that evoke the distant oases of dreams,
Caressing pillows, harvests of gathered flowers.

I know there are eyes like wells of melancholy
That hold no secrets rich as our surmise,
Jewelless coffers, locket-reliquaries,
Deeper and emptier than yourselves, O Skies!

Shall not the semblance alone suffice for me,
To rejoice my heart, since Verity I forswore?
What matters stupidity or indifference?
Hail, mask, dear counterfeit! I bow, adore!

DWIGHT DURLING

## I HAVE NOT FORGOTTEN . . .

### Je n'ai pas oublié . . .

I have not forgotten, neighboring the town,
Our white house, diminutive, yet where peace brims,
Its plaster Pomona and its Venus age-worn
In a mean, wasted shrubbery hiding their naked limbs,
And at evening the sun, pouring light in disdain,
Which, behind the rich window that broke up its grain,
Seemed, great prying eye in the sky's curious urn,
To watch our slow dinners, prolonged and taciturn,
Displaying its fair, waxen rays to the verge
Of the set, frugal cloth and the curtains of serge.

VERNON WATKINS

## MORNING TWILIGHT

### Le Crépuscule du matin

Reveille rang out in the barracks-courts,
And the morning wind blew on the street lamps.

It was the hour when injurious dreams
Twist the brown adolescents on their pillows;
When, like a bleeding, palpitating eye,
The lamp makes a red spot against the day;
When the soul, weighted down with the dull body,
Imitates the struggle of lamp and day.
Like a tear-drenched face dried by the breezes,
The air fills with the shiver of flying things;
Man tires of writing, woman of making love.

Here and there the houses begin to smoke.
Women of pleasure, their eyelids livid,
Slept with open mouths their stupefied sleep;
The beggar girls, dragging their thin, cold breasts,
Blow on their brands and blow on their fingers.
At that hour, with cold and frugality,
The pains of women in labor grow worse;
Like a sob sliced in two by foamy blood
A rooster's far-off cry rends the misty air;
Buildings are bathed in a sea of fog,
And deep in the poorhouses the dying
Give out their last rattle in broken hiccups.
The debauchees come home, spent with their toil.

Dawn, shivering in pink and green garments,
Comes slowly over the deserted Seine,
And, rubbing its eyes, a somber Paris
Takes up its tools like an old laborer.

BARBARA GIBBS

## BEATRICE

### La Béatrice

In a hard, burned land of ash, stripped of leaves,
As I groaned one day to acres of charred trees,
Wandering aimlessly, broken by my thoughts,
Which slowly sharpened daggers at my heart,
I saw descending over me, at noon,
A black cloud, storm-wide, carrying a troop
Of vicious demons, stunted like old dwarves,
Who, cruelly curious, pried into my wounds.
Proudly and coldly they examined me,
And, like pedestrians staring at a madman,
I heard them laugh and whisper savagely.
They made lewd signs and winked disdainfully:

"Let us study well this caricature of man,
This shadow Hamlet, posturing as he moans,
Looking so undecided, letting the wind shake
His locks. Isn't it funny to see this rake,
This tramp, this clown, this laid-off mountebank,
Pretend, because he plays his role with wit,
To interest eagles, flowers, brooks, and crickets
In his stale recitals of imagined pain
And tries beguiling even us with shows,
Tricks that we invented long ago?"

I would have turned my sovereign head aside
(My pride could dominate, as from a mountaintop,
That cloud of demons and their disturbing cries)
Had I not seen among that obscene troop—
Ah, crime that strangely did not stagger the sun!—
The empress of my heart, with crystal eyes,
Who, laughing with them, mocked my black distress
And pitched them, now and then, a lewd caress.

STEPHEN STEPANCHEV

## A VOYAGE TO CYTHERA

*Un Voyage à Cythère*

My heart, like a bird, ahover joyously,
circled the rigging, soaring light and free;
beneath a cloudless sky the ship rolled on
like an angel drunk with blazing rays of sun.

What is that black, sad island? —We are told
it is Cythera, famed in songs of old,
trite El Dorado of worn-out roués.
Look, after all, it's but a paltry place.

—Isle of sweet mysteries and festal loves,
above your waters antique Venus moves;
like an aroma, her imperious shade
burdens the soul with love and lassitude.

Green-myrtled island, fair with flowers in bloom,
revered by every nation for all time,
where sighing hearts send up their fervent praises
afloat like incense over beds of roses

or like a ringdove's endless cooing call!
—Cythera now was but a meager soil,
a flinty desert moiled with bitter cries.
And yet, half-glimpsed, a strange shape met my eyes.

It was no temple couched in shady groves
where the young priestess, lover of flowers, moves,
her body fevered by obscure desires,
her robe half opened to the fleeting airs;

but as we passed, skirting the coast so near
that our white canvas set the birds astir,
we saw it was a three-branched gibbet, high
and black-etched, like a cypress, on the sky.

Perched on their prey, ferocious birds were mangling
with frenzied thrusts a hanged man, ripe and dangling,
each driving like a tool his filthy beak
all through that rot, in every bleeding crack;

the eyes were holes, and from the ruined gut
across the thighs the heavy bowels poured out,
and crammed with hideous pleasures, peck by peck,
his butchers had quite stripped him of his sex.

Beneath his feet, a pack of four-legged brutes
circled and prowled, with upraised avid snouts;
a larger beast was ramping in the midst
like a hangman flanked by his apprentices.

Child of Cythera, born of so fair a sky,
you suffered these defilements silently:
atonement for your impure rituals
and sins that have forbid you burial.

Ridiculous corpse, I know your pains full well.
At sight of your loose-hanging limbs I felt
the bitter-flowing bile of ancient grief
rise up, like a long puke, against my teeth;

poor wretch, so dear-remembered, in your presence
I felt each beak-thrust of those stabbing ravens,
and the black panthers' jaws—each rip and gash—
that once took such delight to grind my flesh.

The sky was suave, and level was the sea,
yet all was blood and blackness then to me,
alas! and my heart in this parable,
as in a heavy shroud, found burial.

On your isle, Venus, I saw but one thing standing,
gallows-emblem from which my shape was hanging . . .
God! give me strength and will to contemplate
heart, body—without loathing, without hate.

FREDERICK MORGAN

## THE VOYAGE

*Le Voyage*

*To Maxime du Camp*

### I

To the child, in love with maps and pictures,
The universe is vast as his appetite.
Ah how immense the world is by lamplight!
How small the world is in recollection!

One morning we set out, our brains full of fire,
Our hearts swollen with rancor and harsh longing,
And we go, following the wave's rhythm,
Cradling our infinite on the seas' finite:

Some are glad to leave a squalid birthplace,
Or their abhorred cradles; some, astrologers
Drowned in a woman's eyes, their tyrannical
Circe of the dangerous perfumes.

Not to be turned to beasts, they make themselves
Drunk on space and light and the flaming skies;
The frost that bites them, the suns that tan them,
Slowly wear away the marks of kisses.

But the true travelers are those who leave
For leaving's sake; light hearts like balloons,
They never swerve from their fatality,
And say, without knowing why: "Let us go on!"

Those whose desires have the shape of clouds,
Who dream, like a recruit of the cannon,
Of boundless, changing, unknown pleasures
Whose name the human mind has never known!

## II

We imitate—horror!—the top and ball,
Waltzing and skipping; even in our sleep
Curiosity torments and rolls us
Like a merciless Angel whipping suns.

Strange lot, in which the goal displaces itself,
And being nowhere may be anywhere!
In which Man, whose hope never flags, goes always
Running like a madman in search of rest!

Our soul's a ship seeking its Icaria;
A voice shouts from the bridge: "Open your eyes!"
From the top, ardent and mad, another cries:
"Love . . . glory . . . happiness!" Hell is a sandbar!

Each island signaled by the man on watch
Is an Eldorado promised by Fate;
Imagination, preparing her feast,
Sees only a reef in the dawning light.

Poor lover of chimerical countries!
Must we toss him in chains, or in the sea, this
Inventor of Americas, this drunken
Sailor whose vision poisons the abyss?

Such is the old vagrant who paws the mud
And dreams, nose in air, of dazzling Edens;
His bewitched eye beholds a Capua
All around, where the candle lights a hovel.

## III

Marvelous travelers! What noble tales
We read in your eyes profound as oceans!
Show us your chests of splendid memories,
Astounding jewels, made of wind and stars.

We will sail without steam or canvas!
Enliven the boredom of our prisons;
Pass across our spirits, stretched like canvases,
Your memories in their frames of horizons.

Tell us, what have you seen?


IV

                    "We have seen stars
And billows; and we have also seen sands;
And, despite shocks and unforeseen disasters,
We were often bored, as you were here.

The sun's splendor above violet seas,
The splendor of cities in the setting sun,
Made our hearts burn with restless ardor
To plunge into a sky of seductive light.

The richest cities, the noblest landscapes,
Never possess the mysterious
Attraction of those chance makes out of clouds.
And desire kept us forever anxious.

—Enjoyment augments the strength of desire.
Desire, ancient tree that thrives on pleasure,
All the while your bark thickens and hardens,
Your branches would look more closely on the sun!

When will you stop growing, great tree, longer
Lived than the cypress? —Yet we were careful
To cull a few sketches for your album,
Brothers who think all that's exotic fair!

We bowed before idols with trunks, and
Thrones constellated with shining jewels,
And carven palaces whose fairy pomp
Would make your bankers ruinous dreams.

Costumes like a drunkenness for the eyes
We say; women with painted teeth and nails,
And skilled fakirs whom the snake caresses."


V


And then, after that what?


VI


           "O childish brains!

Lest we forget the most important thing,
Everywhere, without wishing to, we viewed,
From top to bottom of the fatal ladder,
The dull pageant of everlasting sin:

Woman, conceited slave, neither amused
Nor disgusted by her self-worship;
Man, hot, gluttonous tyrant, hard and grasping,
Slave of a slave, gutter in the sewer;

The hangman enjoying, the martyr sobbing,
The fete that spices and perfumes the blood;
The despot unnerved by power's poison,
The mob in love with the brutalizing whip;

A great many religions like our own,
All scaling heaven; Holiness seeking
Its pleasure in nails and haircloth, as a
Delicate wallows in a feather bed;

Babbling Mankind, drunk with its own genius,
And mad as it ever was, crying out
To God, in its furious agony:
'O my fellow, my master, I curse thee!'

And the less stupid, bold lovers of Madness,
Fleeing the herd fenced in by Destiny,
To take refuge in a vast opium!
—Thus the everlasting news of the whole globe."


VII


A bitter knowledge we gain by traveling!
The world, monotonous and small, today,
Yesterday, tomorrow, reflects our image:
Dreadful oasis in a waste of boredom!

Shall we depart or stay? Stay if you can;
Depart if you must. Some run, others crouch
To deceive the watchful, deadly foe, Time!
There are those, alas! who run without rest,

Like the wandering Jew and the apostles,
Whom nothing suffices, carriage or ship,
To flee that base retiary; others
Wear him out without leaving their cradles.

When at last he has his foot on our backs,
Then we'll be able to hope and cry: on!
Just as we used to set out for China,
Eyes fixed on the horizon and hair streaming,

We will embark on the sea of Darkness
With the joyous hearts of young passengers;
Listen to those charming, mournful voices
Singing: "Come this way, who desire to eat

The perfumed Lotus! Here are gathered the
Miraculous fruits your hearts hunger for;
Come and grow drunk on the strange mildness
Of this afternoon without an ending."

We know the ghost by its familiar speech;
Our Pylades stretch out their arms to us.
"To renew your heart, swim towards your Electra!"
Cries she whose knees we kissed in former days.


VIII


Death, old captain, it's time to weigh anchor!
This country bores us, O Death! Let us set sail!
If the sea and sky are as black as ink,
Our hearts, you know well, are bursting with rays!

Pour your poison on us; let it comfort
Us! We long, so does this fire burn our brains,
To dive into the gulf, Hell or Heaven,
What matter? Into the Unknown in search of the *new!*

BARBARA GIBBS

## LESBOS

*Lesbos*

Mother of the Roman games and Greek pleasures,
Lesbos, where the kisses, gay or languishing,
Burning as suns or cool as watermelons,
Are ornaments for the nights and splendid days;
Mother of the Roman games and Greek pleasures;

Lesbos, where the kisses are like fresh torrents
That cast themselves down bottomless abysses,
And run on, sobbing and cackling fitfully,
Stormy and secretive, turbulent and deep;
Lesbos, where the kisses are like fresh torrents!

Lesbos, where the Phrynes lure one another,
Where no sigh ever went without an echo,
The stars admire you as they do Paphos,
And Venus may well be jealous of Sappho!
Lesbos, where the Phrynes lure one another,

Lesbos, island of those hot, languorous nights
That make, before their mirrors, hollow-eyed girls,
Enamored of their bodies—sterile pleasure!—
Caress the ripe fruits of their nubility;
Lesbos, island of those hot, languorous nights,

Let Plato cast up a disapproving eye;
You win pardon by the excess of your kisses,
Queen of the soft empire, friendly, noble land,
And by your ever-flowering refinements.
Let Plato cast up a disapproving eye;

You win pardon through the eternal martyrdom,
Relentless punisher of ambitious hearts,
That never lets us see the radiant smile
We have glimpsed on the shores of other skies!
You win pardon through eternal martyrdom!

Who among the Gods, Lesbos, will dare judge you,
And condemn the pale forehead of your travail,
If his gold balances have not weighed the torrent
Of tears your rivers emptied into the sea?
Who among the Gods, Lesbos, will dare judge you?

What have laws of right and wrong to do with us?
Noble virgins, pride of the archipelago,
Your religion is august as another,
And love will make mockery of Heaven and Hell!
What have laws of right and wrong to do with us?

For Lesbos has chosen me, of all on earth,
To sing the secret of her virgins in flower,
And from childhood I've known the black mystery
Of frantic laughter mingled with somber tears;
For Lesbos has chosen me, of all on earth.

Since then I've watched from the summit of Leucate,
Like a sentinel with a sure, piercing eye,
Who night and day looks out for tartan or brig,
Whose forms tremble in the blue at a distance;
Since then I've watched from the summit of Leucate,

To learn if the sea is indulgent and good,
And if, while the rocks reverberate with sobs,
One evening there will return to pardoning Lesbos
The adored body of Sappho, who set out
To learn if the sea is indulgent and good!

Of the male Sappho, the lover and poet,
Fairer, with her mournful pallors, than Venus!
The blue eye yields the palm to the black, tarnished
By the dark circle traced by the sorrows
Of the male Sappho, the lover and poet!

Fairer than Venus standing above the world,
Pouring the treasures of her serenity
And all the radiance of her golden youth
On old Ocean, delighted with his daughter;
Fairer than Venus standing above the world!

—Of Sappho who died the day of her blasphemy,
When, insulting the rite and the devised cult,
She let her lovely body be the pasture
Of a brute whose pride punished the impiety
Of her who died the day of her blasphemy.

And it is from that time that Lesbos has mourned,
And despite the admiration of the world
Intoxicates herself each night with the cry
Of torment that escapes from her empty shores!
And it is from that time that Lesbos has mourned!

BARBARA GIBBS

## LETHE

### Le Léthé

Come to my heart, cruel, sullen soul,
Adored tiger, indolent monster;
I would bury my trembling fingers
In the thickness of your heavy mane;

In your skirts laden with your perfume
I would wrap up my aching head,
And inhale the sweet, musty odor,
Like a faded flower, of my dead love.

I long to sleep! sleep sooner than live!
In sleep sweet as death I will lay out
My kisses without remorse upon
Your lovely body, smooth as copper.

Naught so well as the abyss of your couch
Can swallow up my abating sobs;
Oblivion inhabits your mouth,
And Lethe oozes from your kisses.

My destiny, henceforth my delight,
I will obey like one predestined;
Docile martyr, condemned innocent,
Whose fervor excites the tormentor,

I will suck, to deaden my rancor,
Nepenthe and complaisant hemlock
At the tips of that pointed bosom,
Which has never imprisoned a heart.

BARBARA GIBBS


# EPIGRAPH FOR A CONDEMNED BOOK

*Épigraphe pour un livre condamné*

Reader placid and bucolic,
Sober, guileless man of the good,
Fling away this saturnine book,
Orgiastic and melancholic.

Unless with Satan, wily master,
You have studied your rhetoric,
Fling it away! You will understand none of it,
Or think me hysteric.

But if you are able, unenticed,
To plunge your eye in the depths,
Read me, that you learn to love me;

Inquiring soul who suffers
And goes seeking your paradise,
Pity me! . . . If not, be damned!

KATE FLORES

## MEDITATION

*Recueillement*

Be wise, my Sorrow; oh, more tranquil be!
You yearned for day's decline; it comes, is here:
Steeping the town, the darkening atmosphere
Brings peace to some, to some despondency.

While now base human multitudes obey
The torturer's lash of Pleasure, never released,
Go gathering new remorse in the slavish feast,
My Sorrow, give me your hand and come this way—

Come far from them. Now lean the departed years
In outworn robes from the balconies of sky;
Smiling Regret looks out from the waters' deeps;

The dying light under an archway sleeps;
And from the East, the long shroud trailing by—
Listen, my dear—with soft step the night nears.

DWIGHT DURLING

## THE GULF

*Le Gouffre*

Pascal had his gulf, wandering with him.
—Alas! 'Tis all abyss—action, dream, desire,
Word! And oftentimes I sense across my hair,
Arisen all on end, the breath of Fear.

Above, below, on every side: the fathomless, the verge,
Silence, enthralling insidious space . . .
In the pith of my nights God with His knowing finger
Truceless a manifold nightmare shapes.

Sleep gapes appalling as a cave no one knows,
Suffused with impalpable horror, leading endlessly;
Through all the windows I see merely infinity,

And my being, reeling vertiginous ever,
Covets insensible nullity.
—Ah! to leave Numbers and Entities never!

KATE FLORES

## AT ONE O'CLOCK IN THE MORNING

### À Une Heure du matin

At last! Alone! There is no longer anything to be heard but the rattling of a few belated and exhausted cabs. For a few hours we shall possess silence, if not repose. At last! The tyranny of the human face has disappeared, and I shall suffer no longer except by myself.

At last! So it is permitted that I rest in a bath of darkness! First, to double-lock the door. It seems to me that this turn of the key will increase my solitude and strengthen the barricades which separate me now from the world.

Horrible life! Horrible life! Let us sum up the day: to have seen several men of letters, one of whom asked whether it were possible to go to Russia by land (doubtless he was taking Russia for an island); to have argued amiably with the director of a review, who to each objection answered, "We are on the side of the decent people," which implies that all other journals are edited by rascals; to have raised my hat to some twenty people, of whom fifteen are unknown to me; to have shaken hands in the same proportion, and this without having taken the precaution of buying gloves; to have paid a visit, to kill time, to a little dancer who begged me to design a Venus costume for her; to have paid court to a theatrical director, who said upon

dismissing me, "You might do well to speak to Z—; he is the dullest, the stupidest, and the most famous of all my authors; with him you might end up by getting somewhere. Talk to him and then we will see"; to have boasted (why?) about several sordid acts I have never committed, and to have denied like a coward a few other misdeeds committed with joy: the offense of bragging, the crime of respect for men; to have refused a friend an easy service and given a written recommendation to a consummate knave; ah! is it really well over with?

Discontented with everyone and discontented with myself, I should like to redeem myself and rebuild my pride a little in the silence and solitude of the night. Souls of those I have loved, souls of those I have sung, strengthen me, support me, remove from me falsehood and the corruptive mists of the world; and you, oh, Lord my God, accord me the grace to produce a few lovely verses which will prove to me that I am not the last of men, that I am not inferior to those I scorn.

BERT M-P. LEEFMANS

## BE DRUNK

*Enivrez-vous*

Be drunk, always. Nothing else matters; this is our sole concern. To ease the pain as Time's dread burden weighs down upon your shoulders and crushes you to earth, you must be drunk without respite.

Drunk with what? With wine, with poetry, or with virtue, as you please. But be drunk.

And if sometimes, on the steps of palaces, on the green grass in a ditch, in the dreary solitude of your room, you should wake and find your drunkenness half over or fully gone, ask of wind or wave, of star or bird or clock, ask of all that flies, of all that sighs, moves, sings, or speaks, ask them what time it is; and wind, wave, star, bird, or clock

will answer: "It is time to be drunk! To throw off the chains and martyrdom of Time, be drunk; be drunk eternally! With wine, with poetry, or with virtue, as you please."

WILLIAM M. DAVIS

## ANYWHERE OUT OF THE WORLD

### *Anywhere Out of the World*

This life is a hospital where every patient longs desperately to change his bed. This one would like to suffer opposite the stove, and that one is sure he would get well if placed by the window.

Somehow I get the feeling that I should be better elsewhere than where I am, and this question of moving is one which I am always discussing with my soul.

"Tell me, poor chilled soul, how would you like to live in Lisbon? It must be warm there, and you could bask in the sun as blissfully as a lizard. The city is on the coast. They say it is built of marble, and that its people have such a horror of vegetation that they uproot all the trees. Here is a landscape just suited to your taste: a landscape made of light and minerals, with water to reflect them."

My soul makes no reply.

"Since you love tranquillity, and the sight of moving things, do you wish to live in Holland, that heavenly land? Perhaps you will be happy in that land whose image you have so often admired in museums. What do you say to Rotterdam, you who love forests of masts, and ships that are moored at the doors of the houses?"

My soul remains silent.

"Perhaps you would prefer Batavia? There, moreover, we would find the wit of Europe wedded to the beauty of the tropics. Not a word. Can my soul be dead?

"Have you sunk into so deep a stupor that you find satisfaction only in your unhappiness? If such is the case, let us flee to those lands in the likeness of Death. I know just

the place, poor soul! We shall pack our bags for Tornéo.
Let us go even farther, to the utmost limits of the Baltic;
farther still, from life, if possible; let us set up housekeeping
at the Pole. There the sun all but grazes the earth obliquely,
and the slow alternations of light and night make variety
impossible and increase that monotony which is the other
half of nothingness. There we can bathe deep in darkness,
while sometimes, for our diversion, the Aurora Borealis will
send up its rosy sheafs, like reflection of the fireworks of
Hell!"

Finally, my soul explodes, crying: "Anywhere! Any-
where! As long as it be out of this world!"

WILLIAM M. DAVIS

# *Tristan Corbière*

## 1845–1875

# TRISTAN CORBIÈRE

## 1845–1875

Born in Brittany, the son of seafarers and fascinated by the sea, Corbière spent most of his rather short life there. Largely unknown until he was discovered by Verlaine and included among the latter's *Poètes maudits* (1884), Corbière has been and continues to be an influence on modern poetry. Verlaine, Laforgue markedly, and others echo the sardonic view of this curious combination of Bohemian and sailor in the wild seas off his native coast.

These two aspects of Corbière are reflected in his poetry, which is at once a sharp attack, sarcastic and by caricature, upon Romantic sentimentality, Hugo's in particular, and an attempt to return to immediacy, to life itself as it has always been felt and experienced by those more directly involved with it than Corbière could believe the Romantics, and most other poets, ever really were.

Recalling Villon, among others, Corbière was influenced by Baudelaire, but although he sympathized with the latter's attacks on Romantic anti-intellectualism, he felt that Baudelaire went too far in the other direction, that his poetry also became too distant from experience, if in a different way. And Corbière was no defender, either, of art as the highest form of man's endeavor, indeed, in his concerns, no artist. His images, his rhythms, are dynamic and immediate, not literary; his concern is life, not art, and his attempt is to rehabilitate mankind by rejecting the notion that man's creations are somehow superior to man himself.

# AFTER THE RAIN

*Après la pluie*

I love the little rain
   Which dries itself
With a cloth of tattered blue!
I love love and the breeze,
   When it just grazes . . .
And not when it shakes you.

—Like an umbrella of arrows,
   You get dry,
O great sun! wide open . . .
Soon the green parasol
   Wide open!
Of spring—the winter's summer—

Passion is the thunderstorm
   That drenches!
But woman is just a spot:
Beauty spot, spot of madness
   Or of rain . . .
Spot of storm—or of calm—

In a bright spoke of mud
   Fans out her charms
   In great array
—Feather and tail—a chick
   Who splashes;
A sweet dish for the sun!

—"Anne! or whoever you are, dear . . .
   Or not dear,
Who has been had for free . . .
Well . . . Zoé! Nadjejda! Jane!
   Look: I'm strolling here
Lined with gold like the skies!

English spoken? —Spanish? . . .
   Batignolle? . . .
Lift up the canvas
That covers your wares,
   O Marquise
Of Amaëgui! . . . Wiggly!

Monkey-name or archangel's name?
   Or both at once? . . .
Little name in eight parts?
Name that shouts, or name that sings?
   Lover's name? . . .
Or utterly impossible name?

Will you, with a faithful love,
   Eternal!
Adore me for this evening? . . .
For your two little boots
   Which you're getting muddy
Take my heart and the sidewalk!

Aren't you doña Sabine?
   Carbine?
Say: would you like the heaven
Of the Odéon?—extravagant
   Voyage! . . .
They take away your cabbage."

At this point is unsheathed
   The old line:
—"You are mistaken!" Such emotion!
"Let me alone . . . I'm a respectable woman . . ."
   "Not so dumb!"
"—Who do you take me for?" "For me! . . ."

"Wouldn't you take a drink of something
   That's sprinkled
With no matter what . . . some
Pearl juice in cups
   Of gold? . . . You cut!
But me, Mina, will you take me?"

—"Why not? that goes without saying!"—
  "—That smile! . . .
And me, besides! . . .
Hermosa, you seem to me to have a frank-
  ness about your flank!
A pedant would be offended by it!"

—"But my name is Aloïse . . ."
  "Héloise!
Will you, for the love of art
—Abelard without the title—
  Let me
Be a little bit your Abelard?"
. . . . . . . . . . . . . . . . . . .
. . . . . . . . . . . . . . . . . . .
And like a white squall which dies
  The sweet dream
Lay down there, without a dark cloud . . .
Gives to my appeased mouth
  "The dew
Of a rising-kiss— Good night—"

"It is the song of the lark,
  Juliet!
And it's the song of the turkey . . .
I give you, like the dawn
  Which gilds you,
A circle of gold on your eiderdown."

    KENNETH KOCH AND GEORGES GUY

## INSOMNIA

### *Insomnie*

Insomnia, impalpable Creature!
Is all your love in your head
That you come and are ravished to see
Beneath your evil eye man gnaw
His sheets and twist himself with spleen,
Beneath your black diamond eye?

Tell me: why, during the sleepless night,
Rainy like a Sunday,
Do you come to lick us like a dog?
Hope or Regret that keeps watch,
Why, in our throbbing ear
Do you speak low . . . and say nothing?

Why to our parched throat
Do you always tilt your empty cup
And leave us stretching our neck,
Tantaluses, thirsters for chimeras—
Amorous philter or bitter dregs,
Cool dew or melted lead!

Insomnia, aren't you beautiful? . . .
Well, why, lascivious virgin,
Do you squeeze us between your knees?
Why do you moan on our lips,
Why do you unmake our bed,
And . . . not go to bed with us?

Why, impure night-blooming beauty,
That black mask on your face? . . .
To fill the golden dreams with intrigue? . . .
Aren't you love in space,
The breath of Messaline weary
But still not satisfied?

Insomnia, are you Hysteria? . . .
Are you the barrel organ
Which grinds out the hosanna of the elect? . . .
Or aren't you the eternal plectrum
On the nerves of the damned-of-letters
Scraping out their verses—which only they have read?

Insomnia, are you the troubled donkey
Of Buridan—or the firefly
Of hell? —Your kiss of fire
Leaves a chilled taste of red-hot iron . . .
Oh, come perch in my hovel! . . .
We will sleep together a while.

KENNETH KOCH AND GEORGES GUY


## THE TOAD

*Le Crapaud*

A song in a windless night . . .
—The moon plates in metal bright
The cut-out images of dark green.

. . . A song; sudden as an echo, quick,
Buried, there, under the thick
Clump. It stops. Come, it's there, unseen . . .

—A toad! —There in shadow. Why this terror
Near me, your faithful soldier? —Spring!—
Look at him, poet clipped, no wing,
Nightingale of the mud . . . Horror!—

. . . He sings. Horror! —Horror! But why?
Don't you see that eye of light, his own?
No: he goes, chilled, beneath his stone.
Good night. That toad you heard is I.

VERNON WATKINS

## HOURS

*Heures*

Alms to the highwayman in pursuit!
Evil eye to the luring eye!
Blade against blade with the avid swordsman!
—My soul is not in a state of grace!—

I am the fool of Pamplona,
Afraid of the Moon's laughter,
Hypocritical, in black crepe . . .
Horror! is everything, then, beneath a candle snuffer?

I hear a noise like a rattle . . .
It is the evil hour which calls me.
In the pit of nights falls: one knell . . . two knells.

I have counted more than fourteen hours . . .
Each hour a tear. You are weeping,
My heart! . . . Keep singing, go on—— Don't count.

KENNETH KOCH AND GEORGES GUY

## TO MY MOUSE-COLORED MARE

*À ma Jument souris*

No spur or whiplash needed now,
Is there, darling mouse-and-pink?
They're good for prodding some old cow,
But not my gray little mare, I think.

No bridle for that poor mouth of yours:
My love's enough, and my helpful thigh.
I'll put no stirrup, no saddle on:
Just a touch of my boot, and off you fly
On your prettily steel-shod hooves. (Of course,
I'm not a fussy equestrian.)

Whoops! We're off on the dusty track!
My head's lost in your mane somewhere,
My arms are a circlet for your neck.
Whoops! We took that hedge for fair!

Whoops! We're over the hurdle now!
Stay under me, my head's awhirl—
Whoops! and there's the ditch below . . .
We're arsy-varsy! . . . Hold it, girl!

DUDLEY FITTS

## RHAPSODY OF THE DEAF MAN

*Rapsodie du sourd*

The specialist told him: "Fine, let's leave it at that.
The treatment is done: you're deaf. That's how
It is you have quite lost your hearing."
And he understood only too well, not having heard.

—Well, thank you, sir, for deigning to make
   A fine coffin of my head.
Now I shall be able, with legitimate pride,
   To understand all on trust. . . .

Indeed *by eye.** —But watch that jealous eye, serving
For your hocked ear! . . . Ah, no . . . What good is
   showing off?
If I whistle too loudly in ridicule's face,
To my face, and lowly, it can spit in my eye! . . .

* i.e. *free of charge.* This stanza is a series of typical Corbièrian
word-plays dependent on the figurative meanings of phrases in-
volving the eye, ear, and face; they cannot be conveyed when
English lacks the figurative equivalents. In the next stanza *vieux
pot* (old pot) is a friendly appellation, but the French also say
"Deaf as a pot" as we say "Deaf as a post."

A dumb puppet, I, on a banal string! —Tomorrow,
Along the street, a friend could take my hand
And call me old post . . . or, more kindly, nothing;
And I'd come back with: Not bad, thanks, and you!


If someone shouts a word at me, I'm mad for understanding;
If another says nothing: could it be out of pity? . . .
Always, like a rebus, I struggle to catch
A word catercorner . . . No—— They left me out!


Or—reverse of the coin—some officious stuffed shirt,
His lower lip wagging as though he were grazing,
Fancies himself conversing . . . And I, gnawing within,
    keep still:
A grinning idiot—looking intelligent!


—Gray woolen cap pulled down over my soul!
And—the donkey's kick . . . Giddyap! —A good lady,
Old Lemonade Peddler, and of Passion, too!
Might come up to drool her sanctimonious sympathy
In my Eustacian tube—full blast, like a horn—
And I not even able to step on her corn!


—Silly as a virgin, aloof as a leper,
I'm there, but absent . . . Is he a dunce, they want to know,
A muzzled poet, or just a crab? . . .
A shrug of the shoulders, and that means: Deaf.


—Frenzied torment of an acoustic Tantalus!
I see words flying I cannot snatch;
Impotent flycatcher, eaten by a mosquito,
Target-head with free pot shots for all!


O heavenly music: to hear a sea shell
Grate on plaster! A razor, a knife
Scrape in a cork! A couplet on the stage!
A live bone being sawn! A gentleman! A rondeau!

—Nothing—— I babble to myself . . . Words I toss to the
　air
*Off the cuff,* not knowing if I speak Hindu,
Or perhaps duck talk, like the clarinet
Of a blockhead blindman mistaking the stops.

Go then, tipsy pendulum gone loose in my head!
Beat up this fine tom-tom, cracked tinny pianola
That renders a woman's voice a doorbell,
A cuckoo! . . . Sometimes: a buzzing gnat . . .

—Lie down, my heart, and beat your wing no more.
In the dark-lantern let us snuff the candle out,
And all that once vibrated there—I know no longer where—
Dungeon where they come to draw the bolt across the door.

—Be mute for me, pensive Idol.
Both of us, for each other's sake, forgetting to speak,
Say not a word to me: nothing will I answer . . .
And nothing then can mar our understanding.

　　*Silence is golden* (St. John Chrysostom).

　　　　　　　　　　　　　　　　KATE FLORES

## TO MOUNT ÆTNA
### À l'Etna

*Sicelides Musae, paulo majora canamus.*
VIRGIL

Ætna—I've been up Vesuvius . . .
Vesuvius has shrunk, it seems:
There was more heat in me than streams
From that wounded crater in hot pus . . .

—They say you're like a woman. —What?
—Your age, I suppose—? or maybe that cooked
Pebble, your heart? . . . Well, it's a thought . . .
Laugh? I thought I'd come apart!

—That dirty grin of yours, that cough
Thick as the phlegm of a senile lust;
Your old breast cancer draining off
Lava from under its scabby crust.

Comrade, let's go to bed together,
My hide against your sick hide; yes,
I swear by Venus you're my brother,
Vulcan! . . .
      A little more . . . or less . . .

DUDLEY FITTS

## EVIL LANDSCAPE
### Paysage mauvais

Beach of old bones—The tide gasps
Death-knells: croaking sound on sound . . .
—Pale marsh, where the moon swallows
Big worms to make the night pass.

—Calm of plague, where fever
Burns . . . The cursed will-o'-the-wisp fades away.
—Stinking grass where the hare
Is a cowardly sorcerer who flees . . .

—The white Washerwoman spreads out
The dead's dirty linen
In the *sun of wolves* . . . —The toads,

Little melancholy chanters,
With their colics poison
The mushrooms, their stools.

KENNETH KOCH AND GEORGES GUY

## BLIND MAN'S CRIES

*Cris d'aveugle*

To the Low Breton tune: *"Ann hini goz"*

The murdered eye is not dead
A spike still splits it
Nailed up I am coffinless
They drove the nail in my eye
The nailed eye is not dead
And the spike still enters it

*Deus misericors*
*Deus misericors*
The hammer pounds my wooden head
The hammer that will make the cross
*Deus misericors*
*Deus misericors*

The undertaker birds
Are thus afraid of my body
My Golgotha is not over
*Lamma lamma sabacthani*
   Doves of Death
   Be thirsty for my body


   Red as a gun-port
   The sore is on the edge
Like the drooling gum
Of a toothless laughing old woman
   The sore is on the edge
   Red as a gun-port


   I see circles of gold
   The white sun bites me
I've two holes pierced by an iron bar
Reddened in the forge of hell
   I see a circle of gold
   The sky's fire bites me


   In the marrow twists
   A tear which comes out
I see inside paradise
*Miserere de profundis*
   In my skull twists
   A sulfur tear which comes out


   Blessèd the good dead man
   The saved dead man who sleeps
Happy the martyrs the chosen
With the Virgin and her Jesus
   Oh blessèd the dead man
   The judged dead man who sleeps

A Knight outside
Reposes without remorse
In the hallowed cemetery
In his granite siesta
The man of stone outside
Has two eyes without remorse


Oh I feel you still
Yellow moors of Armor
I feel my rosary in my fingers
And Christ in bone on the wood
I gape at you still
O dead Armor sky


Pardon for praying hard
Lord if it is fate
My eyes two burning holy-water fonts
The devil put his fingers inside
Pardon for crying loud
Lord against fate


I hear the north wind
Which bugles like a horn
It is the hunting call for the kill of the dead
I bay enough on my own
I hear the north wind
I hear the horn's knell

KENNETH KOCH AND GEORGES GUY

## LETTER FROM MEXICO
### *Lettre du Mexique*

Veracruz, **February 10**

"You put the kid in my care. —He's dead.
And more than one of his pals with him, poor **dear** soul.
The crew . . . there ain't any more. A few of us,
    Maybe, will get back. —It's fate—

"Nothing as beautiful as that—Sailor—for a man;
They'd all like to be one on land—you bet.
Without the discomfort. Nothing but: You can see
    How already the apprenticeship's tough!

"I weep to be writing it, me, old *Shore-Brother*.
I'd gladly have given my skin, without ado,
To send him back to you . . . Me, it ain't my fault:
    You can't argue with this sickness.

"The fever here is regular as Lent in March.
You go to the cemetery to get your ration.
The Zouave called it—Parisian at that—
    'The Garden of Acclimatization.'

"Console yourselves. They're dropping off here like flies.
. . . I found in his satchel some souvenirs of his heart:
A girl's picture, and two little babouches,
    And: marked—*Gift for my sister.*

"He wants his Mom to be told: that he said his prayers.
And his Dad: that he'd rather have died in a war.
Two angels were with him in his last hour:
    A sailor. An old soldier."

KATE FLORES

## CABIN-KID

*Le Mousse*

Your old man's a sailor, I suppose? . . .
—A fisherman. A long time dead.
He left my mother's side one night,
And sleeps in the breakers now instead.

Up in the graveyard there's a tomb
Ma keeps for him—it's empty, though—
I'm all the husband that she has
To help her while the children grow.

Two little ones. —Nothing was found
Along the beach where he was drowned? . . .
—Only his pipe-case and a shoe . . .

When Sundays come, Mother can stop
And cry for rest . . . But when I grow up
I'll get revenge—a sailor too!

DUDLEY FITTS

# THE END

## *La Fin*

Oh! how many mariners, how many captains
Who set off lighthearted for faraway journeys
Are vanished in this mournful horizon! . . .

. . . . . . . . . . . . . . . . . . . . . . . . . .
How many skippers dead with their crews!
The Ocean took all the pages of their lives
And with one puff scattered them over the waves.
None will know their end sunk in the deep . . .

. . . . . . . . . . . . . . . . . . . . . . . . . .
None will know their names, not even the humble stone
In the narrow cemetery where echoes answer us,
Not even the green weeping willow shedding its leaves in the fall,
Not even the plaintive monotonous song
Of the blindman singing in the corner of an old bridge.

VICTOR HUGO: *Oceano nox*

Well now, these mariners—sailors, captains,
All in their great Ocean swallowed forever . . .
Who left nonchalant for their faraway journeys,
Are dead—as true as they left.

What then! It's their trade; they died with their boots on!
Their snifters to their hearts, all alive inside their ca-
    potes . . .
—*Dead* . . . No thanks: Lady Death has no sea legs;
Let her sleep with you: She's your good wife . . .
—As for them, none of it: Complete! washed away by the
    wave!
        Or lost in a squall . . .

A squall . . . that's death, you think? The lower sail
Pounding across the water! —That's *floundering* . . .
A blast of the leaden sea, then the high mast
Whipping at wave level—and that's *foundering*.

—Foundering. —Fathom this word. Your *death* is mighty
   pale
And nothing much on board, in a raging gale . . .
Nothing much against the great bitter smile
Of the sailor struggling. —Come now, make way!—
Death the windy old phantom changes face:
      The Sea! . . .

Drowned? —Aw, go on! You drown in *fresh* water!
—Sunk! Crew and cargo! And, down to the little ship's-boy,
Defiance in their eyes, in their teeth curses!
Spitting a death-rattle quid to the spume,
And downing without puking *the big salty cup* . . .
     —The way they downed their snifters—
. . . . . . . . . . . . . . . . . . . . . . . . . .
—No six-foot-under for them, or cemetery rats:
Them, they head for the sharks! The soul of a sailor,
Instead of oozing in your potatoes,
      Breathes with every wave!

—See there on the horizon the billow heaving;
      The amorous belly, you'd say,
Of a whore in heat, half-soused . . .
      They're there! —The billow has a cave—

—Listen, listen to the storm bellow! . . .
Their anniversary. —It returns quite often—
O poet, keep your blindman's songs to yourself;
—For them: the *De Profundis* the wind trumpets!

. . . Let them roll eternally in the virgin spaces! . . .
      Let them roll green and bare,
Without pine and without nails, without lid, without
   candles . . .
—O let them roll, parvenu landlubbers!

                        KATE FLORES

# PARIS AT NIGHT

### Paris Nocturne

*It's not a city, it's a world*

—It is the sea: dead calm—and the spring tide
With a far-off roaring has departed.
The surge will come back rolling in its noise—
Do you hear the scratching of the crabs of night?

—It is the Styx run dry: The ragpicker Diogenes,
Lantern in hand, roams about unperturbed.
All along the black stream depraved poets
Fish; from empty skulls they bait their lines.

—It is the field: To glean the dirty rags
The turning flight of hideous Harpies swoops;
The alley cat, on the lookout for rats,
Flees Bondy's criminal sons, nocturnal vintagers.

—It is death: Here lie the police. —Up there, love
Siestas, sucking the meat of a heavy arm
Where the quenched kiss leaves its red mark . . .
The hour is alone—Listen . . . not a dream is moving.

—It is life: Listen: the live stream is singing
The eternal song on the slimy head
Of a sea-god stretching his limbs naked and green
On a bed of the Morgue . . . With his eyes wide open!

KENNETH KOCH AND GEORGES GUY

## RONDEL

*Rondel*

It's dark, child, snatcher of sparks!
No more are there nights, days are no more;
Sleep . . . waiting for everyone to come
Who said: Never! Who told you: Forever!

Do you hear their steps? . . . How far away they are:
Oh, the delicate tread! —Love has wings . . .
It's dark, child, snatcher of sparks!

Do you hear their voices? . . . Coffins have no ears.
Sleep: They weigh but little, all your immortal flowers;
Nor will they be coming, your friends the bears,*
To tumble their cobblestone over your fair ones . . .
It's dark, child, snatcher of sparks!

KATE FLORES

## SLEEP, BABY, SLEEP . . .

*Do, l'Enfant do . . .*

*Buona vespre!* Sleep: Your candle-end,
They set it there, then they left.
You'll not be afraid by yourself, poor little one? . . .
It's the candlestick for your bed at the inn.

Fear no longer the pen-pusher's lash,
Go! . . . To wake no more isn't so reckless.
*Buona sera!* Sleep: Your candle-end . . .

Is dead. —Here no doorkeeper longer attends:
Just the wind from the north, the wind from the south
Comes to quiver a gossamer thread.
Shhh! To the scoundrels, your ground is accursed.
—*Buona notte!* Sleep: Your candle-end . . .

KATE FLORES

* Allusion to La Fontaine's fable "The Bear and the Garden Lover," in which a lonely gardener makes friends with a lonely bear who, attempting to kill a fly on the sleeping gardener's nose, accidentally kills him with a cobblestone.

## KAZOO

### Mirliton

Sleep in love, naughty tuner of cicadas!
Under the quitch-grasses covering you,
The cicada will sing for you too,
Merrily, with his little cymbals.

The dew will have tears in the morning;
And lilies-of-the-valley make a sweet winding-sheet . . .
Sleep in love, naughty tuner of cicadas!

There will be wailing droves of squalls . . .

The Muse of Death will set the pitch.
She will still bring to your darkened lips
Those rhymes that make the pale-faced twitch . . .
Sleep in love, naughty tuner of cicadas!

KATE FLORES

## SMALL DEATH TO LAUGH

### Petit Mort pour rire

Away, airy comber of comets!
The grass in the wind will be your hair;
From your gaping eyes will-o'-wisps
Will rise, prisoners in the poor heads . . .

Graveyard flowers called Little Flirts
Will overgrow your earthy laugh . . .
And forget-me-nots, those flowers of dungeons forgot . . .

Make light of it: poets' coffins
Are but toys to pallbearers,
Violin cases with an empty sound . . .
They'll think you're dead—the bourgeois are dull—
Away, airy comber of comets!

KATE FLORES

# Paul Verlaine

## 1844–1896

## PAUL VERLAINE

### 1844–1896

The key to Verlaine's best poetry is an exquisite music which has never been matched in any verse, an intimate expression of his own nostalgia and his own torment, together at times with a simplicity of vocabulary and an apparent simplicity of form which conceal his mastery both of poetic tradition and of his own means.

Born of a comfortably-off bourgeois family, Verlaine became more and more troubled, his life more and more scandalous, as time went on, despite the fact that his poetic stature and reputation were growing as he escaped the Parnassian influences he had begun by following in order to produce an altogether original sound in French verse. Shortly after the one wholly happy period of his life, his engagement and the first year of his marriage, Verlaine ran off to England with the young Rimbaud, beginning an existence of alternate debauchery and sincere if unavailing attempts at his own rehabilitation. Divorced by his wife while he was in prison for having wounded Rimbaud in a quarrel, Verlaine lost his last steadying influence in 1886 when his mother died. From then on his drinking, which had always been prodigious, led to poverty and illness relieved only by the homage of a younger generation which saw him as the Prince of Poets.

Anything but an intellectual, developer of no system nor of any school, too original to be copied with success, Verlaine left no direct disciples.

# MY RECURRING DREAM

*Mon Rêve familier*

Often I have this strange and penetrating dream
Of an unknown woman I love and who loves me,
And each time she is neither quite the same
Nor quite another, but she loves and understands.

For she does understand, and my heart, lucid
Alas, only for her, is a problem no longer,
But only for her, and the fever of my pale brow
Only by her can be cooled, as she weeps.

Is she dark, fair, or red-haired? I know not.
Her name? I remember it is sweet and singing
Like those of loved ones whom Life has banished.

Her gaze is like the gaze of statues,
And her voice, distant, calm, and low,
Has the inflection of dear voices that are stilled.

MURIEL KITTEL


# ANGUISH

*L'Angoisse*

Nature, nothing in you moves me, not the fruitful
Fields, not the roseate echo of the pastorales
Of Sicily, not the grandeur of the dawns,
Not the solemn ruefulness of sunsets.

I laugh at Art, I laugh at Man too, and at songs,
At verse, at Greek temples and the spiraled towers
Cathedrals spread across the empty sky,
And I see good men and evil with identical eye.

I do not believe in God, I deny and abjure
All thought, and as for Love, that old
Irony, would I might hear of it no more.

Weary of living, fearing to die, like
A lost barque a plaything of the tides,
My soul to dread disaster seems to ride.

KATE FLORES

## THE SHEPHERD'S HOUR

### *L'Heure du berger*

The moon is red through horizon's fog;
In a dancing mist the hazy meadow
Sleeps; by green rushes a frog
Calls, there where movement quivers;

Water flowers fold their petals now;
In the distance, tall and in close array
Poplars outline their shadowy forms;
Towards the thickets the fireflies stray;

The screech owls wake, and soundlessly
Beat the dark air with heavy wings,
And the heaven is filled with muffled light.
Pale, Venus appears, and it is Night.

MURIEL KITTEL

## THE NIGHTINGALE

*Le Rossignol*

Like a clamorous flock of startled birds,
All my memories swoop upon me,
Swoop among the yellow foliage
Of my heart, watching its bent alder-trunk
In the purple foil of the waters of Regret
That flow nearby in melancholy wise;
They swoop, and then the horrid clamor,
That a moist breeze calms as it rises,
Dies gradually in the tree—until
At the end of a moment nothing more is heard,
Nothing but the voice hymning the Absent One,
Nothing but the voice—the languishing voice—
Of the bird that was my Earliest Love,
Singing still as on that earliest day;
And in the sad magnificence of a moon
That rises with pale solemnity, a
Summer night, heavy and melancholy,
Full of silence and obscurity,
Lulls in the sky that a soft wind caresses
The quivering tree and the weeping bird.

MURIEL KITTEL

# IN THE WOODS

*Dans le Bois*

Other people—innocents or lunatics—
Find in the woods only pallid charms,
Fresh breezes and warm scents. They are fortunate!
Others, dreamers, are seized with mystic dread.

They are fortunate! While I, nervous, maddened
By a vague, terrifying, and relentless remorse,
Tremble in the forest: I am like a coward
Who fears an ambush or thinks he sees a corpse.

These huge branches, ever restless as the sea,
Whence dark silence falls with shadows yet
Darker: all this dim, sinister scenery
Fills me with horror at once trivial and profound.

The worst are summer evenings: the red of sunset
Dissolves into gray-blue mists, which it dyes
With fire and blood; the angelus, ringing far off,
Seems an approaching plaintive cry.

The wind rises, heavy and warm; a shiver passes
And repasses, ever increasing, in the denseness
Ever deepening of the tall oaks: it possesses
And is dispersed like a miasma into space.

Night comes, the owl takes flight. This is the moment
When old wives' tales throng into the mind . . .
Under a thicket, over there, over there, spring waters
Sound like waiting assassins plotting to strike.

MURIEL KITTEL

## MOONLIGHT

*Clair de lune*

Your soul is a landscape rare
Where masks and bergamasks charming pass,
Playing the lute and dancing, and almost
Sad beneath their fancy dress.

And while they sing on a minor note
Of conquering love and a favorable life,
They seem not to believe their happy lot,
And their song mingles with the soft moonlight.

With the calm moonlight, beautiful and sad,
That brings dreams to the birds in the trees
And sobs of ecstasy to the fountains,
To the tall fountains, slender among the statuary.

MURIEL KITTEL

## SENTIMENTAL DIALOGUE

*Colloque sentimental*

In the old park, frozen and deserted,
Two shapes have just slipped by.

Their eyes are dead and their lips are limp,
And their words can scarcely be heard.

In the old park, frozen and deserted,
Two wraiths have recalled the past.

"Do you remember our old delight?"
"Whyever should I remember it?"

"Does your heart still throb at my very name?
Do you still see my soul in your dreams?" "No."

"Ah, the fine days of unspeakable joy
When our lips met!" "Perhaps."

"How beautiful the sky was, how great our hope!"
"Hope has fled, defeated, to the dark sky."

They wandered on through the wild oats
And only the night listened to their words.

MURIEL KITTEL

## THE WHITE MOON

### *La Lune blanche*

The white moon
Gleams in the wood;
From every branch
There comes a voice
Beneath the bower . . .

O my love.

The pond reflects,
Shimmering mirror,
The silhouette
Of the dim willow
Where the wind laments . . .

Let us dream, it is the hour.

Vast and tender
An appeasement
Seems to lower
From the firmament
Star-bedecked . . .

Exquisite hour.

KATE FLORES

# THE NOISE OF THE CABARETS . . .

*Le bruit des cabarets . . .*

The noise of the cabarets, the muck of the sidewalks,
The shrunken plane-trees shedding their leaves in the foul
   air,
The omnibus, hurricane of junk-iron and mud,
That grates, badly seated on its four wheels,
And rolls its eyes slowly red and green,
The workers on their way to the club, puffing
Their stubby pipes at the noses of the police,
Leaky roofs, dripping walls, slippery cobblestones,
Worn-out pavements, gutters overflowing the sewers,
That's how my route lies—with paradise at the end.

KATE FLORES

## TEARS FLOW IN MY HEART . . .

*Il pleure dans mon cœur . . .*

*It rains softly on the town*
ARTHUR RIMBAUD

Tears flow in my heart
As rain falls on the town;
What languor is this
That creeps into my heart?

Gentle sound of the rain
On earth and roofs!
For an aching heart
Is the song of the rain!

Tears flow senseless
In this breaking heart.
With no betrayal?
This grief is senseless.

This is the worst sorrow
Not to know why,
Without love or hate,
My heart has all this sorrow.

MURIEL KITTEL

## OH SAD, SAD WAS MY SOUL . . .

*O triste, triste était mon âme . . .*

Oh sad, sad was my soul
Because, because of a woman.

I would not be comforted
Although my heart had fled,

Although my heart, although my soul
Had gone far from this woman.

I would not be comforted
Although my heart had fled.

And my heart, my too sensitive heart
Said to my soul: Is it possible,

Is it possible—could it be true—
This proud exile, this sad exile?

My soul said to my heart: Do I
Myself know the meaning of this snare

Of being here, although in exile,
In spite of fleeing far apart?

MURIEL KITTEL

## IN THE UNENDING TEDIUM . . .

*Dans l'interminable ennui . . .*

In the unending
Tedium of the plain
The uncertain snow
Gleams like sand.

The copper sky
Has no light at all,
You think you can see
The moon live and die.

Like clouds the oaks
Of nearby forests
Are gray, and float
Among the mists.

The copper sky
Has no light at all,
You think you can see
The moon live and die.

Broken-winded crow
And you, gaunt wolves,
What happens to you
In these harsh winds?

In the unending
Tedium of the plain
The indistinct snow
Gleams like sand.

MURIEL KITTEL

## GIVE EAR TO THE VERY FAINT SONG . . .

*Écoutez la chanson bien douce . . .*

Give ear to the very faint song
That weeps but for your delight.
It is discreet, it is light,
Moss a stream runs along!

The voice was familiar (and dear?)
To you, but now it is veiled,
Like a widow loss has paled,
And yet still proud, like her;

And in the long folds of her veil
That lifts in the Autumn wind
It hides and starlike shows to the stunned
Conscience truth like a grail.

It says, that voice in her womb,
That goodness is our life,
And that of envy, hate, and strife
Nothing remains, when death has come.

Then of the glory it sings
Of expecting nothing here,
And of gold nuptials, and the dear
Joy of a peace no victory brings.

The persistent voice bring to bed
In its simple marriage-call.
Come, nothing more profits the soul
Than to make a soul less sad!

It is "in travail" and "with young,"
The soul that suffers without rage,
And how clear is its moral and wage!
Give ear to the very wise song.

VERNON WATKINS

## AND I HAVE SEEN AGAIN THE MARVELOUS CHILD . . .

*Et j'ai revu l'enfant unique . . .*

And I have seen again the marvelous child: it seemed
Then opened in my heart the last wound of my grief,
That whose more tender pain assures me in belief
Of a dear death on some fair day that faith has dreamed.

The patient, pointed spire, and its firm, fresh relief!
In these rare, chosen moments they in me reclaimed
The heavy-lidded dreams of scruple dull and tamed,
And all my Christian blood sang the pure song made chief.

I hear again. I see again. Law of conformity
So sweet! At last I know what means to hear and see,
I hear, I see, always! Voice of dear thoughts at rest,

Innocence, future goodness! Silent, meek, and wise,
How I shall love you now, O you a moment pressed,
Beautiful little hands, hands that will close our eyes!

VERNON WATKINS

## GOD SAID . . .

### *Mon Dieu m'a dit . . .*

God said: "My son you must love me. You see
My pierced side, my heart radiant with blood,
And my injured feet bathed by Magdalene's tears,
My arms that ache under the weight of your

Sins, my hands too! You see the cross,
You see nails, gall, sponge, and all teach you
To love in this bitter world of flesh
Only my Flesh and Blood, my word and voice.

Oh, have I not loved you even unto death,
Brother in my Father, son in the Holy Ghost,
Have I not suffered for you as it was written?

Have I not sobbed for you in your great agony,
Have I not sweated the sweat of your dark nights,
Oh pitiful friend, who seeks me when I am here?"

MURIEL KITTEL

## A GREAT DARK SLEEP . . .

*Un grand sommeil noir . . .*

A great dark sleep
Has fallen on my life:
Sleep, all hope,
Sleep, all want!

I see nothing any more.
I have lost memory
Of good and of bad . . .
O the sad story!

I am a cradle
Rocked by a hand
In the hollow of a crypt:
Silence, silence!

KATE FLORES

## THE SKY ABOVE THE ROOF . . .

*Le ciel est, par-dessus le toit . . .*

The sky above the roof
  Is so blue, so calm!
A tree above the roof
  Sways its fronds.

The bell in the sky we see
  Softly chimes.
A bird in the tree we see
  Sings its lament.

Dear God, dear God, life is there,
  Simple and still.
That peaceful murmur there
  Comes from the town.

What have you done, you who are here
    Weeping endlessly?
Oh, what have you done, you who are here,
    With the days of your youth?

                                MURIEL KITTEL


## I KNOW NOT WHY . . .

*Je ne sais pourquoi . . .*


    I know not why
    My bitter spirit
With wild and restless wing flies over the sea.
    All I hold dear,
    With wing of fear
My love broods over on the waters. Why, oh why?

Seagull of melancholy flight,
My thought follows the waves,
Swayed by all the winds of heaven
And shifting with the turn of the tide,
Seagull of melancholy flight.

    Drunk with sunshine
    And with freedom,
Some instinct guides it across this immensity.
    The summer breeze
    On the vermilion wave
Carries it gently in a warm half-sleep.

At times it utters so sad a cry
That the far-off pilot is perturbed,
Then abandoning itself to the wind's will
It glides, and dives, and with battered wing
Soars again, and again so sadly cries.

I know not why
My bitter spirit
With wild and restless wing flies over the sea.
All I hold dear,
With wing of fear
My love broods over on the waters. Why, oh why?

MURIEL KITTEL

## THE ART OF POETRY

*Art poétique*

*To Charles Morice*

Music must be paramount:
Choose for this an Uneven Rhythm,
More indefinite, more soluble in air,
With nothing to press or bind.

You must not hesitate to choose
Your words without ambiguity:
The best song is a hazy song
Where Vagueness and Precision join.

There, are eyes beautiful and veiled,
And the quivering light of high noon,
There, in a cooled autumnal sky,
Is a blue confusion of bright stars.

For we must have Nuance still,
Not Color—nothing but nuance!
Ah! only nuance can betroth
Dream to dream and flute to horn!

Flee far as possible from deadly Jest,
From cruel Wit and impure Laughter,
That make the eyes of Heaven weep—
Avoid this garlic of low-class kitchens!

Take eloquence and wring its neck!
And while you are in the mood, try
To moderate Rhyme a little more.
If you don't, what limit will it reach?

Who can tell the wrongs that Rhyme has done?
What deaf child or crazy Negro
Fashioned us this bauble from a coin
That rings false and hollow under the file?

Music, always more music!
Let your verse be the winged thing
We feel soaring from a soul on its way
To other loves in other heavens.

Let your verse be a good-luck charm
Scattered on the brisk morning wind
That passes smelling of mint and thyme. . . .
And everything else is mere literature.

MURIEL KITTEL


APATHY

*Langueur*

I am the Empire at the end of its decadence
Watching the tall, fair Barbarians pass,
Meanwhile, I compose idle acrostics
In a golden style where the sun's languors dance.

Intense boredom sickens a soul alone.
Over there, I hear, a long bloody battle rages.
Feeble with too slow desire, there is no power,
There is no will to make this existence flower.

There is no will, no power even to die a little.
Ah, all is drunk, Bathyllus—do you laugh still?
All, all is drunk, all eaten! No more to tell.

Nothing but a stupid poem to throw on the fire,
Nothing but a faithless slave to neglect you,
Nothing but a nameless boredom to afflict you.

MURIEL KITTEL

# *Arthur Rimbaud*

## 1854—1891

# ARTHUR RIMBAUD
## 1854–1891

An extraordinarily precocious genius, Rimbaud completed his career as a poet of striking originality, virtuosity, and influence by the time he was nineteen.

After an apprenticeship involving poetry of revolt, together with some realistically descriptive verse, Rimbaud began upon the task outlined in his famous *Lettres du voyant:* he would be a seer, finding a language capable of translating the absolute. Taking to be sacred the disorder of his own soul, he would comprehend directly his own interior experience, bypassing all the usual categories, exploring with utmost immediacy and without reflection the violent forces he sensed within himself. Thus far poetry had been mere rhymed prose: Rimbaud would write from the soul to the soul, on a plane superior to that of the senses. *The Bateau ivre, The Illuminations,* are among the fruits of this terrifying investigation, and indeed in the striking brilliance and nakedness of his language and his images, Rimbaud comes close to accomplishing his stated intentions. Finally there is *A Season in Hell,* expressing his disillusion as a poet and acknowledging the ultimate impossibility of his quest, and his return from it.

Rimbaud broke with Verlaine shortly before finishing *A Season in Hell* and was henceforth to be a wanderer, on a wild odyssey which was to bring him back to France from time to time, but at ever longer intervals. Teaching at moments, working for a circus, traveling often on foot, he crossed and recrossed Europe, went briefly to the Far East, returned, and finally went to Africa as agent for a coffee merchant, dealer in arms, and explorer of some renown. After a decade there he returned to France to die.

# OPHELIA

*Ophélie*

### I

On the calm black wave where the stars sleep
Floats white Ophelia like a great lily,
Floats very slowly, lying in her long veils . . .
—From the distant woods, the flourish of the kill.

For more than a thousand years sad Ophelia
White phantom, passes, on the long black river.
For more than a thousand years her sweet obsession
Whispers her love to the evening breeze.

The wind embraces her breasts and unfolds her great veils
In a corolla gently rocked by the waters;
Trembling willows weep on her shoulder,
Reeds lean on her lofty pensive brow.

Bruised water lilies sigh about her;
Sometimes in a sleeping alder tree she awakens
A nest; a tiny wing-flutter escapes;
Mysterious sounds fall from the golden stars.

### II

O pale Ophelia! fair as snow!
You died, child, yes, carried off by a river!
Because the winds falling from the great cliffs of Norway
Spoke low to you of fierce freedom;

Because a wind, tearing your long hair,
Bore strange shouts to your dreaming spirit;
Because your heart listened to the strains of Nature
In the wails of the tree and the sighs of the nights.

Because the voice of mad seas, immense rattle,
Bruised your child's heart, too sweet and too human;
Because on an April morning, a handsome pale courtier,
A sorry fool, sat mutely at your feet!

Heaven! Love! Freedom! What a dream, O Foolish girl!
You melted toward him as snow near flame:
Your words were strangled by your great visions
—And the terrible Infinite frightened your blue eyes!

III

And the Poet says you come at night
To gather flowers in the rays of the stars;
And he has seen on the water, lying in her long veils,
White Ophelia floating, like a great lily.

DAISY ALDAN

## MY BOHEMIA

*Ma Bohème*

Fists in torn pockets I departed.
My overcoat grew ideal too.
I walked, your knight, O Muse,
And dreamed, O my! what glorious loves.

My only trousers had a hole.
Little Tom Thumb, I dropped my dreaming rhymes.
My lodging was the Great Bear Inn,
And in the sky my stars were rustling.

I listened, seated by the road—
In soft September—where the dew
Was wine of vigor on my face;

And in weird shadows rhyming, plucked like lyres,
The laces of my martyred shoes,
One foot against my heart.

LOUISE VARÈSE

## POETS SEVEN YEARS OLD

*Les Poètes de sept ans*

And the Mother, closing the exercise book,
Went off satisfied and very proud, not seeing
In the blue eyes and beneath the bumpy forehead
That her child's soul was filled with revulsions.

All day he sweated obedience; very
Intelligent; but certain nasty habits, several traits,
Seemed to show bitter hypocrisies in him.
Passing through dark halls with musty drapes
He would stick out his tongue, his two fists
In his groin, and in his closed eyes see dots.
A door would be open to evening; by lamplight
He could be seen upstairs sulking on the banister
Beneath a gulf of day which hung from the roof. In summer
Above all, vanquished, stupid, he would stubbornly
Lock himself up in the coolness of latrines.
He would think there, tranquil, dilating his nostrils.

When in winter the little garden behind the house,
Washed of the smells of the day, became immooned,
He, stretched out at the foot of a wall, buried in the mud
And pressing his eye flat so as to have visions,
Would listen to the swarming of the scaly trellises.
As for pity! his only intimates were those children—
Feeble, with blank foreheads, eyes fading on their cheeks,
Hiding thin fingers yellow and black with mud
Under clothes stinking of diarrhea and all shabby—
Who conversed with the gentleness of idiots;
And if having discovered him at such filthy pities
His mother became frightened, the deep tenderness
Of the child would overwhelm her surprise.
It was good. She would have the blue look—that lies!

At seven he was writing novels about life
In the great desert where ecstatic Liberty shines,
Forests, suns, banks, savannas! He was aided
By illustrated papers in which, blushing, he looked
At Spanish and Italian women laughing.
When, brown-eyed, mad, in printed cotton dresses
—Aged eight—the daughter of the workers next door,
Had come, the little brute, and when she had jumped
On his back in a corner, shaking her braids,
And he was underneath her, he would bite her buttocks
(For she never wore panties)
And then bruised by her fists and by her heels
He would take the savors of her skin back to his room.

He dreaded the pale Sundays of December
When, all spruced up, at a little round mahogany table
He would read a Bible edged in cabbage-green.
Dreams oppressed him each night in the alcove.
He loved, not God, but the men whom in the russet
    evening,
Dark, in blouses, he would see returning to the suburbs
Where the criers with three rollings of the drum
Make the crowds laugh and groan at proclamations.
He could yearn for the amorous meadow, where luminous
Billows, healthy perfumes, golden pubescences
Make their calm movement and take their flight;

And as he delighted most in somber things,
When, in the bare room with closed shutters,
High and blue, filled with an acrid dampness,
He would read his novel, which he always thought about,
Full of heavy clayey skies and drowned forests,
Of flesh-flowers opened in the depths of celestial woods—
Dizziness, failings, routs, and pity!—
While the din of the neighborhood sounded
Below, alone, lying on pieces of unbleached
Canvas, with a violent premonition of sails! . . .

KENNETH KOCH AND GEORGES GUY

## THE LICE SEEKERS

*Les Chercheuses de poux*

When the child's forehead full of red torments
Begs for the white swarm of indistinct dreams
There come close to his bed two big charming sisters
With frail fingers and silver nails.

They seat the child next to a window
Wide open, where blue air bathes a confusion of flowers
And in his heavy hair where the dew falls
Promenade their delicate fingers, terrible and enchanting.

He hears the singing of their timorous breath
Which bears the scent of long vegetable and rosy honeys
And which a whistling interrupts now and then, salivas
Taken back from the lip or desires for kisses.

He hears their black eyelashes beating beneath perfumed
Silences; and their fingers electric and sweet
Make crackle among his hazy indolences
Beneath their royal fingernails the death of little lice.

Now there is mounting in him the wine of Laziness,
Harmonica's sigh which could be delirious;
The child feels, according to the slowness of the caresses,
Spring up and die unceasingly a wish to cry.

KENNETH KOCH AND GEORGES GUY

## THE DRUNKEN BOAT

*Le Bateau ivre*

As I descended black, impassive Rivers,
I sensed that haulers were no longer guiding me:
Screaming Redskins took them for their targets,
Nailed nude to colored stakes: barbaric trees.

I was indifferent to all my crews;
I carried English cottons, Flemish wheat.
When the disturbing din of haulers ceased,
The Rivers let me ramble where I willed.

Through the furious ripping of the sea's mad tides,
Last winter, deafer than an infant's mind,
I ran! And drifting, green Peninsulas
Did not know roar more gleefully unkind.

A tempest blessed my vigils on the sea.
Lighter than a cork I danced on the waves,
Those endless rollers, as they say, of graves:
Ten nights beyond a lantern's silly eye!

Sweeter than sourest apple-flesh to children,
Green water seeped into my pine-wood hull
And washed away blue wine stains, vomitings,
Scattering rudder, anchor, man's lost rule.

And then I, trembling, plunged into the Poem
Of the Sea, infused with stars, milk-white,
Devouring azure greens; where remnants, pale
And gnawed, of pensive corpses fell from light;

Where, staining suddenly the blueness, delirium,
The slow rhythms of the pulsing glow of day,
Stronger than alcohol and vaster than our lyres,
The bitter reds of love ferment the way!

I know skies splitting into light, whirled spouts
Of water, surfs, and currents: I know the night,
The dawn exalted like a flock of doves, pure wing,
And I have seen what men imagine they have seen.

I saw the low sun stained with mystic horrors,
Lighting long, curdled clouds of violet,
Like actors in a very ancient play,
Waves rolling distant thrills like lattice light!

I dreamed of green night, stirred by dazzling snows,
Of kisses rising to the sea's eyes, slowly,
The sap-like coursing of surprising currents,
And singing phosphors, flaring blue and gold!

I followed, for whole months, a surge like herds
Of insane cattle in assault on the reefs,
Unhopeful that three Marys, come on luminous feet,
Could force a muzzle on the panting seas!

Yes, I struck incredible Floridas
That mingled flowers and the eyes of panthers
In skins of men! And rainbows bridled green
Herds beneath the horizon of the seas.

I saw the ferment of enormous marshes, weirs
Where a whole Leviathan lies rotting in the weeds!
Collapse of waters within calms at sea,
And distances in cataract toward chasms!

Glaciers, silver suns, pearl waves, and skies like coals,
Hideous wrecks at the bottom of brown gulfs
Where giant serpents eaten by red bugs
Drop from twisted trees and shed a black perfume!

I should have liked to show the young those dolphins
In blue waves, those golden fish, those fish that sing.
—Foam like flowers rocked my sleepy drifting,
And, now and then, fine winds supplied me wings.

When, feeling like a martyr, I tired of poles and zones,
The sea, whose sobbing made my tossing sweet,
Raised me its dark flowers, deep and yellow whirled,
And, like a woman, I fell on my knees . . .

Peninsula, I tossed upon my shores
The quarrels and droppings of clamorous, blond-eyed birds.
I sailed until, across my rotting cords,
Drowned men, spinning backwards, fell asleep! . . .

Now I, a lost boat in the hair of coves,
Hurled by tempest into a birdless air,
I, whose drunken carcass neither Monitors
Nor Hansa ships would fish back for men's care;

Free, smoking, rigged with violet fogs,
I, who pierced the red sky like a wall
That carries exquisite mixtures for good poets,
Lichens of sun and azure mucus veils;

Who, spotted with electric crescents, ran
Like a mad plank, escorted by seahorses,
When cudgel blows of hot Julys struck down
The sea-blue skies upon wild water spouts;

I, who trembled, feeling the moan at fifty leagues
Of rutting Behemoths and thick Maelstroms, I,
Eternal weaver of blue immobilities,
I long for Europe with its ancient quays!

I saw sidereal archipelagoes! and isles
Whose delirious skies are open to the voyager:
—Is it in depthless nights you sleep your exile,
A million golden birds, O future Vigor?—

But, truly, I have wept too much! The dawns disturb.
All moons are painful, and all suns break bitterly:
Love has swollen me with drunken torpors.
Oh, that my keel might break and spend me in the sea!

Of European waters I desire
Only the black, cold puddle in a scented twilight
Where a child of sorrows squats and sets the sails
Of a boat as frail as a butterfly in May.

I can no longer, bathed in languors, O waves,
Cross the wake of cotton-bearers on long trips,
Nor ramble in a pride of flags and flares,
Nor swim beneath the horrible eyes of prison ships.

STEPHEN STEPANCHEV

## VOWELS

*Voyelles*

A black, E white, I red, U green, O blue;
Someday I'll tell your latent birth O vowels:
A, a black corset hairy with gaudy flies
That bumble round all stinking putrefactions,

Gulfs of darkness; E, candors of steam and tents,
Icicles' proud spears, white kings, and flutter of parasols;
I, purple blood coughed up, laughter of lovely lips
In anger or ecstatic penitence;

U, cycles, divine vibrations of virescent seas,
Peace of the pastures sown with animals, peace
Of the wrinkles that alchemy stamps on studious brows;

O, Clarion supreme, full of strange stridences,
Silences crossed by Angels and Worlds:
—Omega, the violet ray of His Eyes!

LOUISE VARÈSE

## MEMORY

*Mémoire*

I

Clear water; like the salt of childhood's tears,
whiteness of women's bodies assaulted in the sun;
silk, in mass and lily pure, of oriflammes
under the walls some Maid had defended

frolic of angels. —No . . . the marching current of gold
moves black arms, heavy and supremely cool with grass.
She, dark, with blue Heaven for bed canopy, summons
the shadow of the hill and of the arch for curtains.

II

Eh! the wet pane holding out its limpid bubbles!
With bottomless pale gold the water clothes the waiting
    beds.
And out of the willows—faded green pinafores.
of little girls—hop the unbridled birds.

Yellower than a louis, eyelid warm and pure,
the watchful marigold—your conjugal pledge, O Spouse!
at prompt midday from its tarnished mirror envies,
in the gray-hot sky, the pink and precious Sphere.

III

Madam standing in the meadow too erect,
where snow the sons of toil; poking with sun umbrella
the umbels of the flowers too proud for her;
her children with their book of red morocco

reading in the flowering grass! But He, alas,
like a thousand angels separating on the road,
goes off across the mountain! While She,
all black and cold, hurries after the man's departure!

IV

Regret for arms with pure grass strong and young!
April moons in the heart of the holy bed! Joy
of abandoned lumber yards along the river, prey
to August dusks that made putrescence germinate!

Let her weep now below the ramparts; above,
the poplars' breath is only for the breeze.
Then the gray sheet without reflections or spring
where, in his motionless barge, an old man dredges.

V

Sport of this sad water eye, I cannot reach,
O boat immovable! O arms too short! either this
or the other flower; neither the yellow importuning me,
nor the blue one, friend of the ashy water.

Ah, the powder of the willows that a wing shakes!
The roses of the reeds devoured long ago!
My boat stuck fast; and its chain that drags
On the bottom of this rimless eye . . . in what mud!

LOUISE VARÈSE

## WHAT TO US, MY HEART . . .

*Qu'est-ce pour nous, mon cœur . . .*

What to us, my heart, are the pools of blood,
Embers, and the thousand murders, and the endless cries
Of rage, sobs of all hell overthrowing
All order; and Aquilon still on the ruins;

And all vengeance? Nothing! . . . —Yes, everything,
It's what we're after! Industrialists, princes, senates:
Perish! Down with history, justice, power!
It is our right. Blood! Blood! the golden flame!

All for war, vengeance, and terror.
My spirit! Turn in the wound: Ah! away,
Republics of this world! Emperors,
Regiments, colonizers, peoples: enough!

Who should stir up the blasts of furious fire
But we and those who we imagine are our brothers?
Come, fantastic friends: we're going to like it.
Never will we work, O floods of fire!

Vanish, Europe, Asia, and America.
Our youthful march has overridden everything,
Cities and country! —We shall be crushed!
Volcanoes will explode! And ocean struck . . .

O my friends! O heart, it's sure, they are my brothers!
Black strangers, if we should go? Let's go! Let's go!
Horror! I feel myself trembling, old earth
On me, yours more than ever! The earth melts.

*It is nothing: I am here; I am still here.*

LOUISE VARÈSE

## MICHAEL AND CHRISTINE

*Michel et Christine*

Blast! if the sun desert these shores!
Bright deluge, flee! Look, how the roads darken.
And in the willows and ancient entrance court,
The first big drops fall of the storm.

Blond soldiers of the idyll, O hundred lambs,
From aqueducts and scanty heather,
Away! Horizons, prairies, plains, and heaths
Assist at the red toilet of the storm!

Black shepherd dog and shepherd brown, with billowing
    cloak
Flee from the lightning of the heights,
And when you see the darkness and the sulphur melt,
Seek refuges more sure, white flock, below.

But I, O Lord, see how my spirit soars
Toward the red-iced skies, beneath
Celestial clouds that race and fly
Over a hundred Solognes, long as a railway.

Lo, a thousand wolves and a thousand seeds
Borne by this holy afternoon of storm
(Not without love of the convolvulus)
Over old Europe where a hundred hordes will swarm!

Afterwards, the moonlight! And throughout the land
Warriors on pale chargers slowly ride,
With ruddy faces turned toward the dark skies!
While under the proud band the stones resound!

And shall I see the yellow wood and the bright vale,
Bride with blue eyes and red-faced man, O Gaul!
And white at their feet the Paschal Lamb,
Michael and Christine—and Christ—the idyll's end.

LOUISE VARÈSE

## TEARDROP*

### Larme

Far away from the birds, the flocks, and the girls of the
    village,
Knee-deep in some kind of country heather, I drank,
Surrounded by saplings of a hazelnut wood,
In the haze of an afternoon, warming and green.

What could I have drunk in this young river Oise?
Elms without voice, lawns without flower, lowering sky.
What could I sip from the calabash flask?
Some drop of gold liquor, bland and making one sweat.

* Larme, meaning tear, also means colloquially a drop to drink.
—Translator's Note.

Such as had made me a dreadful sign for a tavern.
Then the storm was changing the skies, till evening came
    on.
It was out of the black country, country of lakes, and of
    poles,
Of colonnades under the blue night, and of mooring-places.

The waters of the woodland sank in the virgin sands.
A gust, God-sent, flung icicles into the swamps . . .
Gold! as if a digger of gold or of mollusks,
To say that I had no need of a drink!

CLAIRE MCALLISTER

## SONG OF THE HIGHEST TOWER

*Chanson de la plus haute tour*

Idle youth
By all availed,
Through delicacy
My life has failed.
Ah! for the time
When hearts entwine.

I told myself: leave,
Let them see you no more:
Nor with the promise
Of higher reward.
Let none impede
Your austere retreat.

I have had patience
Unto forgetting;
Dread and torment
To the heavens are fled,
And thirstings vile
My veins defile.

So does the prairie
Given no heed
Flourish, and blossom
With darnel and weed
To the insensate tone
Of filthy-mouthed drone.

Ah! thousand widowhoods
Of poor soul bereft
Of all but the image
Of Our Lady blessed!
Is it this way
To the Virgin one prays?

Idle youth
By all availed,
Through delicacy
My life has failed.
Ah! for the time
When hearts entwine!

KATE FLORES

ETERNITY

*L'Éternite*

I have recovered it.
What? Eternity.
It is the sea
Matched with the sun.

My sentinel soul,
Let us murmur the vow
Of the night so void
And of the fiery day.

Of human sanctions,
Of common transports,
You free yourself:
You soar according . . .

From your ardor alone,
Embers of satin,
Duty exhales,
Without any one saying: at last.

Never a hope;
No genesis.
Skill with patience . . .
Anguish is certain.

I have recovered it.
What? Eternity.
It is the sea
Matched with the sun.

FRANCIS GOLFFING

## YOUNG COUPLE

*Jeune Ménage*

The room is open to the turquoise sky;
No place at all: coffers and hutches!
And the birthwort on the wall outside
Is all aquiver with hobgoblin gums.

Intrigues of jinn for sure,
This vain disorder and expense!
It's the African fairy who supplies
Mulberry, and cobwebs in the corners.

They enter, godmothers in a huff
In shafts of light on the buffets,
Then stay! And the couple rushes out
Quite scatterbrained, and nothing done.

The bridegroom, like the wind, which
In his absence robs him.
Even the evil water sprites come in,
Roaming around the alcove's province.

At night their friend, Oh the honeymoon!
Will cull their smile and fill
With a thousand copper bands the sky.
There's the sly rat to cope with too.

If only no *ignis fatuus* darts in,
Like the shot of a gun after vespers!
—O holy white Ghosts of Bethlehem
Charm the blue of their window instead!

LOUISE VARÈSE

## BRUSSELS

### *Bruxelles*

*July*                    *Boulevard du Regent*

Amaranthine flower beds stretching to
Jupiter's agreeable palace.
I know it's You, mingling here
Your almost Sahara Blue!

And how enclosed the play
Of the sun's vines and pines and roses,
Cage of the little widow! . . .
                              Listen
What troups of birds, pia, pio, piay! . . .

Mansions calm and ancient passions!
Kiosk of the Madwoman through affection.
And beyond the buttocks of the roses,
Juliet's balcony, shadowy and low.

La Juliette, and we remember Henriette,
O what a charming railway station,
As in an orchard's depth, deep in the mountain,
Where blue devils by the thousand dance in the air.

Green bench where the white Irishwoman sings
To the paradise of storm on her guitar,
And from the dining room Guianan,
Cackling of children and of cages.

The ducal window that makes you think
Of snail's poison and of boxwood
Asleep down here in the sun.
                              But then
It's too too beautiful! Let's be still.

—Boulevard without traffic or trade,
Silent, all drama and comedy too,
Reunion of endless scenes,
I know you and gaze at you in wonder.

LOUISE  VARÈSE

## SHAME

*Honte*

As long as the blade has never
Yet pierced this brain,
This fat and green-white package
Of stagnant vapors,

(Ah! But he ought to cut his lips
His ears, his nose off,
His belly too! and sacrifice—
O marvelous!—both legs!)

But no, I really think
Till over his head the blade,
Over his flank the stones,
Over his gut the flame,

Have not triumphed,
The troublesome child, the feeble fool,
Will not for an instant
Cease his tricks,

And like the Rocky Mountain lion
Will leave his stench behind.
But grant, O God, that when he dies
One prayer should rise!

LOUISE VARÈSE

# A SEASON IN HELL

## Une Saison en Enfer

### ONCE LONG AGO . . .

#### Jadis . . .

Once, long ago—if I remember rightly—my life was a sumptuous feast, where all hearts opened and all wines flowed.

One night, I set Beauty on my lap. —And found her bitter. —And reviled her.

I rebelled against justice.

I fled. Oh witches, oh misery and hatred, *you* have been the guardians of my treasure.

At last I banished all human hope from my mind. Upon each joy, to strangle it, I made the soundless spring of a wild beast. I summoned the executioners so that, dying, I might bite the butts of their guns. I summoned the scourges to choke me with blood and sand. Misfortune was my god. I sprawled in the mire. I dried myself off in the crime-filled air. And I played some fine tricks on madness.

Then spring brought me the idiot's frightful laugh.

Of late, however, since I nearly squawked my last, I have again toyed with the idea of seeking the key to the bygone feast, where perhaps I might revive my appetite.

Charity is the key! —An inspiration which proves I have been dreaming!

"You shall remain a hyena, etc.," shrieks the demon who crowned me with such amiable poppies. "Earn death with all your appetites, and your selfishness and all the capital sins."

Ah! I've had too much already: —But dear Satan, I implore you, don't scowl at me so! And while awaiting my few little misdeeds in arrears, you who love in writers the absence of descriptive or edifying talents, I shall detach for you these sparse hideous pages from my notebook of the damned.

WILLIAM M. DAVIS

## ILL WILL

*Mauvais sang*

. . . . . . . . . . . . . . . . . . . . . . . . . . . . . . . . . . . . . . . . . . . . . . . . .

I await God greedily. . . . Now I am accursed, I detest my country. The best thing is to sleep, dead drunk, on the beach.

. . . . . . . . . . . . . . . . . . . . . . . . . . . . . . . . . . . . . . . . . . . . . . . . .

As a child, I admired the intractable convict who is always being sent behind bars; I would visit the inns and lodgings he might have hallowed with his presence; I saw *with his eyes* the blue sky and the flourishing toil of the countryside; I hounded his destiny into the cities. He had more strength than a saint, more good sense than a traveler —and himself, himself alone! as witness to his glory and his right.

As I trudged along the highways on winter nights, without shelter, clothes, or food, a voice tugged at my frozen heart: "Weakness or strength: there you have it, strength. You know not where you are going nor why, you enter everywhere, and answer everything. No one will kill you any more than if you were a corpse." In the morning I looked so lost and woebegone that those I met *perhaps did not see me.*

In the cities the mud looked suddenly red and black, like a mirror when the lamp shifts in the next room, like a treasure in the forest! Here's to luck, I cried, and saw a sea of flame and smoke up in the sky; and right and left, all kinds of riches flashing like a billion thunderbolts.

But to me the orgies and comradery of women were forbidden. Not even a companion. I saw myself before an exasperated mob, facing the firing squad, weeping over a misfortune they could never understand, and forgiving! —Like Joan of Arc! —"Priests, instructors, schoolmasters, you are wrong to hand me over to justice. I have never belonged to these people; I have never been a Christian; I belong to the race that sang under torture; I do not understand laws; I have no moral sense; I am a brute: you are mistaken . . ."

Yes, my eyes were shut in your light. I am a beast, a Negro. But I can be saved. You, maniacs, butchers, misers,

you are false Negroes. Merchant, you're a Negro; judge, you're a Negro; general, you're a Negro; emperor, you scabby old itch, you're a Negro: you have drunk contraband liquor from Satan's workshop. —This people is inspired by fever and cancer. Cripples and old men are so respectable that they ask to be boiled.—The smartest thing to do is to leave this continent, where madness prowls in search of hostages for these wretches. I enter the true kingdom of the sons of Ham.

Do I still know nature? Do I know myself? —*Speak no more.* I bury the dead in my guts. Shouts, drum, dance, dance, dance, dance! I do not even see the time when, as the white men disembark, I shall fall into nothingness.

Hunger, thirst, shouts, dance, dance, dance, dance!

WILLIAM M. DAVIS

## THE ALCHEMY OF WORDS

### Alchimie du verbe

Listen. The tale of one of my follies.

For a long time I had boasted my mastery of all possible landscapes, and I found ridiculous the celebrities of modern painting and poetry.

I loved absurd paintings, overdoors, décors, side-show backdrops, signboards, popular prints; outmoded literature, church Latin, misspelled erotic books, romances of the days of our grandmothers, fairy tales, little books for children, old operas, childish ditties, naïve rhythms.

I dreamed of crusades, voyages of discovery of which there are no accounts, republics without histories, hushed-up religious wars, revolutions in customs, displacements of races and of continents: I believed in all enchantments.

I invented the colors of the vowels! A black, E white, I red, O blue, U green. I settled the form and the movement of each consonant and, with instinctive rhythms, I flattered myself that I was inventing a poetic language ac-

cessible, one day or another, to all of the senses. I kept back the translation.

In the beginning it was an experiment. I wrote silences, nights, I noted down the inexpressible. I crystallized vertigo.

. . . The bric-a-brac of poetry played a considerable part in my alchemy of words.

I got used to plain hallucination: I saw quite clearly a mosque in place of a factory, a school of drums made by angels, tilburies on the highways of the sky; a parlor at the bottom of a lake; monsters; mysteries; the title of a music-hall comedy raised up horrors before me.

Then I explained the magic of my sophistries by means of the hallucination of words!

I ended by deeming sacred the disorder of my spirit. I was idle, prey to high fever! I envied the beasts their happiness—caterpillars, which symbolize the innocence of limbo; moles, the sleep of virginity!

I became embittered. I bade farewell to society in something like ballads.

. . . . . . . . . . . . . . . . . . . . . . . . . . . . . . . . . . . . . . . . . . . . . . . . .

I became a fabulous opera: I saw that all creatures are destined to a certain contentment: action is not life, but a means of wasting strength, an enervation. Morality is the softening of the brain. It seemed to me that to each creature several *other* lives belonged. This gentleman does not know what he is doing—he is an angel. That family is a litter of pups. With several men I have conversed with a moment from one of their other lives.

"And so . . . I have loved a pig."

None of the sophistries of madness—the madness locked within—have I forgot; I could recite them all, I know the system.

My health was endangered. Terror came. I fell asleep for several days at a stretch and, risen, continued the most depressing dreams. I was ripe for death, and along a highway of danger my weakness led me to the ends of the earth and of Chimmeria, the land of shadow and whirlwinds.

I had to travel, and seek distraction from the spells gathered in my brain. At sea, which I loved as though it should

cleanse me of a stain, I watched the rise of the consoling cross. I had been damned by the rainbows. Happiness was my doom, my remorse, my worm: my life would always be too vast to be given up to strength and beauty.

Happiness! Her tooth, sweet unto death, would warn me at cockcrow—*ad matutinum*, at the *Christus venit*—in the most dismal cities:

> Oh seasons, oh castles!
> What soul is flawless?
>
> I have made the magic study
> Of happiness, that none evades.
>
> Hail to it, each time
> The gallic rooster crows.
>
> Ah! I'll have no cares:
> It manages my life.
>
> This spell, now flesh and soul
> Has put an end to toil.
>
> Oh seasons, oh castles!
>
> Its hour of flight, alas!
> Will be the hour of death.

That is over. Now I know how to greet beauty.

BERT M-P. LEEFMANS—WILLIAM M. DAVIS

## MORNING

*Matin*

. . . . . . . . . . . . . . . . . . . . . . . . . . . . . . . . . . . . . . . . . . . . . . . .

Yet now I think I have finished the tale of my inferno. And inferno it was: the old one, whose gates the Son of Man flung open.

From the same desert, on the same night, my eyes still awake to the silvery star, still, as the Kings of life, the Three Magi, heart, soul, and mind sleep untroubled. When shall we go beyond shores and mountains, to greet the birth of new labors, the new wisdom, the putting to flight of tyrants and demons, the end of superstition, and worship —the very first! —Noel on earth.

The song of the skies, the march of peoples! Slaves, let us not curse life.

WILLIAM M. DAVIS

## ILLUMINATIONS

*Les Illuminations*

### BALLY

*Parade*

Very solid rascals. Several have exploited your worlds. Without needs, and in no great hurry to bring to bear their brilliant abilities and their experience of your consciences. What mature men! Eyes dazed after the manner of the summer night, red and black, tricolored, of steel pricked with golden stars; deformed physiognomies, leaden, blanched, burnt-out; frolicsome hoarsenesses. The cruel gait of tinsel fineries! —There are some young ones—how would they look upon Cherubino?—provided with frightful voices and certain dangerous resources. They are sent into town to gain experience, rigged up with a disgusting *luxury*.

Oh most violent Paradise of the frenzied grimace! Your Fakirs and other scenic buffooneries are not to be compared. In improvised costumes, in the style of a bad dream, they play laments, tragedies of brigands and of demigods witty as history or religions have never been. Chinamen, Hottentots, gypsies, simpletons, hyenas, Molochs, old lunacies, sinister demons, they mingle popular, maternal stunts with bestial poses and caresses. They would interpret new plays and simple-minded ballads. Master jugglers, they transform place and persons and make use of magnetic comedy. The eyes blaze, the blood sings, the bones expand, there is trickling of tears and red filaments. Their banter, their terror lasts a minute, or months on end.

I alone hold the key to this savage ballyhoo.°

FREDERICK MORGAN

## ANTIQUE
### Antique

Graceful son of Pan! About your forehead, crowned with flowerets and berries, your eyes, precious balls, are in motion. Stained with brown sediment, your cheeks deepen in hollows. Your fangs flash. Your chest is like a zither, your blond arms are astir with tinklings. Your heart is beating in that belly where the double sex sleeps. Walk out at night, softly moving that thigh, that second thigh, and that left leg.

FREDERICK MORGAN

° The French word, *parade*, as used in this poem, refers to the little free show given *outside* a tent or booth at a fair or carnival, to induce the public to pay their money and go in. "Bally"— short for "ballyhoo"—is the term used in American circus and carnival talk (this word was originally derived from, or associated with, *Ballyhooly*, a village in County Cork, Ireland).— *Translator's Note.*

## BEING BEAUTEOUS

### Being Beauteous

Standing against the snow, a tall Being of beauty. Rattlings of death and rings of muted music make her adorable body rise, expand, and tremble like a ghost. Scarlet and black wounds burst on the proud flesh. Life's own colors darken, dance, and separate to cluster about the Vision in the market place. Shudders rise and scorn the violent taste of these effects, mingling with the death rattles and raucous music which the world, far behind us, hurls at our mother of beauty—— She draws back, she stands erect. Oh, our bones have put on a new amorous body!

Oh, the ash-colored face, the horsehair escutcheon, the crystal arms! And the cannon I must fall on, in the battle of trees and light air!

ANGEL FLORES

## LIVES

### Vies

I

Oh the enormous avenues of the holy land, the terraces of the temple! What has become of the Brahmin who once taught me Proverbs? Now, further down, I can still see even old women! I recall the silver hours, and sun by the rivers, and my girl's hand on my shoulders, and our caresses as we stood in the peppered heath. A flight of scarlet pigeons thundered in my brain. —Exiled here, I had a stage on which I performed the masterpieces of literatures the world over. I might point out to you incredible riches. I have been following up the history of treasures you might find—and I know what is next! My wisdom is rejected as chaos. What is my void when compared to the surprise awaiting you?

## II

I am an inventor far more deserving of attention than all those who have preceded me; a musician who has moreover discovered something like the key of love. Now a country squire from a lean land with a tranquil sky, I endeavor to throw off lethargy by remembering my mendicant childhood, my years of apprenticeship or my arrival in wooden shoes, my polemics, my five or six widowings, and a few carousals when my level head kept me from emulating my comrades' folly. I do not miss my former share of divine gaiety. The quietude of this harsh countryside feeds my dreadful skepticism rather bountifully. But since this skepticism can no longer be put to use, and since, furthermore, I have devoted myself to a new anxiety, I believe I shall end up as a very dangerous madman.

## III

In an attic where I was locked up when I was twelve I got to know the world—I illustrated the human comedy. In a gin mill I learned history. At some night revel, in a northern city, I met all the women of the Old Masters. In an old Paris arcade I was taught the classical sciences. In a magnificent mansion, reeking with oriental luxury, I completed my exhaustive tasks and spent my luxurious retreat. I have burned up my blood. My duty has been remitted to me. But that need no longer even concern us. I am really from beyond the grave, and accept no new commitments.

ANGEL FLORES

## DEPARTURE

### Départ

Enough seen. The vision has been met in all guises.

Enough heard. Clamor of the towns at night, in the sunlight, at all times.

Enough known. Life's awards. —O Sounds and Visions! Departure in new sympathy amid new sounds.

FRANCIS GOLFFING

## ROYALTY

### Royauté

One fine morning, in a land full of mild-mannered folk, a man and woman, majestic in their bearing, stood on the public square. The man said, "Friends, I want her to be queen!" And the woman said, "I want to be queen!" She laughed and trembled. And the man told his friends of a revelation, of a test completed. Then they swooned into each other's arms, enraptured.

And for one whole morning, as the draperies hung ruby-colored from the houses, and for one whole afternoon, as they walked toward the garden of palms, they were truly kings.

ANGEL FLORES

## WORKERS

### Ouvriers

Ah, that warm February morning! The untimely South wind came rekindling memories of our absurd poverty, our young indigence.

Henrika had a skirt of brown- and white-checked cotton, probably fashionable a century ago, a bonnet trimmed with ribbons, and a silk kerchief. It was much sadder than a bereavement. We took a stroll in the suburbs. The weather

looked ominous and the South wind stirred up all the evil smells of parched fields and ravaged gardens.

And from this, my wife seemed less tired than I. In a puddle left by floods the month before, on a rather high path, she pointed out a school of tiny fish.

The city, with its smoke and noise of men at work, followed us far out along the roads. Ah, the other world, heaven's blessèd dwelling-place, and umbrage! The South wind reminded me of the tawdry events of my childhood, my disappointed summers, and how awfully much fate cheated me out of cleverness and strength. No! We will not spend the summer in this stingy country where we shall never be anything but betrothed orphans. No longer do I want this strong arm to drag a cherished image behind.

ANGEL FLORES

## CITIES

### *Villes*

What cities these! What a people, for whom have been built up these Alleghanies and Lebanons of dream! Chalets of crystal and wood move on invisible rails and pulleys. The old craters rimmed by colossi and copper palms roar melodiously in the fires. On the canals hung behind the chalets, festivals of love ring out. The hunting song of the chimes is hallooing in the gorges. Guilds of giant singers flock together in vestments and oriflammes that glitter like the light on mountain peaks. On platforms, in the midst of chasms, Rolands are blaring their bravura. On the catwalks of the abyss and the roofs of inns the staffs are decked with flags by the hot blaze of the sky. The crumbling of celestial transformations rejoins the fields on high where the seraphic she-centaurs circulate amid the avalanches. Above the level of the highest crests, a sea troubled by the eternal birth of Venus, laden with fleets bearing male-voice choirs and with the confused mutter of precious pearls and conches— the sea darkens at times with deadly glintings. On the declivities bellow harvests of flowers big as our arms and gob-

lets. Processions of Mabs in russet gowns, opaline, ascend from the ravines. High up there, Diana gives suck to stags, their feet in waterfall and brambles. The Bacchantes of the suburbs sob, and the moon burns and howls. Venus enters the caverns of blacksmiths and of hermits. Belfries sing out in clusters the ideas of the peoples. From castles built of bone emerges the unknown music. All the legends circulate, and the elks hurl themselves into the market towns. The paradise of storms caves in. The savages are dancing cease-lessly the Festival of the Night. And, one hour, I descended into the tumult of a boulevard of Bagdad where they sang, in companies, the joy of new work, under a thick breeze, moving about without being able to elude the fabulous phantoms of the mountains where they were to have met again.

What good arms, what beautiful hour will restore to me that region from which come my slumbers and my least movements?

FREDERICK MORGAN

## EVENINGS

### Veillées

It is rest full of light, neither fever nor languor, on the bed or on the road.

It is the friend, neither ardent nor timid. The friend.

It is the loved one, the fond, neither tormenting nor tor-mented. The loved one.

The air and the world all unexplored. Life.

—Was it then this?

—And the dream breaks afresh.

VERNON WATKINS

## DAWN

### Aube

I have kissed the summer dawn.

Before the first faint stirrings on the thresholds of the palaces. The water lay dead. Shadows lingered on by the woodland road. I kept walking, and awoke the brisk warm throbbing air, and stones looked up and wings rose silently.

My first adventure occurred on the path, when a flower, glowing with fresh pale light, told me its name.

I laughed at the waterfall running breathless through the pine trees: At the silvery summit I came upon the goddess.

Then one by one I lifted her veils. In a glade, waving my arms. Across the plain, where I denounced her to the cock. In the city she fled amid belfries and domes; and, fleet as a beggar along the marble quays, I ran, and sought her out.

Further along the road, by a laurel grove, I gathered her veils about her and felt her huge body next to mine. Dawn and the child sank to the depths of the forest.

And when I woke, it was noon.

ANGEL FLORES

## FLOWERS

### Fleurs

From a golden stadium—amid silken cords, gray chiffons, green velvets, and discs of crystal blackening like bronze in the sun—I see the foxglove open on a rug of silver filigree, of eyes, and flowing hair.

Yellow gold-pieces lie strewn over agate, mahogany pil-

lars support a dome of emeralds, bouquets of white satin, and delicate stalks of rubies gird the water lily.

Like a snow-limbed god with enormous blue eyes, sea and sky lure the throng of sturdy young roses to the marble terraces.

ANGEL FLORES

## MARINE

*Marine*

The chariots of silver and copper,
The prows of steel and silver
Beat foam
And lift up the stumps of the bramble.

The currents of the heath
And the immense ruts delved by their reflux
Veer in a circle to the east,
Toward the pillars of the forest,
Toward the piles of the jetty,
Whose angle is struck by the whirlwinds of light.

FRANCIS GOLFFING

# Stéphane Mallarmé

### 1842–1898

# STÉPHANE MALLARMÉ

## 1842–1898

Much influenced initially by Baudelaire, Mallarmé quite
soon developed a poetry which was distinctively his own.
His dedication as a poet and the exquisite finesse of his
verse were enormously important in the genesis of twen-
tieth-century letters.

Obsessed by the ideal of a pure poetry, and well aware
of the impossibility of its achievement by a real poet in the
real world, Mallarmé in a career of more than a third of a
century published hardly more than a thousand lines, many
of them directly concerned with the correlatives which con-
trol his verse: purity as the duty, and sterility as the fate,
of the poet. They include, among the small number of his
longer works, one of the most obscure of poems, *Un Coup
de dés,* and what is certainly one of the most beautiful in
the language, *L'Après-midi d'un faune.* But most are short
and all are musical, evocative, and crystalline with a clarity
which, once perceived, does not fade. If many of them
seem excessively preoccupied with negation, with non-
being, it should be pointed out that Mallarmé represents
—and this is a triumph for purity in art—the ultimate stage
in a development from Flaubert, with his transformation
of the commonplace into art, and Baudelaire, with his al-
chemical transmutation of the ugly into beauty. Mallarmé
converts absence into diamonds.

Difficult to begin with because of extremes of condensa-
tion and displacement—few of the usual syntactical connec-
tives are used and structure itself is of crucial importance
—Mallarmé's poems with their grace and precision are com-
parable only to those of his greatest disciple, Paul Valéry.

# APPARITION

## *Apparition*

The moon was languishing. Dreamy seraphim
Weeping, bow in hand, in the calm of vaporous
Flowers, drew from waning violins white sobs
Gliding down the blue of the corollas.
—'Twas the blessed day of your first kiss.
My reverie, in my martyrdom delighting,
Quaffed deep heady draughts of the perfumes of sadness
Which the gathering of a Dream, even without regret
Or disenchantment, leaves with the questing heart.
I wandered then, my eyes to the worn old pavement joined,
When with the sun in your hair, in the street
And by night, laughing you came before me;
And I seemed to see the fairy of radiant headdress
Who once across my lovely dreams of pampered childhood
Passed, letting always from her loose-clasped hands
White bouquets of perfumed stars snow down.

KATE FLORES

# WINDOWS

## *Les Fenêtres*

Disgusted with the dreary hospital, and the rank fumes
Rising with the banal whiteness of the curtains
Toward the great crucifix tired of the bare wall,
The man destined for death slyly straightens his old spine,

Shuffles, less to warm his rotting body
Than to watch the sun on the stones, to press
His ashen gaunt and skeletal face
To the panes which a clear beautiful ray attempts to tinge,

And his mouth, feverish and greedy for the azure,
As when young, he breathed his prize,
A virginal cheek! soils
With a long bitter kiss the warm golden panes.


Drunk, forgetting the horror of the holy oil,
The herb teas, the clock and the inflicted bed,
The cough, he lives again; and when twilight bleeds on the
    tiles,
His eye on the horizon gorged with light,


Sees golden ships, fine as swans,
On a scented river of purple, sleepily
Rocking the rich faun flash of their lines
In a great calm charged with memory!


In this way, disgusted with the blunt-souled man
Who wallows in contentment, where only his appetites
Devour him, and who insists on fetching this filth
To present to his wife nursing her children,


I flee and I cling to all those windows
From where one turns one's back on life, and hallowed,
In their glass, washed by eternal dews,
Gilded by the chaste morning of the Infinite


I see myself and I brag I am an angel! and I die, and I long
—Let the glass be art, let it be mysticism—
To be reborn, wearing my dream as a crown,
In a past heaven where Beauty flourished!


But, alas! Here—below is master; its curse
Sickens me at times even in this safe shelter,
And the foul vomit of Stupidity
Makes me stop up my nose in face of the azure.

Is there a way for Me who knows bitterness,
To shatter the crystal insulted by the monster
And to escape with my two featherless wings
—Even at the risk of falling in eternity?

DAISY ALDAN

## ANGUISH

*Angoisse*

I come not to conquer your body tonight, O creature
In whom the sins of a nation stream, nor under
The cureless tedium which my kisses pour
To burrow a sad tempest in your impure hair:

I ask of your bed the deep sleep with no dreams
Flitting under unknown drapes of remorse
Which you, after your dark deceits, can enjoy,
You who know more about oblivion than a corpse:

For gnawing at my ingrained morality, Vice
Has marked its sterility in me as in you;
But while there exists in your breast of stone

A heart which the tooth of no crime can wound,
Haunted by my shroud I flee, wan, undone,
In terror of dying while sleeping alone.

KATE FLORES

## SIGH

*Soupir*

Towards your brow where an autumn dreams
freckled with russet scatterings,
calm sister, and towards the sky,
wandering, of your angelic eye
my soul ascends: thus, white and true,
within some melancholy garden
a fountain sighs towards the Blue!
—Towards October's softened Blue
that pure and pale in the great pools
mirrors its endless lassitude
and, on dead water where the leaves
wind-strayed in tawny anguish cleave
cold furrows, lets the yellow sun
in one long lingering ray crawl on.

FREDERICK MORGAN

## WEARY OF BITTER EASE . . .

*Las de l'amer repos . . .*

Weary of bitter ease in which my indolence
Offends a glory for which I fled the charm long since
Of childhood rose-embowered under natural arch
Of blue, and wearier sevenfold of this my harsh
Compact to dig each night a furrow once again
Into the cold and stingy soil of my brain,
Gravedigger with no pity for sterility,
—What can I tell this Dawn, by roses companied,
O Dreams, when out of terror for its ashen rose
The vast graveyard will merge these empty holes?

I would forsake the ravenous Art of cruel lands
And with a smile for all the age-old reprimands

Delivered by my friends and genius and the past
And by my lamp which knows my agony at last,
Would imitate the Chinese of limpid, delicate bent,
Whose purest ecstasy is but to paint the end
Upon his cups of snow new ravished from the moon
Of some exotic flower that constantly perfumed
His life, transparent flower he smelled in infancy,
Grafting itself upon the soul's blue filigree.
And like to death within the sage's only dream,
Serene, I'll choose a landscape young and evergreen
Which I also will paint on cups, preoccupied.
A line of azure, thin and pale, will signify
A lake, amid a sky of naked porcelain;
A shining crescent lost behind a white cloudscape
Will dip its tranquil horn in the water's glassy sheet
Not far from three long emerald eyelashes—reeds.

HUBERT CREEKMORE

## THE AZURE

### L'Azur

In serene irony the infinite azure,
Languidly lovely as the flowers, smites
The impotent poet cursing his genius
Across a barren wilderness of Sorrows.

Fleeing with eyes closed, I feel it probe
Deep as a racking remorse
My empty soul. Where escape? And what eerie night
To hurl, O remains, against this heart-mangling scorn?

O fogs, come forth! Pour your monotonous ashes
In long shreds of haze across the skies,
Drowning the livid quagmire of the autumns
And rearing a vast ceiling of silence!

And you, from the lethal morasses emerge and gather
As you come the slime and the vapid reeds,
Dear Ennui, to stuff with untiring hands
The great blue holes the birds maliciously make.

More! Let the sad chimneys unceasingly
Smoke, and a wandering prison of soot
Blot out in the horror of their murky trails
The sun dying yellowish on the horizon!

—The Sky is dead. —Toward you I run! O matter, give
Oblivion of the cruel Ideal and of Sin
To this martyr who comes to share the straw
Where men's contented cattle lie,

For here I wish, since at the last my brain, empty
As the pot of paint lying at the foot of a wall,
The art to adorn the woeful Idea possesses no more,
To yawn disconsolately to a desolate death . . .

In vain! The Azure triumphs, and in the bells
I hear it sing. My soul, it becomes a voice
Instilling us with fear anew of its awful victory,
And from the living metal comes in bluenesses the Angelus!

It whirls through the mist as of old and cleaves
Like a resolute sword your intrinsic agony;
In the helpless and hopeless revolt what escape?
*I am obsessed.* The Azure! The Azure! The Azure! The
Azure!

KATE FLORES

## GIFT OF THE POEM

*Don du poème*

I bring you the offspring of an Idumæan night!
Dark, with pale and bleeding wing, plumeless.
Through the casement burnished with incense and gold,
Past the frozen panes still bleak, alas!
Dawn burst upon the angel lamp.
Palms! and when it discovered this relic
To this father attempting an inimical smile,
Blue and barren the solitude shuddered.
O cradle-singer, with your child and the innocence
Of your cold feet, welcome a horrible birth:
And your voice reminiscent of viol and clavecin,
Will you press with faded finger the breast
Whence woman in sibylline whiteness flows
For lips in the air of the virgin azure famished?

                              KATE FLORES

## SEA BREEZE

*Brise Marine*

The flesh is sad, alas! and I have read all the books.
To flee! to flee far away! where the birds must be drunk
To be amidst the unknown spray and the skies!
Nothing, not old gardens reflected in eyes
Will keep back this heart drenched in the sea,
O nights! nor the desolate light of my lamp
On the empty paper sheathed in its whiteness,
And neither the young wife nursing her child.
I shall leave! Steamer rocking your masts,
Heave anchor for exotic lands!

An ennui, bereft of cruel hopes,
Yet believes in the ultimate farewell of handkerchiefs!
And, perhaps, the masts, inviting storms,
May be those a wind bends over shipwrecks
Lost, without masts, nor masts nor fertile shores . . .
Still, O my heart, hear the seafarers' song!

KATE FLORES

## HÉRODIADE

### *Hérodiade*

#### FRAGMENT

NURSE:
. . . For whom, consumed
With anguish, do you keep the unseen splendor
And vain mystery of your being?

HÉRODIADE:
For myself.

NURSE:
Poor flower growing alone without a flutter
Save for its shadow seen listless in the water.

HÉRODIADE:
Go, your pity with your irony keep.

NURSE:
Yet explain: O no, innocent child!
This triumphant disdain must one day lessen.

HÉRODIADE:
But who would touch me, by the lions respected?
I want, regardless, nothing human, and if with my eyes
Lost in paradise you see me rapt,
It is with remembering your milk once drunk.

NURSE:
Lamentable victim to her destiny offered!

HÉRODIADE:
Yes, it is for myself, for myself I flower secluded!
You know this, gardens of amethyst, endlessly
Buried in knowing abysses bedazzling,
You, unfathomed gold guarding your ancient luster
Under the dark sleep of a primeval soil,

You, precious stones wherefrom my eyes like
    flawless gems
Borrow their melodious shimmer, and you
Metallics which lend my youthful tresses
Their massive allure and a fatal splendor!
As for you, woman born in centuries iniqui-
    tous
With the sins of sibylline caves
Who of a mortal speak! Who would from the
    calyxes
Of my robes, fragrant of fierce delights,
Have the pale tremor of my nudity emerge,
Foretell that if the tepid azure of summer,
Toward which innately woman unveils,
In my pudency of tremulous star should see
    me,
I die!

       I love the terror of being virgin and I fain
Would live amid the dread my hair instills in
    me
That I may, at evening, retired to my bed,
Inviolate reptile, feel in my useless flesh
The chill scintillation of your pallid light,
You who burn with chastity, who die to
    yourself,
White night of icicles and cruel snow!


And your solitary sister, O my sister eternal
Toward you my dream shall rise: indeed so
    rarely
Limpid this heart brooding on it
I feel I am alone in my monotonous homeland
And all around me dwell in idolatry
Of a mirror which reflects in its changeless
    calm
Hérodiade of the pristine diamond gaze . . .
O final bliss, yes, I feel it, I am alone!

NURSE:          Madame, are you going to die then?
HÉRODIADE:                    No, poor grandam,

Be calm and, taking your leave, forgive this
    hard heart,
But first, if you will, draw to the blinds,
The seraphic azure smiles in the deep win-
    dowpanes,
And I, I detest the beauteous azure!

                                    Yonder
Billows rock, and do you not know of a
    country there
Where the sinister sky has the hated mien
Of Venus burning in the leafage at night:
There would I go.

                        Light again those tapers,
Childishness, you say, whose wax of feeble
    flame
Weeps amid futile gold some foreign tear
And . . .

NURSE:                Now?
HÉRODIADE:            Good night.

                                    O nude flower
Of my lips, you lie.
                        I do wait some thing unknown
Or, perhaps, heedless of the mystery and your
    cries,
You loose the ultimate and wounded sobs
Of a childhood amidst its reveries sensing
Its frigid jewels becoming separate at last.

                                    KATE FLORES

## SAINT

*Sainte*

At the window ledge concealing
The ancient sandalwood gold-flaking
Of her viol dimly twinkling
Long ago with flute or mandore,

Stands the pallid Saint displaying
The ancient missal page unfolding
At the Magnificat outpouring
Long ago for vesper and compline:

At that monstrance glazing lightly
Brushed now by a harp the Angel
Fashioned in his evening flight
Just for the delicate finger

Tip which, lacking the ancient missal
Or ancient sandalwood, she poises
On the instrumental plumage,
Musician of silences.

HUBERT CREEKMORE

# THE AFTERNOON OF A FAUN

*L'Après-midi d'un faune*
### ECLOGUE

### *The Faun*

These nymphs, I would make them endure.

Their delicate flesh-tint so clear,
it hovers yet upon the air
heavy with foliage of sleep.

Was it a dream I loved? My doubt,
hoarded of old night, culminates
in many a subtle branch, that stayed
the very forest's self and proves
alas! that I alone proposed
the ideal failing of the rose
as triumph of my own.   Think now . . .
and if the women whom you gloze
picture a wish of your fabled senses!
Faun, the illusion takes escape
from blue cold eyes, like a spring in tears,
of the purer one: and would you say
of her, the other, made of sighs,
that she contrasts, like the day breeze
warmly astir now in your fleece!
No! through the moveless, half-alive
languor that suffocates in heat
freshness of morning, if it strive,
no water sounds save what is poured
upon the grove sparged with accords
by this my flute; and the sole wind
prompt from twin pipes to be exhaled
before dispersal of the sound
in arid shower without rain
is—on the unwrinkled, unstirred
horizon—calm and clear to the eye,
the artificial breath of in-
spiration, which regains the sky.

Sicilian shores of a calm marsh,
despoilèd by my vanity
that vies with suns, tacit beneath
the flower-sparkle, now RELATE
*how here I cut the hollow reeds*
*that talent tames; when, on pale gold*
*of distant greens that dedicate*
*their vine to fountains, undulates*
*an animal whiteness in repose:*
*and how at sound of slow prelude*
*with which the pipes first come to life*
*this flight of swans, no! naiads flees*
*or plunges . . .*

       Limp in the tawny hour
all is burning and shows no trace
by what art those too many brides
longed-for by him who seeks the *A*
all at once decamped; then shall I wake
to the primal fire, alone and straight,
beneath an ancient surge of light,
and one of all of you, lilies!
by strength of my simplicity.

Other than the soft nothingness
their lips made rumor of, the kiss,
which gives assurance in low tones
of the two perfidious ones,
my breast, immaculate of proof,
attests an enigmatic bite,
imputed to some august tooth;
leave it! such mystery made choice
of confidant: the vast twinned reed—
beneath blue sky we give it voice:
diverting to itself the cheek's
turmoil, it dreams, in a long solo,
that we amused the beauty here-
about by false bewilderments
between it and our naïve song;
dreams too that from the usual dream

of back or flawless flank traced by
my shuttered glances, it makes fade,
tempered to love's own pitch, a vain,
monotonous, sonorous line.

Oh instrument of flights, try then,
cunning Syrinx, to bloom again
by lakes where you await me! I,
proud of my murmur, shall discourse
at length of goddesses; and by
idolatries warmly portrayed
remove more cinctures from their shades:
thus, when from grapes their clarity
I suck, to banish a regret
deflected by my strategy,
laughing, I raise the cluster high
and empty to the summer sky,
and breathing into its bright skins,
craving the grace of drunkenness,
I gaze them through till night begins.

Oh nymphs, let us once more expand
various MEMORIES. *My eye,*
*piercing the reeds, darted at each*
*immortal neck-and-shoulders, which*
*submerged its burning in the wave*
*with a cry of rage to the forest sky;*
*and the splendid shower of their hair*
*in shimmering limpidities,*
*oh jewels, vanishes! I run;*
*when, at my feet, all interlaced*
*(bruised by the languor which they taste*
*of this sickness of being two),*
*I come upon them where they sleep*
*amid their own chance arms alone;*
*and seizing them, together still*
*entwined, I fly to this massed bloom—*
*detested by the frivolous shade—*
*of roses draining all perfume*
*in the sun's heat; where our frisk play*
*may mirror the consumèd day.*

I worship you, oh wrath of virgins,
savage joy of the sacred burden
sliding its nakedness to flee
my lips that drink, all fiery—
like tremor of a lightning-flash!—
the secret terror of the flesh:
from feet of the inhuman one
to her shy sister's heart, who is
forsaken at the instant by
an innocence, moist with wild tears
or humors of a brighter cheer.
*My crime is, that in gaiety*
*of vanquishing these traitor fears*
*I parted the disheveled tuft*
*of kisses which the gods had kept*
*so closely mingled; for I scarce*
*moved to conceal a burning laugh*
*beneath glad sinuosities*
*of one alone (holding the child,*
*naïve and never blushing, by*
*a single finger, that her white-*
*swan candor might take tinge of shame*
*from kindling of her sister's flame):*
*when from my arms, that are undone*
*by obscure passings, this my prey*
*forever thankless slips away*
*unpitying the sob which still*
*intoxicated me.*

                    Ah well!
Others will draw me towards joy,
their tresses knotted to my brow's
twin horns: you know, my passion, how
each pomegranate, purple now
and fully ripened, bursts—and hums
with bees; and our blood, taking fire
from her who will possess it, flows
for the timeless swarm of all desire.
At the hour when this wood is tinged
with ash and gold, a festival

flares up in the extinguished leaves:
Etna! 'tis on your slopes, visited
by Venus setting down her heels
artless upon your lava, when
a solemn slumber thunders, or
the flame expires.        I hold the queen!

Oh certain punishment . . .

                              But no,
the spirit empty of words, and
this weighed-down body late succumb
to the proud silence of midday;
no more—lying on the parched sand,
forgetful of the blasphemy,
I must sleep, in my chosen way,
wide-mouthed to the wine-fostering sun!

Couple, farewell; I soon shall see
the shade wherein you merged as one.

FREDERICK MORGAN


## THE TOMB OF EDGAR POE*

### Le Tombeau d'Edgar Poe

Even as Eternity brings him at last to Himself,
The Poet revives with a naked sword his age
Aghast at having failed to be aware
Of a triumph over death in that strange voice!

They, like a hydra's vile start once having heard
The angel give a purer meaning to the words of the tribe
Loudly proclaimed that witchery imbibed
In the dishonored flow of some foul brew.

* An earlier version of this poem was translated into English by
Mallarmé himself, as follows. The footnotes are his own.

From hostile soil and cloud, O grief!
If our idea cannot carve out a bas-relief
To adorn the dazzling monument of Poe,

Silent stone fallen here below from some dim disaster,
May at least this granite forever be a bourne
To the black flights that Blasphemy may spread hereafter.

DAISY ALDAN

---

Such as into himself at last Eternity changes him,
The Poet arouses with a naked hymn (1)
His century overawed not to have known
That death extolled itself in this (2) strange voice:

But, in a vile writhing of an hydra, (they) once hearing the
     Angel (3)
To give (4) too pure a meaning to the words of the tribe,
They (between themselves) thought (by him) the spell drunk
In the honourless flood of some dark mixture (5)

Of the soil and the ether (which are) enemies, o struggle!
If with it my idea does not carve a bas-relief
Of which Poe's dazzling (6) tomb be adorned,

(A) Stern block here fallen from a mysterious disaster,
Let this granite at least show forever their bound
To the old flights of Blasphemy (still) spread in the future (7)

(1) *naked hymn* meant when the words take in death their
     absolute value.
(2) *this* means his own.
(3) *the Angel* means the above said Poet.
(4) *to give* means giving.
(5) in plain prose: charged him with always being drunk.
(6) *dazzling* means with the idea of such a bas-relief.
(7) *Blasphemy* means against Poets, such as the charge of Poe
     being drunk.

## WHEN WINTER ON FORGOTTEN WOODS . . .

### *Sur les bois oubliés . . .*

"When Winter on forgotten woods moves somber
you, lonely captive of the threshold, sigh
that this twin grave which is to be our pride
alas! but by lack of thick bouquets is cumbered.

Heedless when Midnight cast its vacant number
a vigil vaunts you not to close your eye
until within the ancient armchair, my
Shade is illumined by the final ember.

Who would receive the Visit must not load
too thick with flowers the stone my finger lifts
with ennui of a power that has decayed.

Soul, at the bright hearth trembling to be seated,
I live again, assuming from your lips
my name in murmurs evening-long repeated."

FREDERICK MORGAN

## ANOTHER FAN (OF MADEMOISELLE MALLARMÉ)

### *Autre Éventail (de Mademoiselle Mallarmé)*

That in pristine, unpathed delight,
O dreamer, I may cast,
Know, by an imperceptible guile,
To keep my wing in hand.

To you a sundown coolness
Is wafted with each flutter
Daintily, with tethered draught,
Bowing to the horizon.

Twirling! how the spaces quiver,
As though a mighty kiss,
Wild at being born for no one,
Could be nor breathed nor still.

If you but knew the raging paradise
That like a submerged laugh
Slips from the corner of your lips
To the depths of the unanimous fold!

Sceptre of what roseate shores
Unstirred on nights of gold,
This barred white waving counterposed
Against a bracelet's flame.

KATE FLORES

## THE PRISTINE, THE PERENNIAL AND THE BEAUTEOUS TODAY . . .

*Le vierge, le vivace et le bel aujourd'hui . . .*

The pristine, the perennial, the beauteous today,
May it crack for us with lunge of drunken wing
This hard, forsaken lake haunted beneath its crust
By the crystalline ice of flights not ever flown!

—A quondam swan recalls that it is he,
Magnificent but in despair of extricating himself,
Having left unsung the region where to be
When winter glistened sterile with ennui.

All his neck will be disburdened of this white agony
Imposed by space upon the bird denying it,
But not of his loathing of the ground where trapped his
   plumage lies.

Phantasm to this place consigned by his utter grandeur,
He immures himself in the frigid dream of scorn
Which in his fruitless exile swathes the Swan.

KATE FLORES

## THE WHITE WATER LILY

### Le Nénuphar blanc

I had been rowing for a long time with a sweeping, rhyth-
mical, drowsy stroke, my eyes within me fastened upon
my utter forgetfulness of motion, while the laughter of the
hour flowed round about. Immobility dozed everywhere so
quietly that, when I was suddenly brushed by a dull sound
which my boat half ran into, I could tell that I had stopped
only by the quiet glittering of initials on the lifted oars.
Then I was recalled to my place in the world of reality.

What was happening? Where was I?

To see to the bottom of my adventure I had to go back
in memory to my early departure, in that flaming July,
through the rapid opening and sleeping vegetation of an
ever narrow and absent-minded stream, my search for wa-
ter flowers, and my intention of reconnoitering an estate be-
longing to the friend of a friend of mine, to whom I would
pay my respects as best I could. No ribbon of grass had
held me near any special landscape; all were left behind,
along with their reflections in the water, by the same im-
partial stroke of my oars; and I had just now run aground
on a tuft of reeds, the mysterious end of my travels, in the
middle of the river. There, the river broadens out into a
watery thicket and quietly displays the elegance of a pool,
rippling like the hesitation of a spring before it gushes forth.

Upon closer examination, I discovered that this tuft of
green tapering off above the stream concealed the single
arch of a bridge which was extended on land by a hedge
on either side surrounding a series of lawns. Then it dawned
on me: this was simply the estate belonging to the un-
known lady to whom I had come to pay my respects.

It was an attractive place for this time of year, I thought,
and I could only sympathize with anyone who had chosen

a retreat so watery and impenetrable. Doubtless she had made of this crystal surface an inner mirror to protect herself from the brilliant indiscretion of the afternoons. Now, I imagined, she must be approaching it; the silvery mist chilling the willow trees has just become her limpid glance, which is familiar with every leaf.

I conjured her up in her perfection and her purity.

Bending forward with an alertness prompted by my curiosity, and immersed in the spacious silence of the worlds still uncreated by my unknown lady, I smiled at the thought of the bondage she might lead me into. This was well symbolized by the strap which fastens the rower's shoe to the bottom of the boat; for we are always at one with the instrument of our magic spells.

"Probably just somebody . . ." I was about to say.

Then, suddenly, the tiniest sound made me wonder whether the dweller on this bank was hovering about me —perhaps by the river!—while I lingered there.

The walking stopped. Why?

Oh, subtle secret of feet as they come and go and lead my imagination on, and bend it to the desire of that dear shadow! She is hidden in cambric and in the lace of a skirt flowing on the ground, floating about heel and toe as if to surround her step before she takes it, as (with folds thrown back in a train) she walks forth with her cunning twin arrows.

Has she—herself the walker—a reason for standing there? And yet have I the right, on my side, to penetrate this mystery further by lifting my head above these reeds and waking from that deep imaginative drowse in which my clear vision has been veiled?

"Whatever your features may be, madame (I whisper to myself), I sense that the instinctive, subtle charm created here by the sound of my arrival would be broken if I saw them—a charm not to be denied the explorer by the most exquisitely knotted of sashes, with its diamond buckle. An image as vague as this is self-sufficient; and it will not destroy the delight which has the stamp of generality, which permits and commands me to forget all real faces; for if I saw one (oh, don't bend yours here, don't let me see it on

this ephemeral threshold where I reign supreme!), it would break the spell which is of another world."

I can introduce myself in my pirate dress and say that I happened here by chance.

Separate as we are, we are together. Now I plunge within this mingled intimacy, in this moment of waiting on the water, my revery keeps her here in hesitation, better than visit upon visit could do. How many fruitless talks there would have to be—when I compare them to the one I have had, unheard—before we could find so intimate an understanding as we do now, while I listen along the level of the boat and the expanse of sand now silent!

The waiting moment lasts while I decide.

Oh, my dream, give counsel! What shall I do?

With a glance I shall gather up the virginal absence scattered through this solitude and steal away with it; just as, in memory of a special site, we pick one of those magical, still unopened water lilies which suddenly spring up there and enclose, in their deep white, a nameless nothingness made of unbroken reveries, of happiness never to be—made of my breathing, now, as it stops for fear that she may show herself. Steal silently away, rowing bit by bit, so that the illusion may not be shattered by the stroke of oars, nor the plashing of the visible foam, unwinding behind me as I flee, reach the feet of any chance walker on the bank, nor bring with it the transparent resemblance of the theft I made of the flower of my mind.

But if, sensing something unusual, she was induced to appear (my Meditative lady, my Haughty, my Cruel, my Gay unknown), so much the worse for that ineffable face which I shall never know! For I executed my plan according to my rules: I pushed off, turned, and then skirted a river wave; and so, like a noble swan's egg fated never to burst forth in flight, I carried off my imaginary trophy, which bursts only with that exquisite absence of self which many a lady loves to pursue in summer along the paths of her park, as she stops sometimes and lingers by a spring which must be crossed or by a lake.

BRADFORD COOK

## INSERT MYSELF WITHIN YOUR STORY . . .

*M'introduire dans ton histoire . . .*

Insert myself within your story
it's as a hero all abashed
if with bare toe he has but touched
some grassplot of that territory

Infringer of your glaciers, I
know of no unsophisticated
sin you will not have frustrated
of laughing loud its victory

Say then, if I am not gay
thunder and rubies at the naves
to see in air pierced by these rays

with scattered kingdoms all about
as though in purple death the wheel
of my sole twilight chariot.

FREDERICK MORGAN


## MY OLD BOOKS CLOSED . . .

*Mes bouquins refermés . . .*

My old books closed once more on Paphos' name,
it pleases me to choose by spirit alone
a ruin, blessed by thousand sprays of foam
beneath far hyacinths of its days of fame.

Then let the cold in scything silence leap,
I shall not wail in empty threnodies
if this white frolic skimming the ground denies
each site the honor of the false landscape.

My hunger, feasting on no present fruits,
finds in their learnèd lack an equal zest:
though one of fragrant human flesh would bloom!

Feet on some wyvern (our love warming the room)
longer I muse, distractedly perhaps,
on the other—the ancient amazon's charred breast.

FREDERICK MORGAN

# THE CHASTISED CLOWN

## Le Pitre châtié

Eyes, lakes withal my simple drunkenness to be reborn
Other than actor evoking with gesture
As though of a quill the shameful soot of the lamps,
I bored a window through the curtain wall.

Swimming to my hand and foot sheer traitor,
In numberless bounds, reneging the bad
Hamlet! it's as though in the waves I improvised
A thousand tombs in which to vanish virginal.

Jubilant gold of cymbal irked to fists,
The sun at a fell blow smites the nudity
Breathed forth pure from my nacreous freshness,

Foul night of the skin though you passed upon me,
As if not knowing, ingrate! that it was my sole anointment,
This grease paint drowned in the glacial water of perfidy.

KATE FLORES

## OLD-CLOTHES WOMAN

*La Marchande d'habits*

Your lively look that pierces them
Down to what they hold
Separates my clothes from me
And nude as a god I go.

KATE FLORES

## SALUTE

*Salut*

Nothing, this froth: virgin verse
Delineating naught but the cup;
Such the slip of many a troupe
Of mermaids drowning wrong side up.

We are sailing, oh my divers
Friends: I already on the poop,
You the forward prow that cleaves
The waves of thunderstorms and winters;

Made dauntless even of its lurching
By a sweet inebriation,
Standing up I bear this greeting:

Solitude, reef, star
To whatever it was deserving
Of the white care of our sail.

KATE FLORES

## LITTLE AIR

*Petit Air*

### I

Somehow a solitude
With neither swan nor quay
Surveys its desuetude
With the glance I turned away

Here from the vainglory
Too remote for touch
Bejeweling many a heaven
With the opulence of dusk

But traces languorously
As snowy linen doffed
Such fugitive bird alongside
You exultant one in the surf

To plunge were to become
Your naked jubilation.

**KATE FLORES**


## LITTLE AIR

*Petit Air*

### II

Inexorably bound
As my hope launching high
To shatter there lost
In fury and silence,

Voice strange to the grove
Or by no echo trailed,
The bird in life never
Another time heard.

The weird musician,
The one who leaves in doubt
If from my breast or his
The wilder sob broke out,

May he tear himself away
On some path to stay!

KATE FLORES

## THE TOMB OF CHARLES BAUDELAIRE

*Le tombeau de Charles Baudelaire*

The shrouded temple divulges through its sepulchral
Mouth a running drain of filth and ruby
Abominable as some Anubian idol
The whole snout aflame as a fierce barking.

Or as the recent gas-light twists the dubious wick
Wiped, one knows, of the suffered opprobrium
It lights up, haggard, an immortal pubis
Whose flight, after its reflection, stays out all night

What dry leaves in the cities without evening
Votive, will be able to bless as she who settles herself
   again
Vainly against the marble of Baudelaire

In the veil which circles her, absent, with shivering
She is his own Shade—a tutelary poison
Always to breathe though we perish by it.

THEODORE HOLMES

## STILL BY THE CLOUD STRICKEN . . .

*A la nue accablante tu . . .*

Still by the cloud stricken
Low with lava and ash
Unto its slavish echo
For a worthless blast

What sepulchral shipwreck (spume,
You know, but drool there)
Supreme amid the ruin
Razed its nuded mast

Or can in a rage for want
Of some perdition mighty
All the vain abyss bestrewn

With hair so white bedraggling
Have frugally drowned
A siren limb ungrown.

**KATE FLORES**


## TOMB [OF PAUL VERLAINE]

*Tombeau*

*Anniversary—January, 1897*

The dark rock angered to be blown by the blast
Will not be stilled either under pious hands
Groping its resemblance to human woes
As though in blessing of some dire mold.

Here nearly always if the mourning dove coos
This immaterial grief with many films of cloud
Overcasts the morrows' mellowed star
Destined in brilliance to besilver the crowd.

Who, by pursuing his solitary bourne
Presently external, seeks our vagabond—
Verlaine? He is hid amid the grass, Verlaine

Only to discover naïvely in accord,
Not crossing his lip or quenching his breath,
A stream not very deep and calumniated death.

KATE FLORES

## O SO DEAR FROM FAR AWAY, SO NEAR AND WHITE . . .

*O si chère de loin et proche et blanche . . .*

O so dear from far away, so near and white, so
Deliciously you, Mary, lead me in dream where thrives
A balm so elusive distilled where it revives
On any flower-vase of crystal in shadow.

You know it, yes, for me, here still, as years ago,
Always your blinding smile extenuating contrives
The same rose with its fair Summer that dives
Into lost times and then into the future also.

My heart that in the nights seeks to know itself sometimes
And to call you with what last word most tenderly chimes
Rears nothing in your homage save what a sister sighed

Were it not, great treasure and diminutive head,
That you teach me quite otherwise a sudden delight
Softly by the sole kiss in your hair said.

VERNON WATKINS

# A THROW OF THE DICE

# NEVER WILL ABOLISH

# CHANCE*

*Un Coup de dés jamais n'abolira le hasard*

TRANSLATED BY DAISY ALDAN

* This translation follows faithfully the typographical arrange-
ment designed by Mallarmé. The poem is to be read lengthwise,
from the left side of the page across the fold of the book to the
edge of the opposite page.
   Each page of the poem forms an ideogram—an image of
whiteness of sky and ocean, storm waves, crests, and troughs,

male and female, wing and bird, sail and boat, the Dipper or Septentrion, etc. The four themes introduced by the title are equivalent to the four-phase movement of a symphony. That number, representing many phases of life and time—four divisions of a day, four seasons, four stages of total time, etc., is an important part of the pattern which unifies the poem.

A THROW OF THE DICE/ NEVER/ WILL ABOLISH/ CHANCE in large, bold, Roman caps is the first and major theme, each word group forming the central idea of the four divisions of the work. The secondary theme, in small caps, may be traced through the poem: EVEN WHEN CAST IN ETERNAL CIRCUMSTANCES/ AT THE HEART OF A SHIPWRECK/ LET IT BE/ THE MASTER/ EVEN IF IT EXISTED/ EVEN IF IT BEGAN AND EVEN IF IT CEASED/ EVEN IF SUMMED UP/ EVEN IF IT ENLIGHTENED/ NOTHING/ WILL HAVE TAKEN PLACE/ EXCEPT/ PERHAPS/ A CONSTELLATION. The words in lower case carry out other ideas, and an adjacent theme is carried by those in upper and lower case: Abyss/ Number/ Spirit/ Betrothal. The eight-point type, the italics, all form individual counterpoints.

The central idea is that "Thought" or the creative act, "A Throw of the Dice," will never abolish Death, the Absolute, Chance. The Boatswain, the Master, the Artist, the Poet, Creative Man, stands at the helm of his foundering ship (Life, energy, all the creative forces over which he once held control which now he has lost in a tornado which is pulling him into the whirlpool (the Abyss, the *gouffre*). Driven wild by the indifferent neutrality of the Abyss, he hesitates to make the last throw of the dice which he holds in his clenched fist, which might save the ship (himself); finally realizing that nothing, not even the "unique Number" (the great work of art, the supreme act), can save him from the anonymity of Death (the Absolute, perdition, the final "Chance," the void) in which all reality is dissolved. Yet, a point of light saves the poem from complete darkness. "PERHAPS," in the altitude, beyond human comprehension and perception, there is a last single, dying constellation which retains a point of consciousness which reflects onto the void where he tried to conquer oblivion.—*Translator's Note.*

# A THROW OF THE DICE

# NEVER

EVEN WHEN CAST IN ETERNAL CIRCUMSTANCES

AT THE HEART OF A SHIPWRECK

**LET IT BE**

    that the

                 Abyss

   whitened
            slack
                raging

                        under an incline
                            desperately soars

                                    by its own

                                       wing

beforehand relapsed from wrongly steering the flight
and repressing the outbursts
cleaving the bounds at the root

deep inside weighs

the shadow hidden in the depth by this alternate sail

to adjust
to the spread

its yawning depth as great as the hull

of a ship

careening from side to side

## THE MASTER

arisen
  inferring

    from this conflagration


     which


     as one threatens

   the one Number which can be




     hesitates
    cadaver by his arm
rather
  than
   as the old madman
    play the game
  in behalf of the waves
      one


    direct shipwreck

beyond outworn calculations
where the manoeuvre with age forgotten

once he gripped the helm

at his feet
of the unanimous horizon

prepares itself
is tossed and merges
with the fist which would grip it
destiny and the winds

no other

Spirit
to hurl it
into the tempest
to seal the gap and to go proudly

cut off from the secret he withholds

surges over the chief
flows over the submissive graybeard

of the man

without a ship
no matter
where vainly

ancestrally not to unclench his hand
                              contracted
                    above the worthless head

          legacy on his disappearance

                    to some
                                        unknown
                    the ulterior immemorial demon

having
          from dead lands
                                        led
the  aged  man  toward  this  supreme  conjunction  with
     probability

                                        he
                              the puerile shadow

caressed and polished and drained and washed
               tamed by the wave and freed
          from the unyielding bones lost among the planks

                                        born
                                             of a frolic
the sea by the sire enticed or the sire compelling the sea
               idle fortune
                                             Betrothal
whose
          veil of illusion rekindled their obsession
          as the ghost of a gesture

                              will falter
                              will plummet

                                   madness

# NEVER WILL ABOLISH

AS  IF

A simple

in the silence

into an approaching

hovers

innuendo

encoiled with irony
              or
                   the mystery
                          hurled
                               howled
whirlwind of hilarity and horror

over the abyss
                   neither scattering it
                               nor fleeing

          and rocks therein the virgin symbol

                               AS  IF

*solitary plume lost*

*save*

that a toque of midnight meets or grazes it
and freezes
to the velvet crumpled by a dull guffaw


this stiffened whiteness

derisive
too much
in opposition to heaven
not to weakly
brand
whosoever


bitter prince of the reef


dons the headdress heroic
invincible but curbed
by his limited human mind
in turmoil

*anxious*

      *atoning and pubescent*

                    *mute*

*The lucid and seigneurial aigrette*
*on the invisible brow*
*scintillates*
      *then conceals*
         *a frail gloomy stature*
*in her siren's torsion*

*with impatient end scales*

laugh

                which

                            IF



of vertigo


upright

        time
                for beating
forked

            a rock

        false castle
                suddenly
                    melted into fog

                    which imposed
                        a limit on infinity

IT WAS
*stellar birth*

**THIS WOULD BE**
no
worse
nor better
but as indifferent as

### THE NUMBER

## EVEN IF IT EXISTED
other than as a straggling hallucination of agony

## EVEN IF IT BEGAN AND EVEN IF IT CEASED
hollow as negation and still born
finally
by some profusion spread with rarity

## EVEN IF SUMMED UP

evidence of the sum as small as it is
## EVEN IF IT ENLIGHTENED

# CHANCE

*Falls*
    *the plume*
        *rhythmic suspense of the disaster*
                *to bury itself*
            *in the primitive foam*
  *from where lately his delirium surged to a peak*
                *collapsed*
    *by the indifferent neutrality of the abyss*

**NOTHING**

of the memorable crisis
or the event
might have been

completed with no possible result in view
human

WILL HAVE TAKEN PLACE
an ordinary swell discloses the absence

BUT THE PLACE
any mediocre plashing as if to disperse the empty act
abruptly which otherwise
by its lie
would have justified
the perdition

in these parts
of the void
in which all reality is dissolved

EXCEPT
      in the heights
             PERHAPS
                    at so distant a place

that it fuses with infinity
                    above human interest
              as pointed out to him
                                   in general
by such slant by such slope
                                    of lights


         toward
              what should be
                   the Septentrion or North


                                   A CONSTELLATION

              cold from neglect and disuse
                                   yet not so much
                        that it does not count
              on some empty and superior plane
                        the next collision
                                   sidereally
              of a final reckoning in the making


watching
         doubting
                   revolving
                        blazing and meditating


                             before it halts
              at some final point which consecrates it

              All Thought emits a Throw of the Dice

# Jules Laforgue

## 1860–1887

# JULES LAFORGUE

## 1860–1887

Like Rimbaud, Laforgue had a short career, but he did not have Rimbaud's precocity. If, however, his poetry perhaps suffers from his immaturity, it none the less is remarkable for the eloquence and simplicity with which it deals with the major themes. Laforgue's particular tone of sentimental irony, tender, sincere, colloquial, occasionally sardonic, oppressed at once by the search for perfection and by a sense of the impossibility of finding it in the world in which he lived, is a most engaging and moving one.

Born in Uruguay of French parents, Laforgue went to France for his studies at an early age, lived a lonely life devoted much of the time to literature in one form or another. After a thorough study of philosophy and modern poetry, especially Baudelaire, he went to Germany as reader to the Empress. After five years of exile there, during which he did much of his writing, he married an English girl and settled in Paris once again, only to find there illness, poverty, and death.

In his anti-Romanticism, his departure from grandeur and an elevated tone, and in his irony a descendant of Corbière, and in some respects superior to him, Laforgue eventually quit the classic structures of French poetry for free verse, which he is credited with inventing. If he is a minor poet by comparison with Verlaine, whom he in some ways resembles, Rimbaud, and Mallarmé, still his innovations and his tone were of enormous importance to subsequent poets—notably Apollinaire, Pound, Eliot—and to modern poetry in general.

# LAMENT OF THE ORGANIST OF NOTRE-DAME DE NICE

*Complainte de l'Organiste de Notre-Dame de Nice*

Hark, already the winter crows
Have said their psalm among our bells;
The autumn showers are near, like knells;
Farewell the woods of the casinos.

Last night her cheek had a paler dye
And her body shivered, numbed quite through;
This church of ours is icy, too.
Ah, none loves her down here but I.

I! I shall cut my heart out, tooled
For the sake of a smile so sad from her,
And remain true to her image there
Forever, in this victorious world.

The day that she leaves this world
A *Miserere* I mean to play
So cosmic in its despairing way
That God will have to return me word.

No, I shall stay down here, all dark,
Loyal to my dear phthisic dead,
Rocking my heart too deeply fed
With the eternal fugues of Bach.

And every year, at the new year's birth,
On our anniversary, constant then,
I shall unroll this *Requiem*
I have made for the death of the Earth.

VERNON WATKINS

## SONG OF THE LITTLE HYPERTROPHIC CHILD

*La Chanson du petit hypertrophique*

It is from a heart sickness
She is dead, the doctor says,
        Tra-la-leer!
        Poor mother dear,
And that I'll go below
To play bye-bye with her,
I hear my heartbeat go:
My mother calls me near.

I am laughed at in the streets
For my incongruous hands
        La-lu-lid!
        Of a drunken kid.
Ah God, every step I go
I choke, I rock with fear.
I hear my heartbeat go:
My mother calls me near.

So then through the fields I go
To sob to the sunsets low,
        La-ri-rame!
        It's a silly game.
But the sun seems, I don't know,
Like a heart that is rippling clear.
I hear my heartbeat go:
My mother calls me near.

Ah, if little Gen'vieve took
For my bursting heart one look,
        Pi-lou-less!
        Ah, yes!
I am yellow and sad, I know.
She is rosy, gay, and dear.
I hear my heartbeat go:
My mother calls me near.

No, all the world's all bad,
All but the heart the sunsets had,
        Tra-la-leer!
        And mother dear,
And I must go down there soon
To play bye-bye with her.
My heart beats on, beats on . . .
Is it, Mother, you I hear?

VERNON WATKINS

# APOTHEOSIS

*Apothéose*

In all senses, forever, the silence palpitates
With clusters of gold stars interweaving their rounds.
One might take them for gardens sanded with diamonds,
But each in desolation, very solitary, scintillates.

Now far down, in this corner unknown which vibrates
With a furrow of rubies in its melancholy bounds,
One spark with a twinkle of tenderness astounds:
A patriarch guiding his family with lights.

His family: a swarm of heavy globes; each a star is.
And on one, it is Earth, a yellow point, Paris,
Where a lamp is suspended and, on watch, a poor devil:
In the universal order frail, unique human marvel.
He himself is its mirror of a day and he knows it.
Long he dreams there, then turns to a sonnet to compose it.

VERNON WATKINS

## FOR THE BOOK OF LOVE

*Pour le Livre d'amour*

I can die tomorrow and I have not loved.
My lips never touched a woman's while I lived.
None has given me her soul in a look; none in heat
Has held me, exhausted with love, to her heart.

I have but suffered for all nature, each moment,
For the beings, the wind, the flowers, the firmament,
Suffered through all my nerves minutely, like a knife,
Suffered to have a soul still not yet pure enough.

I spat upon love, and I have killed the flesh.
Mad with pride on this Earth enslaved by Instinct's leash,
I alone stood and stiffened myself against life.
I challenged the Instinct with a bitter laugh.

Everywhere, in the salons, at the theater, in church,
Before these cold great men, these men of finest touch,
And these women with gentle, or jealous, or proud eyes
Whose tender, ravished soul one might virginally rechase,

I thought: all these are come to it. I heard in their rites
The roarings of the unclean coupling of brutes.
So much mire with an access of three minutes in mind!
Men, be correct! O women, keep your smiles refined!

VERNON WATKINS

## WINTER SUNSET

*Couchant d'hiver*

What a sorrowful sunset we had tonight!
In the trees a wind of despair wept,
Blowing dead wood amid the withered leaves.
Across the lace of barren branches
Etched upon the cold and pale-blue sky,
The sovereign of the heavens dropped stark and desolating.
O Sun! In summertime, magnificent in your glory
You set, radiant as a vast ciborium
Inflaming the azure! Now we behold
A sickly saffron disc, bereft of rays,
Die on the vermilion-washed horizon
Bleak in a sinister tubercular décor
Feebly tingeing the rheumy clouds
Dull livid white, splenetic green,
Old gold, wan lilac, leaden gray, tarnished rose.
O, it's finished, finished! The wind is long in its throes!
The days are over with; all is gasping and sere;
Earth's course is run, its loins are able no more.
And its miserable children, thin, bald, and pallid
With pondering the everlasting problems too much,
Shaking and stooped in their burden of shawls,
In the waning yellow gaslight of the misty boulevards
Contemplate their absinthes with mute and empty eyes,
Laughing in bitterness when pregnant women go by
Parading their bellies and their breasts
In the beastly pride of a god's slaves . . .

Unknown tempests of the last debacles,
Come! Unleash your whirlwind floods!
Seize this sordid, gasping globe! Sweep
Its weary heirs and cities' leprosy away!
And fling the unspeakable havoc to the immensity of night!
And in the great innocence of the eternal suns
And the stars of love, may there be nothing known
Of this rotten Brain which was the Earth, one day.

KATE FLORES

## SKEPTIC CHRISTMAS

*Noël sceptique*

Noel! Noel? I hear the bells in the night . . .
And I to these faithless sheets have put my pen:
O memories, sing! All my pride flees me,
And by my vast bitterness I am overcome.

Ah! these voices in the night singing Noel! Noel!
Bringing me from the nave which, out there, is lighted
A motherly reproach so tender, so sweet
That my heart, too full, breaks in my breast . . .

And I listen long to the bells in the night . . .
I am the pariah of the human family,
To whom in his squalid hole the wind
Brings poignant rumor of a far festivity.

KATE FLORES

## THE IMPOSSIBLE

*L'Impossible*

Tonight I may die. Rain, wind, sun
Will scatter everywhere my heart, my nerves, my marrow.
All will be over for me. Neither sleep nor awakening.
I shall not have been out there among the stars.

In every direction, I know, on those distant worlds,
Are similar pilgrims of pale solitudes,
Extending us their hands across the gentle dark,
Sister Humanities dreaming in multitudes.

Yes, brothers everywhere. That I know, I know.
And all alone like us. Trembling with sadness,
They beckon to us at night. Ah, shall we never go?
We would console one another in our great distress.

The stars, it is certain, will one day meet,
Heralding perhaps that universal dawn
Now sung by those beggars with caste marks of thought.
A fraternal outcry will be raised against God.

Alas, before that time, rain, wind, sun
Will have lost in the distance my heart, my nerves, my
  marrow.
All will be done without me. Neither dream nor awakening.
I shall not have been among the gentle stars.

WILLIAM JAY SMITH

## LIGHTNING OF THE ABYSS
### Éclair de gouffre

I was on a tower in the midst of the stars.

Suddenly, stroke of vertigo, a lightning-flash where, cast
Of all its veils, I sounded, thrilling with awe, with fear,
The riddle of the cosmos, in all its depth made clear.
All, all is one? Where am I? Where goes this mass that rolls
Bearing me on? —And I can die, die, take my leave,
Knowing nothing. Speak! O rage! And time flows on and
  tolls
Without return. Stop, stop! And to true joys how cleave?
For I know nothing, I. My hour is there, at least?
I do not know. I was in the night, then I am born.
Why? Whence the universe? Where goes it? For the priest
Is mere man. One knows nothing. Appear to me, take form,
God, witness eternal! Speak: why is there life?
All is silent. Oh, space is without a heart. One moment,
Stars! I do not want to die! I have genius!
Ah, to become nothing again, irrevocably spent!

VERNON WATKINS

## THE FIRST NIGHT

*La Première nuit*

Night falls, soothing to lascivious old men
My cat, Murr, hunched like some heraldic sphinx,
Uneasily surveys, from his fantastic eyeball,
The gradual ascent of the chlorotic moon.

The hour of children's prayers, when whoring Paris
Hurls on to the pavement of every boulevard
Her cold-breasted girls, who wander with searching
Animal eyes under the pale street lights.

With my cat, Murr, I meditate at my window,
I think of the newborn everywhere;
I think of the dead who were buried today.

I imagine myself within the cemetery,
Entering the tombs, going in place
Of those who will spend their first night there.

WILLIAM JAY SMITH

## COMPLAINT OF THAT GOOD MOON

*Complainte de cette bonne lune*

*The Stars are heard*:

On the lap
Of our Master
We are dancing, fast and faster
On the lap
Of our Master
Dancing faster in a ring.

"What about you, little Miss
Moon? Don't take it so amiss!
Come with us and you'll collect
Golden suns around your neck!"

"It's very nice of you to treat
A poor Cinderella so,
But my wardrobe is complete
With my sister planet's glow."

"That reservoir of Thinking mars
The sky! Give up! Come to the ball
And you will turn the heads of all
Our very most distinguished stars!"

"Thanks! I'll stick to the attractions
Of my friend—just now she sighed!"
"You're wrong; that was the cosmic tide
Of weary chemical reactions!"

"Be still! I earn my bread and butter
Keeping watch! Go drag your tails,
You scandalmongers, in the gutter!"

"A first-class Innocence in veils!
Ha! Our Lady of the Soused!
Werewolves, sneak thieves—all for you,
And your prowling cats carouse!
            Cookoo!"

*Exeunt the stars. Silence and Moon. One hears:*

     Under the empty
     Canopy
We are dancing, we are dancing
     Under the empty
     Canopy
Swiftly dancing in a ring.

PATRICIA TERRY

## COMPLAINT OF THE PIANOS OVERHEARD
## IN PROSPEROUS NEIGHBORHOODS

*Complainte des pianos qu'on entend dans les quartiers aisés*

Lead on the soul, well fed by Literature,
Pianos, pianos, in prosperous neighborhoods.
First evenings, without a coat—our walks are pure—
To the tune of nerves, crushed or misunderstood.

Those girls—what dreaming entertains
Their long monotonous refrains?

"Courtyards at night,
The dormitory's Christ!"

"You go away and leave us here,
You leave us here and you are free,
We take down and curl our hair,
And practice our embroidery."

Vague or pretty? sad or wise? and chaste?
O days, is all the same to me? or, world, for *me* now?
And virgins, at least as to that worthy wound;
They know what greasy settings attend the most candid
vow?

Oh, what's behind their dreaming faces?
Rolands, or, perhaps, fine laces?

"Hearts in prisons,
Slow, the seasons!"

"You go away and leave us here,
You leave us and pursue your quests!
Gray convents, choirs of Shulamites,
We cross our arms on our flat breasts."

Then, one day, being's key fatalities;
Psst! heredity's punctual fermentations
Amid the ceaseless dance of our strange streets;
Ah, theaters, dormitories, prose sensations!

Your sterilized refrains annul!
Life is real and criminal.

"Drawn curtains,
May we come in?"

"You go away and leave us,
You leave us and you disappear.
The rose tree soon dries out its spring,
Really! Why isn't he here? . . ."

He'll come! And yours will be the erring heart,
Engaged to remorse, as to a meaningless start,
The adequate heart, insulated and decked
With chiffon and lonely trappings of respect.

Die? Perhaps their needlework engenders
Some wealthy uncle's suspenders?

"Oh, that's not true!
If only you knew!"

"You go away and leave us here,
You leave us here and you won't stay,
But you promised you'd come back and cure
My nice little pain right away?"

And it's true! The Ideal throws them all out of line;
Bohemia flourishes even in well-to-do quarters.
Life is there; the pure flask of living wine
Will be, *as is proper,* baptized with clean waters.

And so, very soon, they'll complain
About some more precise refrain.

    "My one pillow!
    The wall I know!"

"You leave us here and go, alas.
You go untouched by our appeals.
Why couldn't I have died at Mass!
O months, O lingerie, O meals."

PATRICIA TERRY

## ANOTHER LAMENT OF LORD PIERROT

*Autre Complainte de Lord Pierrot*

She, the one who should put me on to Woman!
We will say to her, to begin with, in my least chilly manner:
"The sum of the angles of a triangle, dear heart,
    Is equal to two right angles."

And if this cry escapes her: "God, O God! How I love you!"
—"God will recognize his own." Or, stung to the quick:
—"My keyboards have a soul, you will be my sole theme."
    I: "All is relative."

With both her eyes, then! feeling herself too banal:
"Ah! You do not love me; so many others are jealous!"
And I, with an eye which is carried away toward the
   Unconscious:
    "Thanks, not badly; and you?"

—"Let us play at finding out who is the most faithful!"
  —"What's the use, O Nature!"
"So that the one who loses wins!" Then, another verse:
—"Ah! you will be bored first, I am sure of it . . ."
    —"After you, please."

Finally, if, of an evening, she dies among my books,
Meek; pretending still not to believe my eyes,
I will have a word: "Ah yes, but, we had Enough to live on!
          It was in earnest then?"

JOSEPH BENNETT

## COMPLAINT OF THE KING OF THULE

### Complainte du Roi de Thulé

Once there was a King of Thule,
   An immaculate King was he,
Who far from petticoats and the like
Mourned the metempsychosis
   By which lilies became roses,
   What a palace was his!

On milky nights, past his sleeping flowers,
   He would go, dragging his keys,
To embroider on a high tower
A certain bright-colored sail,
   The stars his only witnesses.

When he had finished hemming the sail,
He departed on the gray seas,
   Far from Thule,
Rowing hard toward the dying sun,
That failing temple of delight,
   And so would wail:

"Dying sun, for one day more
Your beacon light has beckoned forth
All the viviparous holocausts
Of the cult which men call love.

"And now as you feel your strength fail
Before the wild night falls,
You come to bathe the alcove
With one last wave of martyred blood.

"Sun! Sun! See me descending
Now toward your heart-rending
Polar palaces to rock to sleep
    Your bleeding heart
    In this Winding Sheet."

He spoke, and with the sail full-spread,
    Agitated and dismayed,
As handsome as one of the Wise Men,
The King mocked by petticoats,
    Descended then
    To wrecked ships and coral reefs.

Gentle lovers, on milky nights,
    Do not fail to turn the key!
A phantom chilled with pure love
Might come to sing you this old saw:
"Once there was a King of Thule,
    An immaculate King was he . . ."

                    WILLIAM JAY SMITH


COMPLAINT ON THE OBLIVION OF THE DEAD

*Complainte de l'oubli des morts*

        Ladies and gentlemen
        Whose mother is no more,
        The old gravedigger
        Scratches at your door.

Six feet down
Is a dead man's place;
He hardly ever
Shows his face.

You blow smoke into your beer,
You wind up your love affair,
Yonder crows chanticleer,
Poor dead beyond the pale!

His finger at his temple,
Look at Grandpa half asleep,
Sister busy with her knitting,
Mother turning up the lamp.

One who is dead
Is quite discreet,
He goes to bed
Right in the street.

The meal was good, was it?
Now how is everything?
The little stillborn
Get almost no fondling.

On one side of your ledger
Enter the cost of the dance;
On the other, the undertaker's fee
To make your books balance.

Life's a ditty
With a hye-nonny-no.
Eh what, my pretty,
Do you find it so?

Ladies and gentlemen,
Whose sister is no more,
Open up for the gravedigger
Who raps at your door.

Show him no pity,
He will come all the same
To drag you out by the heels
When the moon is full.

Importunate wind,
Howl on.
Where are the dead?
They're gone.

WILLIAM JAY SMITH

## PIERROTS (SOME OF US HAVE PRINCIPLES)

### Pierrots (On a des principes)

She was saying, with the wisdom of the ages,
"I love you just for yourself!" Bravo! A charming device—
Yes, like art! Keep calm, illusory wages
        From capitalist Paradise!

She said, "I'm waiting, here I am, don't know . . ."
Her eyes copied from large and candid moons.
Bravo! Perhaps it wasn't just for prunes
        That we went to school here below?

But she was found one evening, impeccably out of luck,
Deceased! Bravo! A change of key!
We know that you'll revive in three
        Days, if not in person at least

In the perfume, the leaves, the brooks of the spring!
And fools will be entangled, as you flirt,
In the Veil of the Gioconda, in the Skirt!
        I might even be there on your string.

PATRICIA TERRY

# I HEAR MY SACRED HEART BEAT . . .

*J'entends battre mon Sacre-Cœur . . .*

I hear my Sacred Heart beat
Lonely and companionless,
In the twilight of the hour
With little hope, and no retreat.

I hear my youthful blood course
Ambiguous through my arteries
Between the Edens of my verse
And the province of my fathers.

I hear also the flute of Pan.
"Go far, go far afield!" it sings.
"Die, when life demands too much;
But, mark you, he who loses wins."

WILLIAM JAY SMITH

# ROMANCE

*Romance*

HAMLET: *To a nunnery, go.*

A thousand sea birds all pale gray
Nest on the walls of my lovely soul;
And fill the sad halls day by day
With the beat of oars, and the ocean's roll.

Deposit filth on everything,
Flesh, and coral, and sea shells;
And strike the upright paneling
While circling wildly round the walls.

Oh, pallid birds of the roaring waves,
Fashion a necklace of sea shell
To please my lady who arrives,
And spare her not your carrion smell.

So she will say: "My little nose
Can't bear this soul; it's far too strong;
But this lovely necklace, may I take it along?"
What good will it do her, do you suppose?

WILLIAM JAY SMITH

## THE APPROACH OF WINTER

### *L'Hiver qui vient*

Blockade of the senses! Mail steamers from the
    Levant! . . .
O downpour of rain! O downpour of night,
O! the wind! . . .
All Hallow's Eve, Christmas, and the New Year,
Oh, in the drizzling, all my chimneys! . . .
Of factories . . .

It is impossible to sit down any more, all the benches are
    wet;
Believe me, everything is over until next year,
All the benches are wet, the woods are so rusted,
And the horns have so many times sounded your note, your
    sound of *ton* and *taine!* . . .

Ah! storm clouds flocking here from the shores of the
    Channel,
You have spoiled us our last Sunday.

It drizzles;
In the wet forest, spider webs
Bend under the drops of water, and it is their ruin.

Plenipotentiary suns from the washing of golden river-
   sands,
From country fairs,
Where are you buried?
This evening a squandered sun lies helpless at the top of
   the slope,
Lies on the hillside, in the broom, on his cloak.
A sun white as spittle on a barroom floor
Lies in a litter of yellow broom,
The yellow broom-flowers of Autumn.
And the horns call him!
May he come back . . .
May he come to himself again!
Tallyho! Tallyho! and the hunting horn at the kill!
O sad anthem, have you ended! . . . And they play the
   fool! . . .
And he lies there, the sun, like a gland torn out of a neck,
And he shivers, without a friend! . . .

Forward, forward, and the horn at the kill!
It is well-known Winter blowing in;
Oh! the turnings, the bends of the highroads,
And without Little Red Ridinghood making her way! . . .
Oh! their ruts from the wagons of another month,
Ascending like quixotic rails
Towards the patrols of fleeing storm clouds
Which the wind knocks towards the transatlantic sheep-
   folds! . . .
Let us hasten, hasten, it is the well-known season, this time,
And the wind, this night, he has made beautiful clouds!
O havoc, O nests, O modest little gardens!
My heart and my drowsiness: O echoes of hatchets! . . .

All these branches still have their green leaves,
The underbrush is now nothing but a dung heap of dead
   leaves;
Leaves, leaflets, may a fair wind carry you away
In swarms toward the ponds,
Or for the gamekeeper's fire,
Or for the mattresses of ambulances
For soldiers far from France.

It is the season, it is the season, rust overruns the masses,
Rust gnaws in their kilometric spleens
The telegraphic wires on the highroads where no one
   passes.


The horns, the horns, the horns—melancholic! . . .
Melancholic! . . .
They depart, changing their tone,
Changing their tone and their music,
Your note, your sound of *ton* and *taine* and *ton!* . . .
The horns, the horns, the horns! . . .
Have departed with the north wind.


I cannot leave, this tone: such echoes! . . .
It is the season, it is the season, the grape harvest is
   over! . . .
Here come the rains with their angel's patience,
The business is over and done with, adieu grape harvests
   and all the baskets,
All the Watteau baskets of the peasant dances under the
   chestnut trees,
It is the coughing in high-school dormitories which returns,
It is herb tea without a hearth, far from home,
Pulmonary consumption saddening the neighborhood,
And all the misery concentrated in great cities.


But, woolens, rubber overshoes, pharmacy, dream,
Parted curtains on balconies high up above the riverbanks
Facing the sea of roofs of the quarters of the city,
Lamps, engravings, tea, *petits fours,*
Will you not be my only amours! . . .
(Oh! and then, are you versed in, besides the pianos,
The sober and vespertine weekly mystery
Of the sanitation statistics
In the newspapers?)

No, no! it is the season and the planet is curiously quaint!
May the south wind, may the south wind
Ravel out the old shoes which time runs off with!
It is the season, oh rending! it is the season!
Every year, every year,
In chorus I will try to give it its note.

JOSEPH BENNETT


## MOON SOLO

### Solo de lune


On the roof of a coach at night I lie,
My cigarette pointing to the sky;
While my poor bones jostle and roll, up dances my soul
Like some Ariel;
Without malice or solace, my lovely soul,
O roads, O hills, O mists, O vales,
My lovely soul—let's see what it entails.

Yes. We were madly in love, we two,
And with never a word drifted apart;
A sense of disgust held back my heart,
A disgust that was universal, too.

Her eyes said: "Now you see what I mean?
You mean to say that you haven't seen?"
Yet neither would be the first to act;
We longed to kneel *together*, in fact.
(Now you see what I mean?)

So where can she be?
Weeping her heart out bitterly?
So where can she be?
My darling, I beg of you, do take care!

O the woods by the road are cool and clear!
O shawl of sorrow, all things seem to hear,
And all willingly
Would trade places with me!

By hoarding the coin of what must be,
Let us improve upon destiny!
More stars in the sky than pebbles by the sea
Where others than I have watched her bathe;
All goes under Death's dark wave.
No port but the grave.

Years will go by,
And each on his own will grow hardened somehow;
And often—I can already hear myself now—
Say to the other, "Had I but known . . ."
Ah, cursed from the start,
Dead end for the heart—
What an ass was I!

But wild for happiness then in truth,
What shall we do? I with my soul,
She with her fallible youth?
O my aging sinner,
How many evenings after dinner
Shall I turn to infamy to do you honor!

Her eyes would blink: "Now you see what I mean?
You mean to say that you haven't seen?"
But neither would be the first to act—
To kneel together. Ah, in fact! . . .

O see the moon climb,
Dream road beyond time!
We have passed the cotton mills, we have passed the
    sawmills,
And nothing remains but a few road signs.
And little pink cotton-candy clouds
With a thin crescent moon that continues to climb;
Dream road beyond sound, dream road beyond time . . .

What spacious, clean rooms
In these pinewoods where
Since the dawn of time
It is dark as the tomb!
Ah, for an evening of lovely abduction!
I people these rooms, in my mind I am there,
In my mind I behold a loving pair
Whose every gesture breaks the law.


And I pass them by, and I leave them there,
And lie back down
While the road winds on, Ariel, I;
No one waits for me, I am going nowhere:
I have only the friendship of hotel rooms.


O see the moon climb,
Dream road beyond time,
Dream road without end;
Now here at the bend
Is the posthouse where
The lanterns are lit,
And we drink fresh milk,
And change postilion,
While crickets trill
Under the July stars.


O broad moonlight
Like a wedding of torches drowning my sorrow tonight,
The shadows of the poplars along the road . . .
The torrent that listens
As it flows . . .
A river of Lethe that overflows . . .


O Moon Solo, when
Will you answer my pen?
O this night on the road;
Stars—all there, all,
With all you forebode.
O fleeting hour,

Had I but the power
To retain your image until autumn returns! . . .

How cool it is now, how cool,
And what if now at this very hour
She also strolls at the edge of the same wood
Drowning her sorrow
In a wedding of light! . . .
(And how she loves to stroll at night!)
Having forgotten the scarf for her throat tonight,
She is sure to take cold in such cold, clear light!
Oh, my darling, I beg of you, do take care;
That cough is more than one can bear.

Ah, would I had sunk to my knees when I could!
Ah, would you had swooned in my arms as you should!
What a model husband in me you'd have found,
As the swish of your skirt is a model of sound.

WILLIAM JAY SMITH

## SUMMER LANDSCAPE

### Paysage d'été

The hot Sun at its zenith weeps ingots like the clappers
of bells; and thirsty for the breezes of the meadow, and
the smell of water cress, it invisibly absorbs water from the
springs, the springs of the countryside, which have been
writhing with discomfort as they work out their destinies
through this horrid day; from afar, the sun watches flocks
of motes rise through the air, and, cooled and comforted
at the sight, ceases drinking and the water hovers then in
black sheets steaming from this spasmodic christening. In
black sheets thick with storm clouds and fertilized by
latent thunders, sheets that twist like invalids on their mat-
tresses, that drift, stretch themselves, sniff one another
amorously, lustily, and thrust one another back for fear
of final catastrophe . . . Like eyes in death agony the

leaves revolve on their stalks, branches pulsate like arteries
choked by terrible temperatures, the meadow darkens like
an angry peacock's tail, like the comb of a blinded cock, or
the face of some lost balloonist who has sailed beyond the
earth's orbit; inventing inexhaustibly lamentable pretexts,
the winds seek one another out: man feels afflicted. Gone
is the sacramental sun, gone with a wholly somnambulistic
air. Love's simoon makes its round. The pupils of one's eyes
are dilated, moist temples beat like drums, supplications
are choked in burning throats, hands heavy with faith wan-
der idly about, lips mad with thirst come down upon lips
that are even madder with thirst, more withered and dry
. . . Is there no way to set you free, O cool corrosive dew?
Is there no cork your liquid waves can strike against and
thrust out? Poor desperate miners buried underground as
they dug their tunnel, their lamps have gone out, and one
can hear the picks of the pioneers from the other side, with
only one wall remaining between . . . Two lightning flashes
have whistled through the air, interlacing like flashing
snakes, thunder tears the temple veil, and the fan of love's
cloudburst descends upon the breathless meadows like the
speckled hawk upon an ocean wedged with ingots of faith,
descends with a silver sound of rain on a boat lost in a lake.
Water runs down leaves and eyes, dissolving the salt of
sweat, drowning the eyes.

WILLIAM JAY SMITH

## SPRING EVENING ON THE BOULEVARDS

### Soir de printemps sur les boulevards

Sitting on a bench one evening in spring on the great
boulevards, near the Variétés. A café streaming with gas.
A prostitute dressed all in red going from beer to beer. On
the second floor, a room quite somber and quiet with a few
lamps and tables over which heads were bent, a little study.
On the third floor, adazzle with gas, all the windows open,
flowers, perfumes, a dance in progress. One can't hear the

music for the din of the street swarming with cabs and people, with the corridors devouring and vomiting people incessantly, and the hawking of programs in front of the Variétés . . . But one can see, gliding past in front of these ten windows, men in black tails with white shirt fronts, revolving to the music, holding ladies, blue, pink, lilac, white, holding them ever so lightly, so correctly, one can see them pass, repass, with serious, unsmiling faces (but one can't hear the music they follow). Several pimps wander by; one says to the other: "She made ten francs, old boy . . ." From the Variétés a crowd swarms out during intermission; and the hell of the boulevard continues, the cabs, the cafés, the gas, the shopwindows, more and more pedestrians—more prostitutes filing by under the harsh lights of the cafés . . . Near me a newspaper stall and two women chatting; one says: "She certainly won't last the night, that one, and my kid caught it from hers." Busses filled with members of both sexes, each with his or her own feelings, troubles, vices.

And above it all, the gentle, eternal stars.

WILLIAM JAY SMITH

## MID-JULY TWILIGHT, EIGHT O'CLOCK

*Crépuscule de mi-juillet, huit heures*

After a light shower, the pools, muddy green in color, lose their wrinkles and their look of watered silk.

Three distinct monotonous sounds in space: a train whistle, the lively fluting of a blackbird in the low foliage of the terrace, and the tinkle of cowbells.

All the rest is an immobile mass of hills, space, and pale gray sky.

WILLIAM JAY SMITH

## THE END OF A DAY IN THE PROVINCES

*Fin de journée en province*

Passed the end of a day in the provinces.
A gray sort of town, carefully paved, peaceful.
The hotel window looks onto the main square. I watched
a stupid moon rise over there, lighting up this town espe-
cially as though to assure me that this town really existed,
in its insignificance.

A lamplighter carrying a baby in his arms and followed
by a dog who seemed to be used to everything, and who
sniffed at the pavements as though they were very old
friends.

The lamp did not want to light.

Immediately, two, five, six people came along and dis-
cussed it; the lamp lights, the people see that it is lit and
go away slowly. Only one remains. He looks at the lamp
for a moment and then he goes away.

Oh! to live in one of these mollusc beds!

To die! . . . to die.

And the moon is the same here as in Paris, as over the
Mississippi, as in Bombay.

MARGARET CROSLAND

## A HOT STAGNANT EVENING

*Après-diner torride et stagnante*

One's feet are baking, one can feel the arteries throbbing
in one's ankles, under one's chin, in the heart, the wrists;
one raises up hands that are already swollen and wet, the
least little meal weighs one down, one must undo one's
necktie, one breathes so deeply that the cigarette stuck to
the corner of one's mouth is consumed in twelve puffs, one's
skin is wringing wet . . . How unhappy I would be if I
had breasts and were a nurse! Or if I were one of those

military musicians laced tight in a uniform, and had to
blow into a trombone in some bandstand. Ah, to be a fly
on the wet tile floor of some provincial kitchen! Or rather
a passive sponge, a branch of coral encrusted at the bottom
of the sea, watching the parade of submarine nature, or a
blue cornflower on a piece of delft china perched above a
pile of stoles, in the cool, dark back room of an antique
shop on the banks of the Sequana! Or a flower in the chintz
of the bare prim parlor of an old maid in Quimper . . .
or a heron . . .

WILLIAM JAY SMITH

## THUNDERBOLT

### Coup de foudre

I am in love, I am in love: I have drunk a good dizzying
gulp. I with an analytical mind and a shortsighted soul now
feel completely solemn . . . And I walk along the streets.
The Luxembourg Gardens are flooded with a great gaiety
of bells. If she doesn't love me, if she can't be wholly mine,
what difference will it make? I am in love, that's enough;
I feel generous, holy, human, trembling, so filled with
things that I dare not look myself in the eye . . . No joking,
I really mean all that I say.

WILLIAM JAY SMITH

## TWILIGHT

### Crépuscule

Twilight . . . From the houses I pass come the smell of
cooking and the rattle of plates. People are preparing to
dine and then go to bed or to the theater . . . Ah, too long

have I hardened myself against tears; I can be a terrific coward now in the face of the stars!

And all this is without end, without end.

Beaten-down horses drag their heavy carts along the streets—women wander by—gentlemen greet one another with polite smiles . . . And the earth whirls on.

Noon.

One half of the earth lit by the sun, the other half black and spotted with fire, gas, resin, or candle flame . . . In one place people are fighting, there are massacres; in another, there is an execution, in another, a robbery . . . Below, men are sleeping, dying . . . the black ribbons of funeral processions winding toward the yew trees . . . endless. And with all this on its back, how can the enormous earth go on hurtling through eternal space with the terrible rapidity of a lightning flash?

WILLIAM JAY SMITH

# Guillaume Apollinaire

## 1880–1918

# GUILLAUME APOLLINAIRE

## 1880–1918

Immediate predecessor of Dada and the Surrealists in the anti-rational line of descent from Baudelaire–Corbière, Rimbaud, Laforgue–Apollinaire was a very conscious modernist. He strove in his poetry to make use of the new, less in the sense of the search for the unhackneyed or the unknown, as had been the case with Baudelaire and Rimbaud, than of the various phenomena which, before and during the First World War, were revolutionizing the more minor aspects of experience: the automobile, the airplane, moving pictures, and also of course the war itself. At times also even his experiments in form, his surprising images, his omissions of punctuation seem those of the conscious innovator.

As gregarious as Laforgue was shy, Apollinaire knew everyone, was interested in painting and the theater, and the novel, as well as poetry; and, a little like Cocteau shortly afterwards, he served as a kind of clearing house and impresario for new ideas: Futurism, Cubism, every approach which seemed to him to represent the *esprit nouveau*.

His poetry, intimate, casual, unpretentious, was remarkably free and varied, reflecting in its variety the quickly shifting rhythms of the new age which was replacing the relatively stable close of the nineteenth century. Theorist of Cubism in *Les Peintres cubistes*, credited with inventing the term "surrealism," Apollinaire was perhaps as important as the center of an attitude reflecting the modern age as he was because of his two volumes of poetry.

# ZONE

## *Zone*

After all you are weary of this oldtime world

Shepherdess O Eiffel Tower your flock of bridges is bleating
    this morning

You have had enough of this living in a Greek and Roman
    antiquity

Here even the automobiles contrive an ancient aspect
Only religion is still new only religion
Has stayed simple like the Airport hangars

In all Europe you alone are not antique O Christianity
The most up-to-date European is you Pope Pius X
And you whom the windows stare at shame keeps you back
From going into some church and confessing your sins this
    morning
You read the prospectuses the catalogues the public no-
    tices that sing out
Here's the morning's poetry and for prose we have news-
    papers
We've two-bit volumes full of crime adventure
Portraits of the great and a thousand miscellaneous items

This morning I saw a neat street I've forgotten its name
All new and clean a bugle in the sun
Bosses workmen and pretty stenographers
From Monday morning to Saturday night pass along it four
    times a day
Three times each morning the siren moans there
A furious whistle bays along about noon
The slogans the signboards the walls
The plaques the parroty notices nagging
I like the charm of this industrial street
Located in Paris between the Rue Aumont-Thiéville and
    the Avenue des Ternes
Here's your young street and you're only a little child still

Your mother dresses you only in white and blue
You're a religious boy and along with your oldest pal René
    Dalize
You like nothing better than Church ceremonies
It's nine o'clock the gas is all bluey turned down you sneak
    out of the dorm
You pray all night long in the school chapel
While the eternal adorable depth of amethyst
Revolves forever the flamboyant glory of Christ
This is the fair lily that all of us tend
The torch with red hair unquenched by the wind
The pale flushed son of the mother grieving
The tree leafy-thick all over with prayers
The double potency of honor and forever
The six-branched star
God who dies Friday and rises on Sunday
Christ who climbs the sky better than any aviator
He holds the world record for altitude

Pupil Christ of the eye
Twentieth pupil of the centuries he knows his job
And changes into a bird this century goes up into the air
    like Jesus
The devils in their abysses lift up their heads to watch
They call it an imitation of Simon Magus in Judaea
They exclaim if this is flying let's call him fly-by-night
The angels flash around the pretty tightroper
Icarus Enoch Elijah Apollonius of Tyana
Bob about this first airplane
From time to time they step aside for persons transported
    by the Sacrament
Those priests ascending eternally at the Elevation of the
    Host
The plane lands at last with wings outspread
Then the skies are jammed with swallows by the millions
On swooping wings the ravens come the falcons the owls
Ibises from Africa and flamingos and marabouts
The Roc bird celebrated by storytellers and poets
Glides with the skull of Adam the first head in its claws
The eagle plummets from the horizon with a great cry
And from America comes the small colibri

From China the supple long pihis
Who have only one wing and who fly in pairs
And here is the dove immaculate spirit
Escorted by the lyre-bird and the eyey peacock
The phoenix that self-engendering stake
Hides everything for a moment with his burning ashes
The sirens abandon their perilous straits
Arrive all three of them singing at the top of their voices
Eagle phoenix Chinese pihis all combine
To fraternize with the flying machine

You are walking in Paris now all alone in a crowd
Herds of mooing busses pass by as you go
Love's anguish grabs you by the gullet
As if you'd never be loved again
If you lived in the old days you'd enter a monastery
You're ashamed of yourself when you catch yourself pray-
      ing
You sneer at yourself friend your laugh snaps like hell-fire
The sparks of that laugh gild your life's cash reserves
It's a picture hung up in a dusky museum
And every once in a while you get up close to examine it

Today you're taking a walk in Paris the women are bloodied
This was and I did not want to remember it this was in the
      ebb of beauty

Immured in her ancient flames Notre-Dame has seen me at
      Chartres
The blood of your Sacré-Cœur has engulfed me at Mont-
      martre
I am sick of listening to blessed discourse
The love that I suffer is a shameful disease
And the image that owns you keeps you alive in sleepless-
      ness and in agony
It is always near you that transient image

Now you are by the Mediterranean
Under the lemon trees flowering all year long
You go for a sail with some friends of yours

One's from Nice one's from Menton there are two from
    Turbes
We are alarmed by the sight of the cuttlefish far down
And through the seaweed fish swim in the Savior's image

You are in a tavern garden somewhere outside Prague
You are so happy there's a rose on the table
And instead of composing your prose fable
You note the worm asleep in the heart of the rose

In terror you see yourself limned in the agates of Saint Vit
You were deathly sorry the day you saw yourself there
You look like Lazarus struck silly by the daylight
The hands on the ghetto clock move backwards
You too reverse slowly into your life
And going up to Hradchin hearing at nightfall
The tavern songs of the singing Czechs
You're back at Marseille along the watermelons
Back in Coblenz at the Hôtel du Géant
You're in Rome sitting under a Japanese medlar

You're in Amsterdam with a girl you think's pretty but she's
    a fright
She's going to marry a Leyden undergraduate
They rent rooms in Latin there Cubicula locanda
I remember it well I spent three days there and also at
    Gouda

You're in Paris before the examining magistrate
Like a common criminal you are placed in custody
You have made your happy and dolorous journeys
Before taking account of falsehood and age
At twenty and thirty you have suffered from love
I have lived like a madman and I've lost my time
You no longer dare look at your hands and all the time I
    could burst out sobbing
Because of you because of her I love because of everything
    that has frightened you

Eyes full of tears you watch these poor emigrants

They trust in God they pray the women suckle their babies
Their odor fills the concourse of the Saint-Lazare Station
They believe in their star like the Three Wise Men
They look forward to getting rich in the Argentine
And coming back home after their fortune's made
One family transports its red eiderdown just as you trans-
    port your heart
That quilt and our dreams are equally unreal
Certain of these emigrants stay here and take lodgings
In the Rue des Rosiers or the Rue des Écouffes in flopperies
I've often seen them taking the air evenings in the street
They are like chessmen they seldom leave their squares
There are Jews above all their women wear wigs
Drained of blood they sit far back in their shops

You stand before the counter in a rotgut bar
With a five-cent coffee among the down-and-out

You are night in a fine restaurant

These women are not evil they have their troubles never-
    theless
All of them have made some lover unhappy even the
    ugliest
She's the daughter of a Jersey policeman

Her hands I had not seen them are hard and chapped
I've an enormous pity for the stitched scars on her belly

To a poor girl with a horrible laugh I humble my mouth
    now

You are alone morning is coming
The milkmen are clanking their tin cans in the streets

Night takes flight like a fair Médive
It's a faithless Ferdine or a faithful Leah

You drink an alcohol that burns like your life
Your life that you drink down like brandy

You walk toward Auteuil and you would go home on foot
To sleep among your fetishes from Oceania and Guinea
They are Christs in another form Christs of another faith
They are the lesser Christs of obscure yearnings

Good-bye Good-bye

Sun cut throat

DUDLEY FITTS

## THE MIRABEAU BRIDGE

*Le Pont Mirabeau*

Under the Mirabeau Bridge the Seine
Flows and our love
Must I be reminded again
How joy came always after pain

Night comes the hour is rung
The days go I remain

Hands within hands we stand face to face
While underneath
The bridge of our arms passes
The loose wave of our gazing which is endless

Night comes the hour is rung
The days go I remain

Love slips away like this water flowing
Love slips away
How slow life is in its going
And hope is so violent a thing

Night comes the hour is rung
The days go I remain

The days pass the weeks pass and are gone
Neither time that is gone
Nor love ever returns again
Under the Mirabeau Bridge flows the Seine

Night comes the hour is rung
The days go I remain

W. S. MERWIN

## THE SONG OF THE ILL-BELOVED

*La Chanson du mal-aimé*

*To Paul Léautaud*

*And this is the ballad that I sang
In 1903 not knowing then
How like a Phoenix is my love
For if it dies one night the next
Morning sees it born again*

One London night in a half fog
A draggled boy accosted me
So like my love that when I felt
The glance that touched me from his eyes
I dropped my own in modesty

I followed this perverse kid as
He strolled along hands pocketed
And whistling The Red Sea ditch
With houses lining either side
I was Pharaoh he the Jews

Let these brick waves wash down on us
If once I did not love you well
I am great Egypt's sovereign lord
His sister-wife and all his host
If you are not my only love

At the turn of a burning street each house-
front suppurated fiery wounds
Of mist and blood all the façades
In lamentation cried aloud
A woman who resembled him

I knew at once the inhuman eyes
The naked neck with the ragged scar
That came out staggering from some bar
The moment that I recognized
How great a cheat is love itself

When after many a weary year
Ulysses that good man reached home
His ancient dog remembered him
His wife was waiting for him near
A rug she'd woven thick and fine

The royal mate of Sacontale
Bored with his triumphs was well pleased
To find her with love-faded eyes
And face delay had made more pale
Petting her little male gazelle

I thought of those happy royalties
That night when love betraying and
She whom I loved and do love still
Beset me with their sleight of ghosts
Contriving my unhappiness

Hell's built on such regrets as these
A Heav'n of forgetfulness revealed
For a kiss from her all the world's kings
Would have gladly died poor famous things
And bartered their own shades willingly

I have been wintering in my past
O Easter sunlight come again
To warm a heart more frozen than
Sebastus' was by forty such
My life has suffered briefer pain

Fair ship O Memory have we two
Sailed long enough upon a sea
Too sour for drinking and gone astray
From sweet dawn to nagging night
Mindless heedless of our way

O false farewells O love involved
In her who takes her leave of me
The loved woman whom I lost
That last year in Germany
And whom I shall not again see

O Galaxy O luminous
Sister of the white Canaan rills
And the white flesh of girls in love
Shall we not swim in death along
That course toward systems further still

I call to mind another year
The dawning of an April day
I sang my darling pleasure I
Sang as a man sings of his love
In the love-rising of the year

### AUBADE SUNG AT LAETARE A YEAR SINCE

*Spring's come again Arise Pâquette*
*And walk with me in the pretty woods*
*The hens go cluckcluck in the yard*
*Dawn hangs the sky up in pink folds*
*Love's on the march to take you dear*

*Mars and Venus have come back*
*To drink each other's lips in love*
*There in the open where roses lean*
*Leafing shelteringly above*
*The naked dance of the rose gods*

*Oh come this is my love's domain*
*The heavy flowers yield to love*
*Nature is all immediacy*
*Pan plays his woodland pipes again*
*The damp frogs have begun their song*


Those gods are mostly dead For them
It is the weeping willows weep
The great god Pan Love Jesus Christ
Utterly dead and tomcats wail
In Paris courtyards I too weep


I who have lays fit for a queen
And love-compleynts for all my years
The choruses of fisher slaves
The ballad of the ill-beloved
And such songs as the Sirens sing


For love's dead and I shake therefore
Idols of him I now adore
Mementoes in his likeness made
Thus like Mausolus' wife I droop
Faithful in grief forevermore


For I am true as a bull-pup
To his master or as ivy to the trunk
Or the Zaporozhian Cossacks drunk
Brigandish and full of prayers
To their native steppes and the Decalogue


Under the Crescent bow your necks
That Crescent that the Mages quiz
I am the Sultan King of Kings
Zaporozhian Cossacks *Ecce Rex*
Your Sovereign your Dazzling Lord

Subjects swear fealty to me
Thus he had written to them once
But when they'd got his words aright
They laughed and sat down cheerfully
To answer him by candlelight


REPLY OF THE ZAPOROZHIAN COSSACKS
TO THE SULTAN OF CONSTANTINOPLE

*You are worse news than Barabbas was*
*Horn'd like the Angels of the Pit*
*Are you there you old Beelzebub*
*Suckled on drainage and filthy mud*
*We must decline Walpurgisnacht*

*Spoilt fishfood from Saloniki*
*Interminable necklace of bad nights*
*Of eyes gouged out and speared on spikes*
*Your mother let a squishy fart*
*And of her gut-cramp you were born*

*Podolian hangman Fancier*
*Of gashes ulcers and scab-crust*
*Arse of horse and snout of hog*
*Keep whatever gold you've got*
*To pay the druggist for your drugs*

O Galaxy O luminous
Sister of the white Canaan rills
And the white flesh of girls in love
Shall we not swim in death along
Your course toward systems further still

The hurt that troubles a whore's eyes
Lovely as a panther is
Your kisses Love were Florentine
And tasted of such bitterness
As canceled both our destinies

An evening rout of trembling stars
Trailed from those eyes and Sirens swam
Therein and our quick kisses bit
Deep into blood our fury moved
Our fairy godmothers to tears

Surely I wait for her return
I wait with all my heart and soul
And on Come-back-to-me-dear Bridge
If we must never meet again
I'll tell her That's all right by me

My heart is drained and so's my head
All heaven it seems runs out of them
To fill my Danaïd casks Shall I
Ever find happiness instead
The innocence of a small child

I would not drive her from my mind
O dove O roadstead calm and white
Daisy exfoliate Isle remote
My land of dreaming My Cockayne
My gillyflower and my rose

Satyrs and pyralidês
Aegipans and will-o'-the-wisps
Fates frustrate or fates fortunate
A Calais choke-string round my neck
What holocaust of miseries

O sorrow multiplying fate
The unicorn the capricorn
My soul and wavering body fly
From you Torment divine adorned
With all the morning's flower stars

Unhappiness pale god with eyes
Of ivory your mad priests bring
Your victims wrapped in robes of black
And have they shed their tears in vain
God in whom no man need have faith

And you that follow after me
Cringing god of my gods that died
In autumn You mark off the hours
Of earth that still are left to me
My Shade and my inveterate Snake


We walked together in the sun
Because remember you love it so
Shadowy wife I love you too
You are mine for ever nothing you
My ghost wears mourning for myself


Winter with all its snow is dead
The gleaming hives are all burnt down
Birds on branches overhead
Sing springtime light sing April bright
For orchard plot and garden bed


Argýraspids undying strike
The silver-targèd snow gives way
Before the pale Dendróphori
Of spring that simple people like
And wet eyes learn to smile again


And me my heart's as thumping fat
As the arse of a wife from the Middle East
I loved you too much O my love
I have found too much hurt in love
Now seven swords leap from the sheath


Seven subtle blades of grief
Transfix my heart O lucent pain
My foolish mind would justify
My plight but the excuse is vain
Forget you say But how can I

### THE SEVEN SWORDS

The first sword is pure silver and
Pâline they call its vibrant name
Its blade a wintry snowing sky
Ghibelline blood its destiny
When he had forged it Vulcan died

The second blade is named Noubosse
Oh rainbow of delight The gods
Handle it at their wedding feasts
It's killed thirty Bé-Rieux at least
Its power came from Carabosse

The third is all a woman's blue
But Cypriape for all of that
They call it Lul de Faltenin
And Hermês Ernest a midget now
Brings it in on a tablecloth

The fourth is known as Malourène
A river running green and gold
And river girls at evening bathe
The worship of their bodies in
That stream and singing boatmen pass

The fifth sword's name is Sainte-Fabeau
Prettiest of the distaff kind
A cypress shadowing a tomb
Where the four winds fall to their knees
And every night's a torch ablaze

A glory of metal is the sixth
Our friend with such small hands from whom
Each morning forces us to part
Good-bye that's the road you must take
Crowing has drained the cock's shrill heart

*The seventh lies exhausted here*
*A woman a dead rose also*
*Thank you the last man to appear*
*Shut the door upon my love*
*I have not known you all these years*


O Galaxy O luminous
Sister of the white Canaan rills
And the white flesh of girls in love
Shall we not swim in death along
That course toward systems further still


The quiring firmament declares
That dicing devils guide our steps
The scrape of those lost fiddles cheers
Our human dance as we descend
Backwards into the abyss


What fate inscrutable is this
The shaking madness of great kings
A sky of stiff stars shivering
Faithless women for your beds
In deserts crushed by history


The old Prince Regent Leopold
Male nurse of two mad Heads of State
Does he sob himself to sleep for them
While fireflies flash their sparkling light
Gilded for Midsummer's Night


A château without a chatelaine
And a barque with barcarolles near by
On a lake of white touched by the breath
Of delicate breezes It was like
A Siren sailing a dying swan

One day the King drowned in that flood
Of silver but floated up again
Mouth wide open and lay down
Upon the bank to sleep awhile
Face up beneath the fickle sky

Your sun O June your ardent lyre
Scorches the fingers of my hand
Pain-singing ecstasy of fire
I stroll through my fine Paris and
Have no heart for dying there

Each Sunday is eternity
Barrel organs creak their grief
In dingy courtyards flowers lean
From these Parisian balconies
Like towers in a Pisan scene

Nights in Paris drunk on gin
Aflare with electricity
Trams trail green fire along their spines
Take the long rails melodiously
Musicking the insane machine

Paunchy with smoke the cafés grunt
Love love love from the gypsy dance
Love from siphons sniffly-nosed
Love from the apron'd waiter-boys
Love from you love whom I loved

I who have lays fit for a queen
And love-compleynts for all my years
The choruses of fisher slaves
The ballad of the ill-beloved
And such songs as the Sirens sing

DUDLEY FITTS

## DUSK

*Crépuscule*

*To Mademoiselle Marie Laurencin*

Brushed by the shadows of the dead
On grass where failing daylight falls
The lady harlequin's stripped bare
Admiring herself in a still pool

A twilight juggler a charlatan
Boasts tricks that he knows how to play
Pale as milk the studding stars
Stand in the tall uncolored air

Harlequin pallid on his small stage
Greets the audience first of all
Bohemian sorcerers a train
Of fairies and prestidigitals

Reaching up to unhook a star
He whirls it round with outstretched arm
While cymbals mark a measured beat
Hanging from a hanged man's feet

The sightless one croons to a child
The hind and her troop of fawns pass by
The dwarf sulks at the growing thrust
Of Harlequin the Trismegist

**DUDLEY FITTS**

## ANNIE

*Annie*

On the Texas coast
Between Mobile and Galveston there's
A large garden full of roses
And the villa there
Is one great rose

Time and again a woman walks
In that garden all alone
And when I pass by on the lime-shaded road
Our eyes lock

As this woman is a Mennonite
Her rosebushes and her frocks are buttonless
There are two missing from my coat
The lady and I profess almost the same rite

DUDLEY FITTS

## MARIZIBILL

*Marizibill*

Along the high-street in Cologne
back and forth she walked at night
a slick little piece for all to own
then tired of sidewalks she'd stay on
in shady barrooms drinking late

She went down and out, she gave her all
for a redheaded pimp with a bloodshot eye
a Jew he was with a garlic smell
who'd come from Formosa once and hauled
her out of some whorehouse in Shanghai

People I know of every sort
to match their fates they lack the force
like dead leaves they're irresolute
their eyes are fires just half put out
their hearts sway open like their doors

FREDERICK MORGAN

## WHITE SNOW

*La Blanche neige*

Angels angels in the sky
One's dressed as an officer
One as a cook
And the others are singing

Smart officer color of the sky
Long after Christmas soft spring will bring
A shining sun to medal you
A shining sun

And now the cook is plucking geese
Ah! fall of snow
Falling and no
Darling girl in my arms' embrace

DUDLEY FITTS

## SALOME

*Salomé*

To bring a smile once more to John Baptist's lips
Sire I would outdance the Seraphim
In your countess' finery why are you so sad
As you sit by the Prince Mother and look at him

My heart leaped up leaped up to hear him speak
That day I was dancing on the fennel ground
Lilies I worked in silken embroidery
For a streamer to bind the tip of his staff around

Now King Herod for whom will you have me sew
His staff bloomed with new flowers at Jordan River
And when your soldiers carried him away
The lilies in my garden died forever

Come down come down with me to the quincunx glade
    Silly pretty King your tears are told
Instead of that gewgaw of yours take this head and dance
But do not touch the brow my mother is cold

Go before us Sire and you pikemen march behind
We'll dig in the earth and bury him and he
Shall have our flowers our dancing in a round
Until my garter drops from my dancing knee
                From the king his snuffery
                From the princess her rosary
                From the parson his breviary

                        **DUDLEY FITTS**

## AUTUMN

*Automne*

A bowlegged peasant and his ox receding
Through the mist slowly through the mist of autumn
Which hides the shabby and sordid villages

And out there as he goes the peasant is singing
A song of love and infidelity
About a ring and a heart which someone is breaking

Oh the autumn the autumn has been the death of summer
In the mist there are two gray shapes receding

                                                W. S. MERWIN

## RHENISH AUTUMN

*Rhénane d'Automne*

                        *To Toussaint Luca*

The children of the dead are going to play
In the graveyard
Martin Gertrude Hans and Henri
No cock has crowed today
Kikiriki

The old women
All in tears are proceeding
And the good burros
Bray heehaw and start to munch the flowers
Of the funeral wreaths

This is the day of the dead and of all their souls

The children and the old women
Light candles and tapers
On each catholic grave
The veils of the old women
The clouds in the sky
Are like the beards of she-goats

The air trembles with flames and prayer

The graveyard is a beautiful garden
Full of hoary willows and rosemary
Often they are friends who are buried here
Ah! how blessed you are in the beautiful graveyard
You beggars who died drunkards
You who are eyeless as Fate
And you children who died as you prayed

Ah! how blessed you are in the beautiful graveyard
You burgomasters you seamen
And you counselors of state
And you gypsies without passport
Life is rotting your belly
We stumble on the cross at our feet

The owls hoot and the moaning wind from the Rhine
Blows out the tapers which the children light again and
   again
And the dead leaves
Come to cover the dead

Dead children now and then speak with their mother
And dead women now and then long to come back

Oh! I do not want you to return
The autumn is full of disembodied hands
No no these are dead leaves
They are the hands of the dear dead
They are your disembodied hands

We have wept so much today
With these dead their children and the old women
Under a sunless sky
In the graveyard full of flames

Then we had to turn back into the wind
At our feet the chestnuts rolled
And their burrs were
Like the wounded heart of the Madonna
We wondered if her skin
Was the color of the autumn chestnuts

DAISY ALDAN

## I HAD THE COURAGE . . .

*J'ai eu le courage . . .*

I had the courage to look backward
The ghosts of my days
Mark my way and I mourn them
Some lie moldering in Italian churches
Or in little woods of citron trees
Which flower and bear fruit
At the same time and in every season
Other days wept before dying in taverns
Where ardent odes became jaded
Before the eyes of a mulatto girl who inspired poetry
And the roses of electricity open once more
In the garden of my memory

DAISY ALDAN

## HUNTING HORNS

*Cors de chasse*

Our history is exalted tragic
Like the masque of some despot
No drama of high exploit or magic
No detail that matters or does not
Can make this love of ours pathetic

Thomas De Quincey drinking down
His opium sweet poison demure
Went in a dream to his poor Anne
Pass by pass by since nothing's sure
Often I'll come back again

Memory is a hunting horn
Its tone dies out along the wind

DUDLEY FITTS

## VENDÉMIAIRE

*Vendémiaire*

Remember me you men in years to come
My lifetime saw the passing away of kings
Silent and glum they perished one by one
Who were thrice brave reduced to conjuring

In Paris how charmingly September closed
Each night grew like a vine whose branches spread
Light upon that city while overhead
Ripe stars pecked at by my glory's tipsy birds
Hung waiting to be gathered in the dawn

Passing the shadowy empty quays one night
As I came back to Auteuil I heard a voice
Singing a grave song phrased with silences
Through which there rose from all along the Seine
Farther voices in distant pure lament

Long I stood listening to these cries and songs
Stirred by the voice of Paris in the night

Cities of France of Europe of all the world
I am thirsty drain into my deep throat

Then I saw that Paris already drunk in the vine
Was gathering the sweetest grape that the world knows
The marvelous fruit singing from the trellises

And Rennes answered for Quimper and for Vannes
We are here O Paris Our houses our citizens

These grapes of our senses engendered by the sun
Perish to quench your thirst too urgent a prodigy
To all of you we bring minds graveyards and walls
And cradles filled with cries that you will not hear
Upstream or down O rivers our thoughts are yours
The ears of the schools and our joined hands
Fingers pricked up like parish steeples
We bring you the lithe power of reason too
Mystery that shuts as a door shuts the house
The gallant mystery of ancient courtesy
Mystery fatal fatal in another life

Double reason existing beyond beauty
Unknown to Greece unknown to the Orient
The double reason of Brittany where wave by wave
The ocean slowly gelds the continent

Gaily the cities of the North replied

O Paris we are yours your lively drinks

The virile cities where metallic saints
Talk and sing in our consecrated mills
Sky-open our chimneys fill the clouds
As once Ixion good mechanic did
And our numberless hands
Shops mills factories hands
Where workers naked as our fingers fashion
Reality for whatever wage an hour
All that we give you

And Lyon answered as the angels of Fourvières
Wove a new heaven with the silk of prayer

Refresh your thirst Paris with the divine words
Murmured by my two lips the Rhône and the Saône
The same cult rising always from its death
Puts saints asunder here and rains down blood
Fortunate rain O tepid drops O pain
A child watches windows opening wide
And grapes yielding themselves to drunken birds

And then the cities of the South replied

Great Paris last refuge of living reason
Ordering our moods as your destiny compels
And you O Mediterranean drawing back
Divide our bodies as it were the broken Host
These lofty loves and this orphan dance of theirs
Shall be the pure wine O Paris that you love

An endless death-rattle rose from Sicily
Composing words in a long whir of wings

All the grapes have been gathered from our vines
And this fruit of the dead whose flattened seeds
Taste of the blood of earth and of its salt
All is yours for your thirst Paris beneath
A sky curtained by hungry clouds
Petted by Ixion that indirect creator
And all the crows of Africa hatch in this sea

O grapes And these leaden and domestic eyes
Future and life mope in the trellises

But where are the sirens with gleaming stare
That trapped the mariners whom these birds loved
There is no gleam now from the Skyllan rock
Where once serene and soft three voices sang

Suddenly the aspect of the strait had changed
Faces of wave-flesh or of
Whatever else the mind can summon up
You are only masks imposed upon faces masked

He smiled that young swimmer in midstream
Among the drowned floating on that new flood
And the plaintive singers fled in pursuit of him

They said farewell to whirlpool and to rock
To their pale husbands stretched on the terraces
Then set their flight toward the burning sun
Along the wave where the great stars plunge down

When night returned covered with open eyes
To wander where the hydra hissed this winter
And suddenly I heard your imperious voice
O Rome
Damn with one breath all my accustomed thoughts
And the sky where love shepherds our destinies

The sprung iron bands on the tree of the Cross
And even the fleur-de-lis dying in the Vatican
Compounded in this wine I offer you having
A taste of the pure blood of one familiar
With a vegetal liberty you do not know
For the essential power that it is

The triple crown is fallen on the flagstones
And hierarchs kick it with their sandaled feet
O democratic splendor fading now
Let the royal night descend and the beasts be killed

Wolf-bitch and lamb eagle and mild dove
A crowd of kings hostile and merciless
Thirsting like you in the eternal vine
Shall spring from the ground and come down from the air
For a drink of my twice millenary wine

In silence now the Moselle meets the Rhine
At Coblenz it is Europe praying night and day
And I who lingered on the Auteuil quay
As the spaced hours drifted down like leaves
I heard the timely prayer of the vine stock
Joining the liquid purity of the rivers

O Paris your own wine is better than this
Grown on our banks but on branches from the north

All the grapes are ripe for this terrible thirst
My masculine strong grapes bleeding in the press
You will drink down in long draughts all of Europe's blood
Because you are beautiful because only you are noble
And because it is in you that God becomes
And these vintners of mine in their elegant houses
That flash fire each evening across our waters
In these fine houses stark white and black
Not knowing the real you they chant your glory
But we join our liquid hands in prayer
Leading the restless floods down to the brine
And the city lying between our two blades
Sheds no light on its two waters as it sleeps
While from time to time a far-off whistle
Troubles the sleeping daughters of Coblenz

And now the cities were answering by the hundreds
I could no longer distinguish their distant speech
And Trier that venerable city
Joined its voice with theirs

All the universe centered in this wine
Containing seas animals plants
Cities and their fate and the singing stars

Men kneeling on Heaven's bank
And docile iron our good companion
And fire lovable as one's own self
All the haughty dead united behind my brow
The lightning flash quick as a newborn thought
All names six by six all numbers one by one
Tons of paper twisting like flame
And those coming someday to whiten our bones
The good immortal worms so demurely bored
Armies ranged as for battle
Crucifix forests and the lacustrine dwellings
Along the shores of her eyes whom I love so
And flowers crying out of mouths
And everything that I can not say
Everything that I shall never know
All of it all of it changed into this pure wine

For which Paris thirsted
Then was revealed to me

Accomplishments pleasant days horror nights
Vegetation Couplings eternal music
Motions Adorations divine regret
Worlds self-mirroring mirroring us
I have drunk you without being slaked

But I have known since how the universe tastes

I am drunk from drinking the whole universe
On the dock by the river flood and the sleeping barges

Oh hear me I am the gullet of Paris
If I like I will drink the universe again

Listen to my song of cosmic drunkenness

The September night was ending slowly
The red bridge-fires were dying in the Seine
With the fading stars Dawn was about to break

DUDLEY FITTS

## STAR

### *Étoile*

I think of Gaspard that certainly was not
His real name he is traveling he has left the town
Of Blue Lanchi where all the children called him Papa
At the foot of the calm gulf facing the seven islands
Gaspard walks on and longs for the rice and the tea
          The milky way
At night since naturally he is walking
Only at night often catches his eye
          But Gaspard
Knows full well that one must not follow it

W. S. MERWIN

## HILLS

### *Les Collines*

Overhead in the Paris sky
Two airplanes fought it out one day
And one was red and one was black
And all the while in the zenith flamed
The everlasting sun-airplane

And one of them was my whole youth
The other was my days to come
The fury of their fight was like
The Archangel's with radiant wings
The day he fought with Lucifer

Set the sum against the problem thus
And the night thus against the day
Thus what I love makes its attack
Upon my love thus a great storm
Tears up the roots of a crying tree

There is such sweetness everywhere
Paris like a waking girl
Rises languid from her sleep
Shakes out the long coils of her hair
Singing and what she sings is fair

My youth has fallen where is it now
See all my future is in flames
Let the whole world hear me today
When I pronounce that now at last
Prophecy is an art newborn

You will find men who stand like hills
Towering from the run of men
Seeing the distant future's shape
Better than what surrounds them now
Clearer than what is past and gone

Adornment of roadways and of times
Passing and lasting without stay
Let us give the serpents leave to hiss
Vainly against the southern wind
The Psylli and the wave are gone

Schedule of days if our machines
Should set themselves to think at last
Waves of gold would comb and break
On stretches of a jeweled shore
The foam would be a womb once more

An eagle's pitch is less than man's
Man's is the joy that the sea knows
He frees himself in that upper air
From shadows and the muzzying blues
And so the spirit regains the dream

This is the time of sorcery
It's ours again prepare to see
A thousand million prodigies
Beyond the scope of myth itself
Since none has yet imagined them

The inner depths of consciousness
Tomorrow they will be explored
Who knows what living entities
Will be drawn up from that abyss
What new and whole cosmologies

Prophets rising up to speak
On the blue line of the distant hills
Will know the certitude of things
That learned men pretend to know
And they will carry us where they will

Desire is the greatest force
Come let me kiss you on the brow
Ah you are light as a tongue of flame
All of whose suffering you know
All of whose fervor burning bright

The time will come when we shall know
All that's to know of suffering
An age neither of taking heart
Nor of letting what we cherish go
Nor of doing all that we can do

In man himself we shall seek out
More than was ever sought before
And we shall weigh with no machines
Or instruments the will of man
And the drive engendered by that will

·And even those who most would help
Are wrong in their ministering to us
Since the times that made us one
Nothing is ended nothing's begun
Look on your finger there's a ring

Time of deserts and crossroads
Time of hills and of city squares
I am here for a stroll or two
Where a talisman enacts his role
Dead and more subtile than life itself

At last I've set myself apart
From every natural concern
Die I may but I cannot sin
And whatever any man has touched
My hands have touched my hands have felt

I have investigated un-
imagined things and many times
I have taken the very weight
Of life unweighable and now
I can perish with a smile

How often I have soared so high
So high that everything disappeared
Good-bye bizarreries ghosts good-bye
Then how shall I be imposed upon
By a small boy's pantomime of fear

Farewell my youth jasmine of time
I have breathed that fresh perfume
At Rome upon the floral floats
Gay with masks and tinkling bells
And the bright wreaths of carnival

Pure Christmas farewell now my youth
When all life was a single star
And I could see it mirrored in
The Mediterranean water far
Pearlier than a meteor

Downy as an archangelical
Nest with a garland made of clouds
Brighter than halos are and all
Splendors and emanating fires
Single sweetness Harmonies

But now I make a halt to watch
Upon the incandescent grass
A straying snake and it is I
I am the flute I play upon
I am the whip I am the lash

There is a time for suffering
There is a time for goodness too
My youth farewell the time has come
To know what it is the future holds
To know and not to die of it

This is the time of burning grace
When only a man's will can act
Seven years of tests beyond belief
Will bring him back to his true self
More pure more wise and more alive

He will discover worlds beyond
Now his mind shrivels like those flowers
That bring to birth delicious fruits
And we shall see them ripening
Upon the hill in the thick sun

I sing of very life and I
Alone am fit to sing this song
My music falls like scattered seed
You other singers be still You shall
Not mingle your tares with my wheat

A vessel came into the port
A great ship fine with all her flags
On her we found no one at all
But a woman she was rosy fair
And she lay murdered at our feet

I was begging another time
And all they gave me was a flame
That burnt me to the lips I could
Not say a single word of thanks
Torch that nothing can put out

And where are you dear friend of mine
Withdrawn so deep into yourself
That only a pit was left behind
For me to hurl myself into
Down to the neutral shades below

I hear my footsteps coming back
Along those pathways that no foot
Has ever taken I hear my steps
Always passing there below
Slow or swift as they come and go

Winter you with your whiskered chin
It's snowing I am out of sorts
I have traversed a glory of skies
Where human life is music and
The sun is too white for my eyes

Become familiar as I have
With the wonders that I proclaim
The goodness that is to prevail
The suffering that I endure
Then you will know what is to come

From suffering with goodness joined
A purer beauty shall be born
Than any beauty found before
In balanced counterweight of forms
Snow falls I shudder and I burn

Here at my table I write down
Whatever it may be I have felt
Whatever I have sung up there
A thrusting tree that sways against
The wind and its light streaming hair

A silk hat on the tablecloth
In a jumble of fruit the gloves lie dead
Beside an apple a lady cranes
Her neck to see the gentleman
Stands next her and engulfs himself

The dance whirls on at the back of time
I have killed the handsome band leader
And for the pleasure of my friends
I peel an orange now whose taste
Is a marvel of fireworks in the sky

They are all dead the headwaiter comes
And pours them an unreal champagne
That bubbles as though it were a snail
Or as though it were a poet's brain
A rose was singing all the while


The slave raises a naked sword
Like rivers and their springing wells
And every time he lowers it
The guts of a universe are drawn
And new worlds issue forth from it


The chauffeur hangs on to the wheel
And every time along the road
He honks at a corner there beyond
Just at the edge of his eye's reach
A virgin universe recedes


Third on the program's the lady who
Takes the elevator up
Up she goes forever up
And light streams round about her and
She stands transfigured in that light


But these are minor secrets There
Are others you'll find more profound
To be disclosed in a little while
And they will cut you through and through
With a thought forever unparalleled


Weep then and weep and weep again
What though the moon is full tonight
Or only crescent in the sky
Ah weep and weep and weep again
We have laughed so long in the sunlight

Arms of gold support this life
The golden secret must be pierced
There's nothing but a rapid flame
Touched by a rose adorably
And all the fragrance of the rose

DUDLEY FITTS

## ALWAYS

*Toujours*

*To Madame Faure-Favier*

Always
We'll go further without ever advancing
And from planet to planet

From nebula to nebula
The Don Juan of a thousand-and-three comets
Without even stirring from the earth
Looks for new forces
And takes phantoms seriously

And so much universe forgets itself
What are the great forgetters
Who then will know how to make us forget such and such
    a part of the world
Where is the Christopher Columbus to whom one will owe
    the forgetting of a continent

To lose
But to lose truly
To give way to discovery
                To lose
Life to find Triumph

R. G. STERN

## COMPANY COMMANDER

### *Chef de section*

My mouth will flame the sulphurs of the Pit
You will find my mouth a hell of sweetness and seduction
My mouth's angels will hold sway in your heart
My mouth's soldiers will take you by storm
The priests of my mouth will cense your beauty
Your soul will shake like a terrain in an earthquake
Your eyes will be charged with all the love that humanity
    has stored up in its eyes since the beginning
My mouth will be an army against you a stumbling
    awkward army
Tricky as a magician with his sleight of changing shapes
The choirs and orchestra of my mouth will tell you my love
It murmurs to you now from far away
While I stand here eyes fastened to my watch waiting for
    the exact moment to go over the top

DUDLEY FITTS

## THE PRETTY REDHEAD

### *La Jolie Rousse*

Here I am before all a man of sense
Knowing life and of death as much as a human being can
    know
Having experienced the pangs and the joys of love
Having known at times how to impose his ideas
Acquainted with several languages
Having traveled not a little
Having seen war in the Artillery and the Infantry
Wounded in the head trepanned under chloroform
Having lost his best friends in the frightful struggle
I know of the old and the new as much as one man can
    know of the two
And without being disturbed today by this war

Between us and for us my friends
I judge this long quarrel about tradition and invention
           About Order and Adventure


You whose mouth is made in the image of God's
Mouth which is order itself
Be indulgent when you compare us
With those who were the perfection of order
We who seek adventure everywhere


We are not your enemies
We strive to give you vast and strange domains
Where mystery flowers for all who would gather it
There are new fires of colors there never seen before
A thousand imponderable phantasms
To which reality must be given
We strive to explore kindness enormous country where all
     is still
There is also time which can be banished or recaptured
Pity us who struggle ever on the frontiers
Of the limitless and the future
Pity us our errors pity us our sins


Here now comes summer the violent season
And my youth as well as the spring is dead
O Sun this is the time of ardent Reason
           And I expect
To follow ever the sweet and noble form
Which she takes that I may love only her
She comes and draws me as a magnet iron
     She has the charming aspect
     Of an adorable redhead


Her hair is of gold one might say
A lovely flash of lightning that endures
Or those flames which flaunt
In tea roses that wither

But laugh laugh at me
Men everywhere especially people here
For there are so many things that I do not dare tell you
So many things that you would not permit me to say
Have pity on me

KATE FLORES

# Paul Valéry

## 1871–1945

## PAUL VALÉRY

### 1871–1945

Valéry is without question the pre-eminent French poet of
the twentieth century. Like Mallarmé, whose leading dis-
ciple he was, he produced relatively little poetry and was
silent altogether from the mid-nineties until 1917, when
what he had planned as the short valedictory to a reprint-
ing of his scattered poems turned into *La Jeune Parque*,
his major work in verse and, it has been said, the most dif-
ficult poem in the language. Neither its difficulty, however,
nor the time of its publication prevented the immediate rec-
ognition of it as a masterpiece. Within a few years Valéry's
stature as a literary figure was to be compared only with
that of Proust and Gide.

Echoing Mallarmé's preoccupation with the relation of
potentiality to action, Valéry moved this concern from the
world of art, of the poem, to the world of experience, of
such experience, at any rate, as involved the intellect. His
world is divided into a pure, potential, contemplated as-
pect, where all is absolute, and one which is impure, ac-
tual, acted, where all is relative. Creativity, the creation of
the poem—or the process of any action involving intellect
—is an oscillation between these aspects. What may serve
to control activity, to keep it as near perfection as can be,
what may demonstrate the poet's mastery of the actual, is
the skill with which he works, the rigidity of the control
he exerts as he works. At the opposite pole from the Ro-
mantic notion of inspiration, as it is from the Surrealist's
automatic writing, Valéry's emphasis upon technique and
the function of the mind produces in his poetry a remarka-
ble contrast with its delicate but none the less striking
sensuality.

# HELEN

## *Hélène*

Azure! behold me . . . I come from the caverns of death
To hear once more the measured sounding of waves,
And once more I see long galleys in the dawn
Revive from darkness in a file of golden oars.

My solitary hands call forth those monarchs
Whose beards of salt entwined my simple fingers.
I wept. They sang of their obscure triumphs
And of buried seas in the wake of their barques.

I hear deep hollow shells and the compelling
Clarions of war, pacing the flight of the oars—
The clear song of the oarsmen chains this tumult.

And gods raised high on the heroic prow,
Their ancient smile insulted by the spray,
Hold forth toward me forgiving sculptured arms.

ANDREW CHIAPPE

# THE FRIENDLY WOOD

## *Le Bois amical*

Meditations pure were ours
Side by side, along the ways;
We held each other's hand without
Speaking, among the hidden flowers.

Alone we walked as if betrothed,
Lost in the green night of the fields;
We shared this fruit of fairy reels,
The moon, to madmen well disposed.

And then, we were dead upon the moss,
Far, quite alone, among the soft
Shades of this intimate, murmuring wood;

And there, in the vast light aloft,
We found ourselves with many a tear,
O my companion of silence dear!

                    VERNON WATKINS

# THE CEMETERY BY THE SEA

*Le Cimetière marin*

This tranquil roof, with walking pigeons, looms
Trembling between the pines, among the tombs;
Precise midday the sea from fire composes—
The sea, the sea, forever rebegun!
What recompense after a thought is one
Look on the calm of gods the sea disposes!

Pure energies of lightning-flash consume
What diamond of evanescent spume!
And how is peace conceived in this pure air!
When the sun rests at noon above the abyss,
Pure work of an eternal cause is this,
And dream is knowledge, here in trembling air.

Temple unto Athena, quiet curve,
Ponderous calm and visible reserve,
Enchanting water, sleeping eye, aloof
Beneath a flaming veil, enduring bowl,
O silence! Like a tower within the soul,
But summit of a thousand gold tiles, Roof!

Temple of Time that one sigh may resume,
I climb this point and habitude assume,
Surrounded by the sea's enclosing sight.
As though an altar flamed and smoke arose,
My offering, the scintillation sows
A sovereign disdain along the height.

And as the hungry mouth obscures the fresh
Contour of fruit, translating thus its flesh
Into enjoyment, which the form abhors,
My future I inhale, in smoke unbound;
And to the soul consumed the heavens sound
The hollow alteration of seashores.

Fair sky, true sky, consider how I change!
After so much of pride, so much of strange
Indolence, yet full of power, unspent,
I abandon myself to this bright space,
Over the tombs my shadow runs its race,
Taming myself to its fragile movement.

My soul exposed to torches of the sun,
I can sustain you, just and forthright one,
Unerring light, pitilessly arrayed!
Pure to your primal place I have restored
You: comtemplate yourself! But light outpoured
Presumes one somber moiety of shade.

O for myself, within myself alone,
Near to the poem's source, against the bone,
Between the void and pure contingency,
I wait the echoing greatness from within,
Like some sonorous, bitter cistern's din,
Sounding some chasm in the soul to be.

Do you know, subtle prisoner of leaves,
Devourer of the grills the foliage weaves,
The shining mystery on my closed eyes,
What flesh impels me to its slothful end,
What forehead to this bony earth I bend?
A spark dreams of my absent loyalties.

Closed, sacred, filled with fire of nothing spun,
Terrestrial fragment offered to the sun,
This place by torches governed pleases me,
Composed of gold, of stone and somber glades,
Where so much marble trembles over shades;
Over the tombs there sleeps the faithful sea!

Resplendent bitch! Keep off the idolator,
While I with shepherd's smile lay out the store
Of earth for these, my white, mysterious sheep,
My tranquil tombs, the strange, white, herded things.
Vain dreams, and angels with inquiring wings,
And prudent pigeons at a distance keep!

Once here the future becomes idleness;
The clean insect scratches the aridness;
Everything burns and is undone, the sere
Grasses like fire invade the splitting wood . . .
Now drunk with absence, life's infinitude,
And bitterness is sweet and mind is clear.

The hidden dead are well within this clay
That warms them, burns their mystery away.
Midday above, high noontide without motion,
Thinks in itself and is its proper stem . . .
O complete head and perfect diadem,
I am in you the secret alteration.

You have but me to hold your fearful taint!
My penitence and doubt and my constraint
In your great diamond comprise the flaw! . . .
But in their night of marble-weighted cold,
A shadowy people of the rooted mold,
Slow, hesitating, to your party draw.

Into heavy absence they are blended,
White species unto the red clay descended;
The gift of life is passing to the flowers.
Where are the well-known phrases of the dead,
The personal art, the souls distinguishèd?
The source of tears the tracking worm devours.

Of flattered girls the eager, sharpened cries,
The moistened eyelids and the teeth and eyes,
The charming breasts that parley with the flame,
The shining blood at lips that pleasure rifts,
The fingers that defend the final gifts,
All go beneath the earth, rejoin the game.

Do you, great soul, still hope to find a dream
Without these colors of a lying scheme
That wave and gold display here to the eye?
When you are changed to breath, then will you sing?
My presence is porous! All is flying!
But holy eagerness must also die!

You, black and gold, gaunt immortality,
Death's head wreathed with the broken laurel tree,
Who say that where we end we but begin—
O lovely lie! O cunning, pious ruse!
Who does not know them—who does not refuse
The empty skull and the eternal grin!

Deep fathers, uninhabited heads, now dull,
Who, weighted by so many shovelsful,
Become the earth, and who confound our steps,
The gnawing and unanswerable worm's
Not yours, beneath the table. He confirms
My flesh, he lives on life, he keeps my steps.

What name I call him does not signify,
As love, or self-contempt; his tooth must pry,
Ever, so near my life no name him wrongs!
What matter! He can see, will, dream, and touch!
He likes my flesh, and even on my couch
My passing life to him, who lives, belongs.

Ah Zeno! Cruel Zeno of Elea!
Who pierce my body with your winged idea,
Arrow that flying denies motion's press!
The sound brings me to birth, the arrow slays!
Ah Sun! What shadow of a tortoise stays
The soul, Achilles running motionless!

No, no! . . . Arise and enter the next state!
This thoughtful pose, my body, dissipate!
Drink, my breast, of the wind, a rising bourn!
A freshness breathed from off the quickening sea
Gives back my soul . . . O salty potency!
I'll run to the wave and from it be reborn!

Yes! great sea with delirium endowed,
O torn chlamys and hide of panther proud,
With thousand thousand idols of the sun,
Absolute hydra, drunk with your blue flesh,
Who tail in mouth eternally enmesh
In turbulence that is with silence one,

The wind awakes! . . . I must presume to live!
The immense air in my book is tentative;
The wave dares spout in powder from the rocks!
Flee, dazzled pages! Chase time and the hour!
Break, waves, and shatter with exultant power
This tranquil roof where jib-sails peck in flocks!

BARBARA GIBBS

## SONG OF THE COLUMNS

*Cantique des colonnes*

Sweet columns, with
Chaplets adorned with day,
Crowned with true birds, no myth,
That walk the stone-fledged way,

Sweet columns, O
The bobbins' orchestra!
Each one confides its own
Hush to the unison.

—What do you bear so high
Equal in radiance?
—For desire's faultless eye
Our studious elegance.

We sing by mutual choice
That we bear up the skies.
O sage and single voice
Singing for the eyes!

See what clear hymns!
What sonority
Our light-enamoured limbs
Draw from limpidity!

So chill, chased with dawn,
We from our beds early
By the chisel were drawn
To become these lilies!

From our beds of cold crystal
We were awakened,
Talons of metal
Gripped us and slackened.

To face the moon,
The moon and sunglow,
We were polished each one
Like a nail of the toe!

Servant-maids inflexuous,
Smiles with no viewer,
The girl before us
Feels her legs pure.

Piously matched peers,
The nose beneath the stringcourse
And our rich ears
Deaf to the white load's force,

A temple on our eyes,
Dark for eternity,
Without the gods we rise
To that divinity!

Our antique youths,
Dull flesh, fair shades of mirth,
Are bright with subtle truths
Which numbers bring to birth.

Girls of the golden numbers,
Strong with heaven's laws and rod,
On us there falls and slumbers
A honey-colored god.

He sleeps at ease, the Day,
Whom every day with vows
We on love's table lay,
Slack-tided on our brows.

Incorruptible sisters,
Half fire, half cool as eves,
We took for dancers
Breezes and dry leaves,

And the centuries, by ten,
And the past peoples' tide,
It is a deep-found Then,
Then never satisfied!

Beneath our loves that raise
A weight than Earth more grave
Silent we cross the days
Like a stone the wave!

We walk in time, and these
Our dazzling bodies
Have steps ineffable
That mark in fable . . .

VERNON WATKINS

## INSINUATION

*L'Insinuant*

Oh Curves, meanderings,
Tricks of the liar,
What skill more gentle
Than this delay?

May I be your guide?
I know what I do,
And my fell design
Will not injure you . . .

(Although she smiles
So confidently,
Such liberty
Bewilders her!)

Oh Curves, meanderings,
Tricks of the liar,
I will make you wait
For the gentlest word.

BARBARA HOWES

## THE BURIED LADY

*La Fausse morte*

Tenderly, humbly, upon the charming tomb,
        The unconscious monument
Formed by your overweary grace from shade,
        Surrenderings, wasteful love,
I die, I throw myself upon you, drop, despond,

But hardly have I fallen to the sepulcher
Whose sealed expanse invites me on to dust,
Than her seeming corpse, in which the life revives,
Stirs, fires me with her glance, and sinks her teeth
In my flesh—and ever tears from me a new
        Death far dearer than life.

                                    BARBARA HOWES


# POMEGRANATES

## *Les Grenades*

Hard pomegranates sundered
By excess of your seeds,
You make me think of mighty brows
Aburst with their discoveries!

If the suns you underwent,
O pomegranates severed,
Wrought your essence with the pride
To rend your ruby segments,

And if the dry gold of your shell
At instance of a power
Cracks in crimson gems of juice,

This luminous eruption
Sets a soul to dream upon
Its secret architecture.

                                    KATE FLORES

## THE LOST WINE

*Le Vin perdu*

One day into the sea I cast
(But where I cannot now divine)
As offering to oblivion,
My small store of precious wine . . .

What, oh rare liquor, willed your loss?
Some oracle half understood?
Some hidden impulse of the heart
That made the poured wine seem like blood?

From this infusion of smoky rose
The sea regained its purity,
Its usual transparency . . .

Lost was the wine, and drunk the waves!
I saw high in the briny air
Forms unfathomed leaping there.

BARBARA HOWES

## INTERIOR

*Intérieur*

With narrow eyes below soft chains, a slave
Empties my vases, in the mirror dives,
Extends to the secret bed her pure, white hands:
Within these walls a modest woman moves
Who in my reverie cuts through my vision,
Never once endangering abstraction,
As by a simple glass the sun is caught
Without the apparatus of pure thought.

BARBARA HOWES

PALM

*Palme*

*To Jeannie*

An angel sets at my place
—Barely screening the accolade
Of his formidable grace—
Fresh milk, new-baked bread;
With his lids he makes a sign
That is like a petition
That says to my vision:
Calm, calm, be calm,
Know the heaviness of a palm
Bearing its profusion!

Even as it bends
Under abundant good things
The shape perfectly rounds,
The heavy fruits are strings.
Wonder how it sheds
Vibrancy, how a slow thread
That parcels out the moment
Adjudicates without mystery
The heaviness of the sky
And the earth's enticement!

This fair mobile arbitress
Between shadow and sunlight
Wears the sibyl's dress,
Wisdom of day, sleep of night.
All round the one spot
The wide palm wearies not
Of welcomes and farewells . . .
How noble and soft it is
And worthy to dispose
The comforts of immortals!

The faint gold it sighs
Rings like a mere finger of air
Burdening the desert skies
With a silken signature.
An imperishable sound
Which it gives to the sandy wind
That waters it with its grains
Serves it as oracle
And foretells the miracle
Of the chanting pain.


Between sand and sky,
Ignorant of its own nature,
Each brightening day
Adds honey to its store.
This gentleness is ordered by
The divine continuity
Which does not mark passing time
But rather hides it
In a juice wherein secretes
All of love's perfume.


If you sometimes despond—
If the ardored rigor
In spite of tears responds
Under a shadow of languor—
Never blame of avarice
A Wisdom that is nurse
To so much gold and authority:
An everlasting hope
Rises through the dark sap
To maturity!

These days that seem effete,
Lost to the universal will,
Have thirsty roots that penetrate
The desert soil.
Fibrous substances,
The elect of shades,
They will never cease to try,
Short of the world's bowels,
To uncover the deep wells
For which the heights cry.

Patience, patience,
Patience in the blueness!
Every atom of silence
Is a seed of ripeness!
The glad surprise will come,
Quietest commotion,
A dove, a fresh breeze,
A woman leaning in languor
Will bring the downpour
That makes you fall on your knees!

Let multitudes pass away
Palm! . . . Let them abandon
Themselves, wallow in the clay
At the fruitfulness of creation!
These hours have not been lost,
So lightly you rest,
Like one contemplative
After lovely surrender,
Whose soul is spendthrift
To grow with what it gives!

BARBARA GIBBS

## ASIDES

### *Chanson à part*

What do you do? Why, everything.
What are you worth? Worth, well,
The worth of mastery and disgust,
Presentiment and trial . . .
What are you worth? Worth, well . . .
What do you want? Nothing, all.

What do you know? Boredom.
What can you do? Dream.
And with the power of the mind
Can turn the morning into night.
What can you do? Dream,
And so drive boredom from the mind.

What do you want? My own good.
What must you do? Learn.
Learn and master and foresee,
All, of course, to no good.
What do you fear? The will.
Who are you? Nothing, nothing at all.

Where are you going? To death.
What will you do there? Die;
Nor ever return to this rotten game,
Forever and ever and ever the same.
Where are you going? To die.
What will you do there? Be dead.

WILLIAM JAY SMITH

# French Texts

# Gérard de Nerval

## FANTAISIE

Il est un air pour qui je donnerais
Tout Rossini, tout Mozart et tout Weber
Un air très vieux, languissant et funèbre,
Qui pour moi seul a des charmes secrets.

Or, chaque fois que je viens à l'entendre,
De deux cents ans mon âme rajeunit:
C'est sous Louis-Treize . . . —Et je crois voir s'étendre
Un coteau vert que le couchant jaunit;

Puis un château de brique à coins de pierre,
Aux vitraux teints de rougeâtres couleurs,
Ceint de grands parcs, avec une rivière
Baignant ses pieds, qui coule entre des fleurs.

Puis une dame, à sa haute fenêtre,
Blonde aux yeux noirs, en ses habits anciens . . .
Que, dans une autre existence peut-être,
J'ai déjà vue—et dont je me souviens!

## LES CYDALISES

Où sont nos amoureuses?
Elles sont au tombeau!
Elles sont plus heureuses
Dans un séjour plus beau!

Elles sont près des anges
Dans le fond du ciel bleu,
Et chantent les louanges
De la mère de Dieu!

O blanche fiancée!
O jeune vierge en fleur!
Amante délaissée,
Que flétrit la douleur!

L'éternité profonde
Souriait dans vos yeux . . .
Flambeaux éteints du monde,
Rallumez-vous aux cieux!


## LE POINT NOIR

Quiconque a regardé le soleil fixement
Croit voir devant ses yeux voler obstinément
Autour de lui, dans l'air une tache livide.

Ainsi, tout jeune encor et plus audacieux,
Sur la gloire un instant j'osai fixer les yeux:
Un point noir est resté dans mon regard avide.

Depuis, mêlée à tout comme un signe de deuil,
Partout, sur quelque endroit que s'arrête mon œil,
Je la vois se poser aussi, la tache noire!

Quoi, toujours! Entre moi sans cesse et le bonheur?
Oh! c'est que l'aigle seul—malheur à nous! malheur!—
Contemple impunément le Soleil et la Gloire.


## EL DESDICHADO

Je suis le ténébreux,—le veuf,—l'inconsolé,
Le prince d'Aquitaine à la tour abolie:
Ma seule *étoile* est morte,—et mon luth constellé
Porte le *soleil noir* de la *Mélancolie.*

Dans la nuit du tombeau, toi qui m'as consolé,
Rends-moi le Pausilippe et la mer d'Italie,
La *fleur* qui plaisait tant à mon cœur désolé
Et la treille où le pampre à la rose s'allie.

Suis-je Amour ou Phébus, Lusignan ou Biron?
Mon front est rouge encor du baiser de la reine;
J'ai rêvé dans la grotte où nage la sirène . . .

Et j'ai deux fois vainqueur traversé l'Achéron:
Modulant tour à tour sur la lyre d'Orphée
Les soupirs de la sainte et les cris de la fée.

## MYRTHO

Je pense à toi, Myrtho, divine enchanteresse,
Au Pausilippe altier, de mille feux brillant,
A ton front inondé des clartés d'Orient,
Aux raisins noirs mêlés avec l'or de ta tresse.

C'est dans ta coupe aussi que j'avais bu l'ivresse,
Et dans l'éclair furtif de ton œil souriant,
Quand aux pieds d'Iacchus on me voyait priant,
Car la Muse m'a fait l'un des fils de la Grèce.

Je sais pourquoi là-bas le volcan s'est rouvert . . .
C'est qu'hier tu l'avais touché d'un pied agile,
Et de cendres soudain l'horizon s'est couvert.

Depuis qu'un duc normand brisa tes dieux d'argile,
Toujours, sous les rameaux du laurier de Virgile,
Le pâle hortensia s'unit au myrte vert!

## HORUS

Le dieu Kneph en tremblant ébranlait l'univers:
Isis, la mère, alors se leva sur sa couche,
Fit un geste de haine à son époux farouche,
Et l'ardeur d'autrefois brilla dans ses yeux verts.

"Le voyez-vous, dit-elle, il meurt, ce vieux pervers.
Tous les frimas du monde ont passé par sa bouche;
Attachez son pied tors, éteignez son œil louche:
C'est le dieu des volcans et le roi des hivers!

"L'aigle a déjà passé, l'esprit nouveau m'appelle,
J'ai revêtu pour lui la robe de Cybèle . . .
C'est l'enfant bien-aimé d'Hermès et d'Osiris!"

La déesse avait fui sur sa conque dorée,
La mer nous renvoyait son image adorée,
Et les cieux rayonnaient sous l'écharpe d'Iris.

## ANTÉROS

Tu demandes pourquoi j'ai tant de rage au cœur
Et sur un col flexible une tête indomptée;
C'est que je suis issu de la race d'Antée,
Je retourne les dards contre le dieu vainqueur.

Oui, je suis de ceux-là qu'inspire le Vengeur,
Il m'a marqué le front de sa lèvre irritée,
Sous la pâleur d'Abel, hélas! ensanglantée,
J'ai parfois de Caïn l'implacable rougeur!

Jéhovah! le dernier, vaincu par ton génie,
Qui, du fond des enfers, criait: "O tyrannie!"
C'est mon aïeul Bélus ou mon père Dagon . . .

Ils m'ont plongé trois fois dans les eaux du Cocyte,
Et protégeant tout seul ma mère Amalécyte,
Je ressème à ses pieds les dents du vieux dragon.

## DELFICA

La connais-tu, Dafné, cette ancienne romance,
Au pied du sycomore, ou sous les lauriers blancs,
Sous l'olivier, le myrte ou les saules tremblants,
Cette chanson d'amour . . . qui toujours recommence?

Reconnais-tu le temple, au péristyle immense,
Et les citrons amers où s'imprimaient tes dents?
Et la grotte, fatale aux hôtes imprudents,
Où du dragon vaincu dort l'antique semence!

Ils reviendront, ces dieux que tu pleures toujours!
Le temps va ramener l'ordre des anciens jours;
La terre a tressailli d'un souffle prophétique . . .

Cependant la sibylle au visage latin
Est endormie encor sous l'arc de Constantin:
—Et rien n'a dérangé le sévère portique.

## ARTÉMIS

La Treizième revient. . . . C'est encore la première;
Et c'est toujours la seule,—ou c'est le seul moment;
Car est-tu reine, ô toi! la première ou dernière?
Es-tu roi, toi le seul ou le dernier amant? . . .

Aimez qui vous aima du berceau dans la bière;
Celle que j'aimai seul m'aime encore tendrement:
C'est la mort—ou la morte. . . . O délice! ô tourment!
La rose qu'elle tient, c'est la Rose trémière.

Sainte napolitaine aux mains pleines de feux,
Rose au cœur violet, fleur de sainte Gudule:
As-tu trouvé ta croix dans le désert des cieux?

Roses blanches, tombez! vous insultez nos dieux,
Tombez, fantômes blancs, de votre ciel qui brûle:
—La sainte de l'abîme est plus sainte à mes yeux!

## VERS DORÉS

Homme, libre penseur! te crois-tu seul pensant
Dans ce monde où la vie éclate en toute chose?
Des forces que tu tiens ta liberté dispose,
Mais de tous tes conseils l'univers est absent.

Respecte dans la bête un esprit agissant:
Chaque fleur est une âme à la nature éclose;
Un mystère d'amour dans le métal repose;
Tout est sensible! Et tout sur ton être est puissant.

Crains, dans le mur aveugle, un regard qui t'épie:
A la matière même un verbe est attaché! . . .
Ne la fais pas servir à quelque usage impie!

Souvent dans l'être obscur habite un dieu caché;
Et, comme un œil naissant couvert par ses paupieres,
Un pur esprit s'accroît sous l'écorce des pierres!

# *Charles Baudelaire*

## AU LECTEUR

La sottise, l'erreur, le péché, la lésine,
Occupent nos esprits et travaillent nos corps,
Et nous alimentons nos aimables remords,
Comme les mendiants nourrissent leur vermine.

Nos péchés sont têtus, nos repentirs sont lâches;
Nous nous faisons payer grassement nos aveux,
Et nous rentrons gaiement dans le chemin bourbeux,
Croyant par de vils pleurs laver toutes nos taches.

Sur l'oreiller du mal c'est Satan Trismégiste
Qui berce longuement notre esprit enchanté,
Et le riche métal de notre volonté
Est tout vaporisé par ce savant chimiste.

C'est le Diable qui tient les fils qui nous remuent!
Aux objets répugnants nous trouvons des appas;
Chaque jour vers l'Enfer nous descendons d'un pas,
Sans horreur, à travers des ténèbres qui puent.

Ainsi qu'un débauché pauvre qui baise et mange
Le sein martyrisé d'une antique catin,
Nous volons au passage un plaisir clandestin
Que nous pressons bien fort comme une vieille orange.

Serré, fourmillant, comme un million d'helminthes,
Dans nos cerveaux ribote un peuple de Démons,
Et, quand nous respirons, la Mort dans nos poumons
Descend, fleuve invisible, avec de sourdes plaintes.

Si le viol, le poison, le poignard, l'incendie,
N'ont pas encor brodé de leurs plaisants dessins
Le canevas banal de nos piteux destins,
C'est que notre âme, hélas! n'est pas assez hardie.

Mais parmi les chacals, les panthères, les lices,
Les singes, les vautours, les scorpions, les serpents,
Les monstres glapissants, hurlants, grognants, rampants,
Dans la ménagerie infâme de nos vices,

Il en est un plus laid, plus méchant, plus immonde!
Quoiqu'il ne pousse ni grands gestes ni grands cris,
Il ferait volontiers de la terre un débris
Et dans un bâillement avalerait le monde;

C'est l'Ennui!—l'œil chargé d'un pleur involontaire,
Il rêve d'échafauds en fumant son houka.
Tu le connais, lecteur, ce monstre délicat,
—Hypocrite lecteur,—mon semblable,—mon frère!


## BÉNÉDICTION

Lorsque par un décret des puissances suprêmes,
Le Poète apparaît en ce monde ennuyé,
Sa mère épouvantée et pleine de blasphèmes
Crispe ses poings vers Dieu, qui la prend en pitié:

—"Ah! que n'ai-je mis bas tout un nœud de vipères,
Plutôt que de nourrir cette dérision!
Maudite soit la nuit aux plaisirs éphémères
Où mon ventre a conçu mon expiation!

Puisque tu m'as choisie entre toutes les femmes
Pour être le dégoût de mon triste mari,
Et que je ne puis pas rejeter dans les flammes,
Comme un billet d'amour, ce monstre rabougri,

Je ferai rejaillir ta haine qui m'accable
Sur l'instrument maudit de tes méchancetés,
Et je tordrai si bien cet arbre misérable,
Qu'il ne pourra pousser ses boutons empestés!"

Elle ravale ainsi l'écume de sa haine,
Et, ne comprenant pas les desseins éternels,
Elle-même prépare au fond de la Géhenne
Les bûchers consacrés aux crimes maternels.

Pourtant, sous la tutelle invisible d'un Ange,
L'Enfant déshérité s'enivre de soleil,
Et dans tout ce qu'il boit et dans tout ce qu'il mange
Retrouve l'ambroisie et le nectar vermeil.

Il joue avec le vent, cause avec le nuage,
Et s'enivre en chantant du chemin de la croix;
Et l'Esprit qui le suit dans son pèlerinage
Pleure de le voir gai comme un oiseau des bois.

Tous ceux qu'il veut aimer l'observent avec crainte,
Ou bien, s'enhardissant de sa tranquillité,
Cherchent à qui saura lui tirer une plainte,
Et font sur lui l'essai de leur férocité.

Dans le pain et le vin destinés à sa bouche
Ils mêlent de la cendre avec d'impurs crachats;
Avec hypocrisie ils jettent ce qu'il touche,
Et s'accusent d'avoir mis leurs pieds dans ses pas.

Sa femme va criant sur les places publiques:
"Puisqu'il me trouve assez belle pour m'adorer,
Je ferai le métier des idoles antiques,
Et comme elles je veux me faire redorer;

Et je me soûlerai de nard, d'encens, de myrrhe,
De génuflexions, de viandes et de vins,
Pour savoir si je puis dans un cœur qui m'admire
Usurper en riant les hommages divins!

Et, quand je m'ennuierai de ces farces impies,
Je poserai sur lui ma frêle et forte main;
Et mes ongles, pareils aux ongles des harpies,
Sauront jusqu'à son cœur se frayer un chemin.

Comme un tout jeune oiseau qui tremble et qui palpite,
J'arracherai ce cœur tout rouge de son sein,
Et, pour rassasier ma bête favorite,
Je le lui jetterai par terre avec dédain!"

Vers le Ciel, où son œil voit un trône splendide,
Le Poète serein lève ses bras pieux,
Et les vastes éclairs de son esprit lucide
Lui dérobent l'aspect des peuples furieux:

—"Soyez béni, mon Dieu, qui donnez la souffrance
Comme un divin remède à nos impuretés
Et comme la meilleure et la plus pure essence
Qui prépare les forts aux saintes voluptés!

Je sais que vous gardez une place au Poète
Dans les rangs bienheureux des saintes Légions,
Et que vous l'invitez à l'éternelle fête
Des Trônes, des Vertus, des Dominations.

Je sais que la douleur est la noblesse unique
Où ne mordront jamais la terre et les enfers,
Et qu'il faut pour tresser ma couronne mystique
Imposer tous les temps et tous les univers.

Mais les bijoux perdus de l'antique Palmyre,
Les métaux inconnus, les perles de la mer,
Par votre main montés, ne pourraient pas suffire
A ce beau diadème éblouissant et clair;

Car il ne sera fait que de pure lumière,
Puisée au foyer saint des rayons primitifs,
Et dont les yeux mortels, dans leur splendeur entière,
Ne sont que des miroirs obscurcis et plaintifs!"

## L'ALBATROS

Souvent, pour s'amuser, les hommes d'équipage
Prennent des albatros, vastes oiseaux des mers,
Qui suivent, indolents compagnons de voyage,
Le navire glissant sur les gouffres amers.

A peine les ont-ils déposés sur les planches,
Que ces rois de l'azur, maladroits et honteux,
Laissent piteusement leurs grandes ailes blanches
Comme des avirons traîner à côté d'eux.

Ce voyageur ailé, comme il est gauche et veule!
Lui, naguère si beau, qu'il est comique et laid!
L'un agace son bec avec un brûle-gueule,
L'autre mime, en boitant, l'infirme qui volait!

Le Poète est semblable au prince des nuées
Qui hante la tempête et se rit de l'archer;
Exilé sur le sol au milieu des huées,
Ses ailes de géant l'empêchent de marcher.

## CORRESPONDANCES

La Nature est un temple où de vivants piliers
Laissent parfois sortir de confuses paroles;
L'homme y passe à travers des forêts de symboles
Qui l'observent avec des regards familiers.

Comme de longs échos qui de loin se confondent
Dans une ténébreuse et profonde unité,
Vaste comme la nuit et comme la clarté,
Les parfums, les couleurs et les sons se répondent.

Il est des parfums frais comme des chairs d'enfants,
Doux comme les hautbois, verts comme les prairies,
—Et d'autres, corrompus, riches et triomphants,

Ayant l'expansion des choses infinies,
Comme l'ambre, le musc, le benjoin et l'encens,
Qui chantent les transports de l'esprit et des sens.

## L'ENNEMI

Ma jeunesse ne fut qu'un ténébreux orage,
Traversé çà et là par de brillants soleils;
Le tonnerre et la pluie ont fait un tel ravage,
Qu'il reste en mon jardin bien peu de fruits vermeils.

Voilà que j'ai touché l'automne des idées,
Et qu'il faut employer la pelle et les râteaux
Pour rassembler à neuf les terres inondées,
Où l'eau creuse des trous grands comme des tombeaux.

Et qui sait si les fleurs nouvelles que je rêve
Trouveront dans ce sol lavé comme une grève
Le mystique aliment qui ferait leur vigueur?

—O douleur! ô douleur! Le Temps mange la vie,
Et l'obscur Ennemi qui nous ronge le cœur
Du sang que nous perdons croît et se fortifie!

## LA VIE ANTÉRIEURE

J'ai longtemps habité sous de vastes portiques
Que les soleils marins teignaient de mille feux,
Et que leurs grands piliers, droits et majestueux,
Rendaient pareils, le soir, aux grottes basaltiques.

Les houles en roulant les images des cieux,
Mêlaient d'une façon solennelle et mystique
Les tout-puissants accords de leur riche musique
Aux couleurs du couchant reflété par mes yeux.

C'est là que j'ai vécu dans les voluptés calmes,
Au milieu de l'azur, des vagues, des splendeurs
Et des esclaves nus, tout imprégnés d'odeurs,

Qui me refraîchissaient le front avec des palmes,
Et dont l'unique soin était d'approfondir
Le secret douloureux qui me faisait languir.


## LA BEAUTÉ

Je suis belle, ô mortels! comme un rêve de pierre,
Et mon sein, où chacun s'est meurtri tour à tour,
Est fait pour inspirer au poète un amour
Éternel et muet ainsi que la matière.

Je trône dans l'azur comme un sphinx incompris;
J'unis un cœur de neige à la blancheur des cygnes;
Je hais le mouvement qui déplace les lignes,
Et jamais je ne pleure et jamais je ne ris.

Les poètes, devant mes grandes attitudes,
Que j'ai l'air d'emprunter aux plus fiers monuments,
Consumeront leurs jours en d'austères études;

Car j'ai, pour fasciner ces dociles amants,
De purs miroirs qui font toutes choses plus belles:
Mes yeux, mes larges yeux aux clartés éternelles!


## REMORDS POSTHUME

Lorsque tu dormiras, ma belle ténébreuse,
Au fond d'un monument construit en marbre noir,
Et lorsque tu n'auras pour alcôve et manoir
Qu'un caveau pluvieux et qu'une fosse creuse;

Quand la pierre, opprimant ta poitrine peureuse
Et tes flancs qu'assouplit un charmant nonchaloir,
Empêchera ton cœur de battre et de vouloir,
Et tes pieds de courir leur course aventureuse,

Le tombeau, confident de mon rêve infini
(Car le tombeau toujours comprendra le poète),
Durant ces grandes nuits d'où le somme est banni,

Te dira: "Que vous sert, courtisane imparfaite,
De n'avoir pas connu ce que pleurent les morts?"
—Et le ver rongera ta peau comme un remords.


## JE TE DONNE CES VERS . . .

Je te donne ces vers afin que si mon nom
Aborde heureusement aux époques lointaines,
Et fait rêver un soir les cervelles humaines,
Vaisseau favorisé par un grand aquilon,

Ta mémoire pareille aux fables incertaines,
Fatigue le lecteur ainsi qu'un tympanon,
Et par un fraternel et mystique chaînon
Reste comme pendue à mes rimes hautaines;

Être maudit à qui, de l'abîme profond
Jusqu'au plus haut du ciel, rien, hors moi, ne répond!
—O toi qui, comme une ombre à la trace éphémère,

Foules d'un pied léger et d'un regard serein
Les stupides mortels qui t'ont jugée amère,
Statue aux yeux de jais, grand ange au front d'airain!


## LE FLACON

Il est de forts parfums pour qui toute matière
Est poreuse. On dirait qu'ils pénètrent le verre.
En ouvrant un coffret venu de l'Orient
Dont la serrure grince et rechigne en criant,

Ou dans une maison déserte quelque armoire
Pleine de l'âcre odeur des temps, poudreuse et noire,
Parfois on trouve un vieux flacon qui se souvient,
D'où jaillit toute vive une âme qui revient.

Mille pensers dormaient, chrysalides funèbres,
Frémissant doucement dans les lourdes ténèbres,
Qui dégagent leur aile et prennent leur essor,
Teintés d'azur, glacés de rose, lamés d'or.

Voilà le souvenir enivrant qui voltige
Dans l'air troublé; les yeux se ferment; le Vertige
Saisit l'âme vaincue et la pousse à deux mains
Vers un gouffre obscurci de miasmes humains;

Il la terrasse au bord d'un gouffre séculaire,
Où, Lazare odorant déchirant son suaire,
Se meut dans son réveil le cadavre spectral
D'un vieil amour ranci, charmant et sépulcral.

Ainsi, quand je serai perdu dans la mémoire
Des hommes, dans le coin d'une sinistre armoire
Quand on m'aura jeté, vieux flacon désolé,
Décrépit, poudreux, sale, abject, visqueux, fêlé,

Je serai ton cercueil, aimable pestilence!
Le témoin de ta force et de ta virulence,
Cher poison préparé par les anges! liqueur
Qui me ronge, ô la vie et la mort de mon cœur!


## L'INVITATION AU VOYAGE

Mon enfant, ma sœur,
Songe à la douceur
D'aller là-bas vivre ensemble!
Aimer à loisir,
Aimer et mourir
Au pays qui te ressemble!
Les soleils mouillés
De ces ciels brouillés
Pour mon esprit ont les charmes
Si mystérieux
De tes traîtres yeux,
Brillant à travers leurs larmes.

Là, tout n'est qu'ordre et beauté,
Luxe, calme et volupté.

Des meubles luisants,
Polis par les ans,
Décoreraient notre chambre;
Les plus rares fleurs
Mêlant leurs odeurs
Aux vagues senteurs de l'ambre,
Les riches plafonds,
Les miroirs profonds,
La splendeur orientale,
Tout y parlerait
A l'âme en secret
Sa douce langue natale.

Là, tout n'est qu'ordre et beauté,
Luxe, calme et volupté.

Vois sur ces canaux
Dormir ces vaisseaux
Dont l'humeur est vagabonde;
C'est pour assouvir
Ton moindre désir
Qu'ils viennent du bout du monde.
—Les soleils couchants
Revêtent les champs,
Les canaux, la ville entière,
D'hyacinthe et d'or;
Le monde s'endort
Dans une chaude lumière.

Là, tout n'est qu'ordre et beauté,
Luxe, calme et volupté.

## LA MUSIQUE

La musique souvent me prend comme une mer!
Vers ma pâle étoile,
Sous un plafond de brume ou dans un vaste éther,
Je mets à la voile;

La poitrine en avant et les poumons gonflés
Comme de la toile,
J'escalade le dos des flots amoncelés
Que la nuit me voile;

Je sens vibrer en moi toutes *les* passions
D'un vaisseau qui souffre;
Le bon vent, la tempête et ses convulsions

Sur l'immense gouffre
Me bercent. D'autres fois, calme plat, grand miroir
De mon désespoir!

## LA CLOCHE FÊLÉE

Il est amer et doux, pendant les nuits d'hiver,
D'écouter, près du feu qui palpite et qui fume,
Les souvenirs lointains lentement s'élever
Au bruit des carillons qui chantent dans la brume.

Bienheureuse la cloche au gosier vigoureux
Qui, malgré sa vieillesse, alerte et bien portante,
Jette fidèlement son cri religieux,
Ainsi qu'un vieux soldat qui veille sous la tente!

Moi, mon âme est fêlée, et lorsqu'en ses ennuis
Elle veut de ses chants peupler l'air froid des nuits,
Il arrive souvent que sa voix affaiblie

Semble le râle épais d'un blessé qu'on oublie
Au bord d'un lac de sang, sous un grand tas de morts,
Et qui meurt, sans bouger, dans d'immenses efforts!

## SPLEEN

Quand le ciel bas et lourd pèse comme un couvercle
Sur l'esprit gémissant en proie aux longs ennuis,
Et que de l'horizon embrassant tout le cercle
Il nous verse un jour noir plus triste que les nuits;

Quand la terre est changée en un cachot humide,
Où l'Espérance, comme une chauve-souris,
S'en va battant les murs de son aile timide
Et se cognant la tête à des plafonds pourris;

Quand la pluie étalant ses immenses traînées
D'une vaste prison imite les barreaux,
Et qu'un peuple muet d'infâmes araignées
Vient tendre ses filets au fond de nos cerveaux,

Des cloches tout à coup sautent avec furie
Et lancent vers le ciel un affreux hurlement,
Ainsi que des esprits errants et sans patrie
Qui se mettent à geindre opiniâtrément.

—Et de longs corbillards, sans tambours ni musique,
Défilent lentement dans mon âme; l'Espoir,
Vaincu, pleure, et l'Angoisse atroce, despotique,
Sur mon crâne incliné plante son drapeau noir.

## L'HÉAUTONTIMOROUMÉNOS

*A J. G. F.*

Je te frapperai sans colère
Et sans haine, comme un boucher,
Comme Moïse le rocher!
Et je ferai de ta paupière,

Pour abreuver mon Saharah,
Jaillir les eaux de la souffrance.
Mon désir gonflé d'espérance
Sur tes pleurs salés nagera

Comme un vaisseau qui prend le large,
Et dans mon cœur qu'ils soûleront
Tes chers sanglots retentiront
Comme un tambour qui bat la charge!

Ne suis-je pas un faux accord
Dans la divine symphonie,
Grâce à la vorace Ironie
Qui me secoue et qui me mord?

Elle est dans ma voix, la criarde!
C'est tout mon sang, ce poison noir!
Je suis le sinistre miroir
Où la mégère se regarde!

Je suis la plaie et le couteau!
Je suis le soufflet et la joue!
Je suis les membres et la roue,
Et la victime et le bourreau!

Je suis de mon cœur le vampire,
—Un de ces grands abandonnés
Au rire éternel condamnés,
Et qui ne peuvent plus sourire!


## PAYSAGE

Je veux pour composer chastement mes églogues,
Coucher auprès du ciel, comme les astrologues,
Et, voisin des clochers, écouter en rêvant
Leurs hymnes solennels emportés par le vent.
Les deux mains au menton, du haut de ma mansarde,
Je verrai l'atelier qui chante et qui bavarde;

Les tuyaux, les clochers, ces mâts de la cité,
Et les grands ciels qui font rêver d'éternité.

Il est doux, à travers les brumes, de voir naître
L'étoile dans l'azur, la lampe à la fenêtre,
Les fleuves de charbon monter au firmament
Et la lune verser son pâle enchantement.
Je verrai les printemps, les étés, les automnes,
Et quand viendra l'hiver aux neiges monotones,
Je fermerai partout portières et volets
Pour bâtir dans la nuit mes féeriques palais.
Alors je rêverai des horizons bleuâtres,
Des jardins, des jets d'eau pleurant dans les albâtres,
Des baisers, des oiseaux chantant soir et matin,
Et tout ce que l'Idylle a de plus enfantin.
L'Émeute, tempêtant vainement à ma vitre,
Ne fera pas lever mon front de mon pupitre;
Car je serai plongé dans cette volupté
D'évoquer le Printemps avec ma volonté,
De tirer un soleil de mon cœur, et de faire
De mes pensers brûlants une tiède atmosphère.

## LE CYGNE

*A Victor Hugo*

I

Andromaque, je pense à vous! Ce petit fleuve,
Pauvre et triste miroir où jadis resplendit
L'immense majesté de vos douleurs de veuve,
Ce Simoïs menteur qui par vos pleurs grandit,

A fécondé soudain ma mémoire fertile,
Comme je traversais le nouveau Carrousel.
Le vieux Paris n'est plus (la forme d'une ville
Change plus vite, hélas! que le cœur d'un mortel);

Je ne vois qu'en esprit tout ce camp de baraques,
Ces tas de chapiteaux ébauchés et de fûts,
Les herbes, les gros blocs verdis par l'eau des flaques,
Et, brillant aux carreaux, le bric-à-brac confus.

Là s'étalait jadis une ménagerie;
Là je vis, un matin, à l'heure où sous les cieux
Froids et clairs le Travail s'éveille, où la voirie
Pousse un sombre ouragan dans l'air silencieux,

Un cygne qui s'était évadé de sa cage,
Et, de ses pieds palmés frottant le pavé sec,
Sur le sol raboteux traînait son blanc plumage.
Près d'un ruisseau sans eau la bête ouvrant le bec

Baignait nerveusement ses ailes dans la poudre,
Et disait, le cœur plein de son beau lac natal:
"Eau, quand donc pleuvras-tu? quand tonneras-tu, foudre?"
Je vois ce malheureux, mythe étrange et fatal,

Vers le ciel quelquefois, comme l'homme d'Ovide,
Vers le ciel ironique et cruellement bleu,
Sur son cou convulsif tendant sa tête avide,
Comme s'il adressait des reproches à Dieu!

II

Paris change! mais rien dans ma mélancolie
N'a bougé! palais neufs, échafaudages, blocs,
Vieux faubourgs, tout pour moi devient allégorie,
Et mes chers souvenirs sont plus lourds que des rocs.

Aussi devant ce Louvre une image m'opprime:
Je pense à mon grand cygne, avec ses gestes fous,
Comme les exilés, ridicule et sublime,
Et rongé d'un désir sans trêve! et puis à vous,

Andromaque, des bras d'un grand époux tombée,
Vil bétail, sous la main du superbe Pyrrhus,
Auprès d'un tombeau vide en extase courbée;
Veuve d'Hector, hélas! et femme d'Hélénus!

Je pense à la négresse, amaigrie et phtisique,
Piétinant dans la boue, et cherchant, l'œil hagard,
Les cocotiers absents de la superbe Afrique
Derrière la muraille immense du brouillard;

A quiconque a perdu ce qui ne se retrouve
Jamais, jamais! à ceux qui s'abreuvent de pleurs
Et tettent la Douleur comme une bonne louve!
Aux maigres orphelins séchant comme des fleurs!

Ainsi dans la forêt, où mon esprit s'exile
Un vieux Souvenir sonne à plein souffle du cor!
Je pense aux matelots oubliés dans une île,
Aux captifs, aux vaincus! . . . à bien d'autres encor!

## LES SEPT VIEILLARDS

*A Victor Hugo*

Fourmillante cité, cité pleine de rêves,
Où le spectre, en plein jour raccroche le passant!
Les mystères partout coulent comme des sèves
Dans les canaux étroits du colosse puissant.

Un matin, cependant que dans la triste rue
Les maisons, dont la brume allongeait la hauteur,
Simulaient les deux quais d'une rivière accrue,
Et que, décor semblable à l'âme de l'acteur,

Un brouillard sale et jaune inondait tout l'espace,
Je suivais, roidissant mes nerfs comme un héros
Et discutant avec mon âme déjà lasse,
Le faubourg secoué par les lourds tombereaux.

Tout à coup, un vieillard dont les guenilles jaunes
Imitaient la couleur de ce ciel pluvieux,
Et dont l'aspect aurait fait pleuvoir les aumônes,
Sans la méchanceté qui luisait dans ses yeux,

M'apparut. On eût dit sa prunelle trempée
Dans le fiel; son regard aiguisait les frimas,
Et sa barbe à longs poils, roide comme une épée,
Se projetait, pareille à celle de Judas.

Il n'était pas voûté, mais cassé, son échine
Faisait avec sa jambe un parfait angle droit,
Si bien que son bâton, parachevant sa mine,
Lui donnait la tournure et le pas maladroit

D'un quadrupède infirme ou d'un juif à trois pattes.
Dans la neige et la boue il allait s'empêtrant,
Comme s'il écrasait des morts sous ses savates,
Hostile à l'univers plutôt qu'indifférent.

Son pareil le suivait: barbe, œil, dos, bâton, loques,
Nul trait ne distinguait, du même enfer venu,
Ce jumeau centenaire, et ces spectres baroques
Marchaient du même pas vers un but inconnu.

A quel complot infâme étais-je donc en butte,
Ou quel méchant hasard ainsi m'humiliait?
Car je comptais sept fois, de minute en minute,
Ce sinistre vieillard qui se multipliait!

Que celui-là quit rit de mon inquiétude,
Et qui n'est pas saisi d'un frisson fraternel,
Songe bien que malgré tant de décrépitude
Ces sept monstres hideux avaient l'air éternel!

Aurais-je, sans mourir, contemplé le huitième,
Sosie inexorable, ironique et fatal,
Dégoûtant Phénix, fils et père de lui-même?
—Mais je tournai le dos au cortège infernal.

Exaspéré comme un ivrogne qui voit double,
Je rentrai, je fermai ma porte, épouvanté,
Malade et morfondu, l'esprit fiévreux et trouble,
Blessé par le mystère et par l'absurdité!

Vainement ma raison voulait prendre la barre;
La tempête en jouant déroutait ses efforts,
Et mon âme dansait, dansait, vieille gabarre
Sans mâts, sur une mer monstrueuse et sans bords!


## LES PETITES VIEILLES

*A Victor Hugo*

I

Dans les plis sinueux des vieilles capitales,
Où tout, même l'horreur, tourne aux enchantements,
Je guette obéissant à mes humeurs fatales,
Des êtres singuliers, décrépits et charmants.

Ces monstres disloqués furent jadis des femmes,
Eponine ou Laïs! Monstres brisés, bossus
Ou tordus, aimons-les! ce sont encor des âmes.
Sous des jupons troués et sous de froids tissus

Ils rampent, flagellés par les bises iniques,
Frémissant au fracas roulant des omnibus,
Et serrant sur leur flanc, ainsi que des reliques,
Un petit sac brodé de fleurs ou de rébus;

Ils trottent, tous pareils à des marionnettes;
Se traînent, comme font les animaux blessés,
Ou dansent sans vouloir danser, pauvres sonnettes
Où se pend un Démon sans pitié! Tout cassés

Qu'ils sont, ils ont des yeux perçants comme une vrille,
Luisants comme ces trous où l'eau dort dans la nuit;
Ils ont les yeux divins de la petite fille
Qui s'étonne et qui rit à tout ce qui reluit.


—Avez-vous observé que maints cercueils de vieilles
Sont presque aussi petits que celui d'un enfant?
La Mort savante met dans ces bières pareilles
Un symbole d'un goût bizarre et captivant,


Et lorsque j'entrevois un fantôme débile
Traversant de Paris le fourmillant tableau,
Il me semble toujours que cet être fragile
S'en va tout doucement vers un nouveau berceau;


A moins que, méditant sur la géométrie,
Je ne cherche, à l'aspect de ces membres discords,
Combien de fois il faut que l'ouvrier varie
La forme de la boîte où l'on met tous ces corps.


—Ces yeux sont des puits faits d'un million de larmes,
Des creusets qu'un métal refroidi pailleta . . .
Ces yeux mystérieux ont d'invincibles charmes
Pour celui que l'austère Infortune allaita!


II


De Frascati défunt Vestale enamourée;
Prêtresse de Thalie, hélas! dont le souffleur
Enterré sait le nom; célèbre évaporée
Que Tivoli jadis ombragea dans sa fleur,


Toutes m'enivrent! mais parmi ces êtres frêles
Il en est qui, faisant de la douleur un miel,
Ont dit au Dévouement qui leur prêtait ses ailes:
Hippogriffe puissant, mène-moi jusqu'au ciel!


L'une, par sa patrie au malheur exercée,
L'autre, que son époux surchargea de douleurs,
L'autre, par son enfant Madone transpercée,
Toutes auraient pu faire un fleuve avec leurs pleurs!

### III

Ah! que j'en ai suivi, de ces petites vieilles!
Une, entre autres, à l'heure où le soleil tombant
Ensanglante le ciel de blessures vermeilles,
Pensive, s'asseyait a l'écart sur un banc,

Pour entendre un de ces concerts, riches de cuivre,
Dont les soldats parfois inondent nos jardins,
Et qui, dans ces soirs d'or où l'on se sent revivre,
Versent quelque héroïsme au cœur des citadins.

Celle-là, droite encor, fière et sentant la règle,
Humait avidement ce chant vif et guerrier;
Son œil parfois s'ouvrait comme l'œil d'un vieil aigle;
Son front de marbre avait l'air fait pour le laurier!

### IV

Telles vous cheminez, stoïques et sans plaintes,
A travers le chaos des vivantes cités,
Mères au cœur saignant, courtisanes ou saintes,
Dont autrefois les noms par tous étaient cités.

Vous qui fûtes la grâce ou qui fûtes la gloire,
Nul ne vous reconnaît! un ivrogne incivil
Vous insulte en passant d'un amour dérisoire;
Sur vos talons gambade un enfant lâche et vil.

Honteuses d'exister, ombres, ratatinées,
Peureuses, le dos bas, vous côtoyez les murs;
Et nul ne vous salue, étranges destinées!
Débris d'humanité pour l'éternité mûrs!

Mais moi, moi qui de loin tendrement vous surveille,
L'œil inquiet fixé sur vos pas incertains,
Tout comme si j'étais votre père, ô merveille!
Je goûte à votre insu des plaisirs clandestins:

Je vois s'épanouir vos passions novices;
Sombres ou lumineux, je vis vos jours perdus;
Mon cœur multiplié jouit de tous vos vices!
Mon âme resplendit de toutes vos vertus!

Ruines! ma famille! ô cerveaux congénères!
Je vous fais chaque soir un solennel adieu!
Où serez-vous demain, Èves octogénaires,
Sur qui pèse la griffe effroyable de Dieu?

## L'AMOUR DU MENSONGE

Quand je te vois passer, ô ma chère indolente,
Au chant des instruments qui se brise au plafond
Suspendant ton allure harmonieuse et lente,
Et promenant l'ennui de ton regard profond;

Quand je contemple, aux feux du gaz qui le colore,
Ton front pâle, embelli par un morbide attrait,
Où les torches du soir allument une aurore,
Et tes yeux attirants comme ceux d'un portrait,

Je me dis: Qu'elle est belle! et bizarrement fraîche!
Le souvenir massif, royale et lourde tour,
La couronne, et son cœur, meurtri comme une pêche,
Est mûr, comme son corps, pour le savant amour.

Es-tu le fruit d'automne aux saveurs souveraines?
Es-tu vase funèbre attendant quelques pleurs,
Parfum qui fait rêver aux oasis lointaines,
Oreiller caressant, ou corbeille de fleurs?

Je sais qu'il est des yeux des plus mélancoliques,
Qui ne recèlent point de secrets précieux;
Beaux, écrins sans joyaux, médaillons sans reliques,
Plus vides, plus profonds que vous-mêmes, ô Cieux!

Mais ne suffit-il pas que tu sois l'apparence,
Pour réjouir un cœur qui fuit la vérité?
Qu'importe ta bêtise ou ton indifférence!
Masque ou décor, salut! J'adore ta beauté.


## JE N'AI PAS OUBLIÉ . . .

Je n'ai pas oublié, voisine de la ville,
Notre blanche maison, petite mais tranquille;
Sa Pomone de plâtre et sa vieille Vénus
Dans un bosquet chétif cachant leurs membres nus,
Et le soleil, le soir, ruisselant et superbe,
Qui, derrière la vitre où se brisait sa gerbe,
Semblait, grand œil ouvert dans le ciel curieux,
Contempler nos dîners longs et silencieux,
Répandant largement ses beaux reflets de cierge
Sur la nappe frugale et les rideaux de serge.

## LE CRÉPUSCULE DU MATIN

La diane chantait dans les cours des casernes,
Et le vent du matin soufflait sur les lanternes.

C'était l'heure où l'essaim des rêves malfaisants
Tord sur leurs oreillers les bruns adolescents;
Où, comme un œil sanglant qui palpite et qui bouge,
La lampe sur le jour fait une tache rouge;
Où l'âme, sous le poids du corps revêche et lourd,
Imite les combats de la lampe et du jour.
Comme un visage en pleurs que les brises essuient,
L'air est plein du frisson des choses qui s'enfuient,
Et l'homme est las d'écrire et la femme d'aimer.

Les maisons çà et là commençaient à fumer.
Les femmes de plaisir, la paupière livide,
Bouche ouverte, dormaient de leur sommeil stupide;
Les pauvresses, traînant leur seins maigres et froids,
Soufflaient sur leurs tisons et soufflaient sur leurs doigts.
C'était l'heure où parmi le froid et la lésine
S'aggravent les douleurs des femmes en gésine;
Comme un sanglot coupé par un sang écumeux
Le chant du coq au loin déchirait l'air brumeux;
Une mer de brouillards baignait les édifices,
Et les agonisants dans le fond des hospices
Poussaient leur dernier râle en hoquets inégaux.
Les débauchés rentraient, brisés par leurs travaux.

L'aurore grelottante en robe rose et verte
S'avançait lentement sur la Seine déserte,
Et le sombre Paris, en se frottant les yeux,
Empoignait ses outils, vieillard laborieux.

## LA BÉATRICE

Dans des terrains cendreux, calcinés, sans verdure,
Comme je me plaignais un jour à la nature,
Et que de ma pensée, en vaguant au hasard,
J'aiguisais lentement sur mon cœur le poignard,
Je vis en plein midi descendre sur ma tête
Un nuage funèbre et gros d'une tempête,

Qui portait un troupeau de démons vicieux,
Semblables à des nains cruels et curieux.
A me considérer froidement ils se mirent,
Et, comme des passants sur un fou qu'ils admirent,
Je les entendis rire et chuchoter entre eux,
En échangeant maint signe et maint clignement d'yeux:

—"Contemplons à loisir cette caricature
Et cette ombre d'Hamlet imitant sa posture,
Le regard indécis et les cheveux au vent.
N'est-ce pas grand'pitié de voir ce bon vivant,
Ce gueux, cet histrion en vacances, ce drôle,
Parce qu'il sait jouer artistement son rôle,
Vouloir intéresser au chant de ses douleurs
Les aigles, les grillons, les ruisseaux et les fleurs,
Et même à nous, auteurs de ces vieilles rubriques,
Réciter en hurlant ses tirades publiques?"

J'aurais pu (mon orgueil aussi haut que les monts
Domine la nuée et le cri des démons)
Détourner simplement ma tête souveraine,
Si je n'eusse pas vu parmi leur troupe obscène,
Crime qui n'a pas fait chanceler le soleil!
La reine de mon cœur au regard nonpareil,
Qui riait avec eux de ma sombre détresse
Et leur versait parfois quelque sale caresse.

## UN VOYAGE À CYTHÈRE

Mon cœur, comme un oiseau, voltigeait tout joyeux
Et planait librement à l'entour des cordages;
Le navire roulait sous un ciel sans nuages,
Comme un ange enivré d'un soleil radieux.

Quelle est cette île triste et noire?—C'est Cythère,
Nous dit-on, un pays fameux dans les chansons,
Eldorado banal de tous les vieux garçons.
Regardez, après tout, c'est une pauvre terre.

—Ile des doux secrets et des fêtes du cœur!
De l'antique Vénus le superbe fantôme
Au-dessus de tes mers plane comme un arome,
Et charge les esprits d'amour et de langueur.

Belle île aux myrtes verts, pleine de fleurs écloses,
Vénérée à jamais par toute nation,
Où les soupirs des cœurs en adoration
Roulent comme l'encens sur un jardin de roses

Ou le roucoulement éternel d'un ramier!
—Cythère n'était plus qu'un terrain des plus maigres,
Un désert rocailleux troublé par des cris aigres.
J'entrevoyais pourtant un objet singulier!

Ce n'était pas un temple aux ombres bocagères,
Où la jeune prêtresse, amoureuse des fleurs,
Allait, le corps brûlé de secrètes chaleurs,
Entre-bâillant sa robe aux brises passagères;

Mais voilà qu'en rasant la côte d'assez près
Pour troubler les oiseaux avec nos voiles blanches,
Nous vîmes que c'était un gibet à trois branches,
Du ciel se détachant en noir, comme un cyprès.

De féroces oiseaux perchés sur leur pâture
Détruisaient avec rage un pendu déjà mûr,
Chacun plantant, comme un outil, son bec impur
Dans tous les coins saignants de cette pourriture;

Les yeux étaient deux trous, et du ventre effondré
Les intestins pesants lui coulaient sur les cuisses,
Et ses bourreaux, gorgés de hideuses délices,
L'avaient à coups de bec absolument châtré.

Sous les pieds, un troupeau de jaloux quadrupèdes,
Le museau relevé, tournoyait et rôdait;
Une plus grande bête au milieu s'agitait
Comme un exécuteur entouré de ses aides.

Habitant de Cythère, enfant d'un ciel si beau,
Silencieusement tu souffrais ces insultes
En expiation de tes infâmes cultes
Et des péchés qui t'ont interdit le tombeau.

Ridicule pendu, tes douleurs sont les miennes!
Je sentis, à l'aspect de tes membres flottants,
Comme un vomissement, remonter vers mes dents
Le long fleuve de fiel des douleurs anciennes;

Devant toi, pauvre diable au souvenir si cher,
J'ai senti tous les becs et toutes les mâchoires
Des corbeaux lancinants et des panthères noires
Qui jadis aimaient tant à triturer ma chair.

—Le ciel était charmant, la mer était unie;
Pour moi tout état noir et sanglant désormais,
Hélas! et j'avais, comme en un suaire épais,
Le cœur enseveli dans cette allégorie.

Dans ton île, ô Vénus! je n'ai trouvé debout
Qu'un gibet symbolique où pendait mon image . . .
—Ah! Seigneur! donnez-moi la force et le courage
De contempler mon cœur et mon corps sans dégoût!

## LE VOYAGE

*A Maxime du Camp*

### I

Pour l'enfant, amoureux de cartes et d'estampes,
L'univers est égal à son grand appétit.
Ah! que le monde est grand à la clarté des lampes!
Aux yeux du souvenir que le monde est petit!

Un matin nous partons, le cerveau plein de flamme,
Le cœur gros de rancune et de désirs amers,
Et nous allons, suivant le rhythme de la lame,
Berçant notre infini sur le fini des mers:

Les uns, joyeux de fuir une patrie infâme;
D'autres, l'horreur de leurs berceaux, et quelques-uns,
Astrologues noyés dans les yeux d'une femme,
La Circé tyrannique aux dangereux parfums.

Pour n'être pas changés en bêtes, ils s'enivrent
D'espace et de lumière et de cieux embrasés;
La glace qui les mord, les soleils qui les cuivrent,
Effacent lentement la marque des baisers.

Mais les vrais voyageurs sont ceux-là seuls qui partent
Pour partir; cœurs légers, semblables aux ballons,
De leur fatalité jamais ils ne s'écartent,
Et, sans savoir pourquoi, disent toujours: Allons!

Ceux-là dont les désirs ont la forme des nues,
Et qui rêvent, ainsi qu'un conscrit le canon,
De vastes voluptés, changeantes, inconnues,
Et dont l'esprit humain n'a jamais su le nom!


## II

Nous imitons, horreur! la toupie et la boule
Dans leur valse et leurs bonds; même dans nos sommeils
La Curiosité nous tourmente et nous roule,
Comme un Ange cruel qui fouette des soleils.

Singulière fortune où le but se déplace,
Et, n'étant nulle part, peut être n'importe où!
Où l'Homme, dont jamais l'espérance n'est lasse,
Pour trouver le repos court toujours comme un fou!

Notre âme est un trois-mâts cherchant son Icarie;
Une voix retentit sur le pont: "Ouvre l'œil!"
Une voix de la hune, ardente et folle, crie:
"Amour . . . gloire . . . bonheur!" Enfer! c'est un écueil!

Chaque îlot signalé par l'homme de vigie
Est un Eldorado promis par le Destin;
L'imagination que dresse son orgie
Ne trouve qu'un récif aux clartés du matin.

O le pauvre amoureux des pays chimériques!
Faut-il le mettre aux fers, le jeter à la mer,
Ce matelot ivrogne, inventeur d'Amériques
Dont le mirage rend le gouffre plus amer?

Tel le vieux, vagabond, piétinant dans la boue,
Rêve, le nez en l'air, de brillants paradis;
Son œil ensorcelé découvre une Capoue
Partout où la chandelle illumine un taudis.


## III

Etonnants voyageurs! quelles nobles histoires
Nous lisons dans vos yeux profonds comme les mers!
Montrez-nous les écrins de vos riches mémoires,
Ces bijoux merveilleux, faits d'astres et d'éthers.

Nous voulons voyager sans vapeur et sans voile!
Faites, pour égayer l'ennui de nos prisons,
Passer sur nos esprits, tendus comme une toile,
Vos souvenirs avec leurs cadres d'horizons.

Dites, qu'avez-vous vu?

IV

"Nous avons vu des astres
Et des flots; nous avons vu des sables aussi;
Et, malgré bien des chocs et d'imprévus désastres,
Nous nous sommes souvent ennuyés, comme ici.

La gloire du soleil sur la mer violette,
La gloire des cités dans le soleil couchant,
Allumaient dans nos cœurs une ardeur inquiète
De plonger dans un ciel au reflet alléchant.

Les plus riches cités, les plus grands paysages,
Jamais ne contenaient l'attrait mystérieux
De ceux que le hasard fait avec les nuages.
Et toujours le désir nous rendait soucieux!

—La jouissance ajoute au désir de la force.
Désir, vieil arbre à qui le plaisir sert d'engrais,
Cependant que grossit et durcit ton écorce,
Tes branches veulent voir le soleil de plus près!

Grandiras-tu toujours, grand arbre plus vivace
Que le cyprès?—Pourtant nous avons, avec soin,
Cueilli quelques croquis pour votre album vorace,
Frères qui trouvez beau tout ce qui vient de loin!

Nous avons salué des idoles à trompe;
Des trônes constellés de joyaux lumineux;
Des palais ouvragés dont la féerique pompe
Serait pour vos banquiers un rêve ruineux;

Des costumes qui sont pour les yeux une ivresse;
Des femmes dont les dents et les ongles sont teints,
Et des jongleurs savants que le serpent caresse."

V

Et puis, et puis encore?

VI

"O cerveaux enfantins!

Pour ne pas oublier la chose capitale,
Nous avons vu partout, et sans l'avoir cherché,
Du haut jusques en bas de l'échelle fatale,
Le spectacle ennuyeux de l'immortel péché:

La femme, esclave vile, orgueilleuse et stupide,
Sans rire s'adorant et s'aimant sans dégoût;
L'homme, tyran goulu, paillard, dur et cupide,
Esclave de l'esclave et ruisseau dans l'égout;

Le bourreau qui jouit, le martyr qui sanglote;
La fête qu'assaisonne et parfume le sang;
Le poison du pouvoir énervant le despote,
Et le peuple amoureux du fouet abrutissant;

Plusieurs religions semblables à la nôtre,
Toutes escaladant le ciel; la Sainteté,
Comme en un lit de plume un délicat se vautre,
Dans les clous et le crin cherchant la volupté;

L'Humanité bavarde, ivre de son génie,
Et, folle maintenant comme elle était jadis,
Criant à Dieu, dans sa furibonde agonie:
'O mon semblable, ô mon maître, je te maudis!'

Et les moins sots, hardis amants de la Démence,
Fuyant le grand troupeau parqué par le Destin,
Et se réfugiant dans l'opium immense!
—Tel est du globe entier l'éternel bulletin."


VII

Amer savoir, celui qu'on tire du voyage!
Le monde, monotone et petit, aujourd'hui,
Hier, demain, toujours, nous fait voir notre image:
Une oasis d'horreur dans un désert d'ennui!

Faut-il partir? rester? Si tu peux rester, reste;
Pars s'il le faut. L'un court, et l'autre se tapit
Pour tromper l'ennemi vigilant et funeste,
Le Temps! Il est, hélas! des coureurs sans répit,

Comme le Juif errant et comme les apôtres,
A qui rien ne suffit, ni wagon ni vaisseau,
Pour fuir ce rétiaire infâme; il en est d'autres
Qui savent le tuer sans quitter leur berceau.

Lorsque enfin il mettra le pied sur notre échine,
Nous pourrons espérer et crier: En avant!
De même qu'autrefois nous partions pour la Chine,
Les yeux fixés au large et les cheveux au vent,

Nous nous embarquerons sur la mer des Ténèbres
Avec le cœur joyeux, d'un jeune passager.
Entendez-vous ces voix charmantes et funèbres,
Qui chantent: "Par ici! vous qui voulez manger

Le Lotus parfumé! c'est ici qu'on vendange
Les fruits miraculeux dont votre cœur a faim;
Venez vous enivrer de la douceur étrange
De cette après-midi qui n'a jamais de fin"?

A l'accent familier nous devinons le spectre;
Nos Pylades là-bas tendent leurs bras vers nous.
"Pour rafraîchir ton cœur nage vers ton Electre!"
Dit celle dont jadis nous baisions les genoux.

### VIII

O Mort, vieux capitaine, il est temps! levons l'ancre.
Ce pays nous ennuie, ô Mort! Appareillons!
Si le ciel et la mer sont noirs comme de l'encre,
Nos cœurs que tu connais sont remplis de rayons!

Verse-nous ton poison pour qu'il nous réconforte!
Nous voulons, tant ce feu nous brûle le cerveau,
Plonger au fond du gouffre, Enfer ou Ciel, qu'importe?
Au fond de l'Inconnu pour trouver du *nouveau!*

## LESBOS

Mère des jeux latins et des voluptés grecques,
Lesbos, où les baisers, languissants ou joyeux,
Chauds comme les soleils, frais comme les pastèques,
Font l'ornement des nuits et des jours glorieux;
Mère des jeux latins et des voluptés grecques;

Lesbos, où les baisers sont comme les cascades
Qui se jettent sans peur dans les gouffres sans fonds,
Et courent, sanglotant et gloussant par saccades,
Orageux et secrets, fourmillants et profonds;
Lesbos, où les baisers sont comme les cascades!

Lesbos, où les Phrynés l'une l'autre s'attirent,
Où jamais un soupir ne resta sans écho,
A l'égal de Paphos les étoiles t'admirent,
Et Vénus à bon droit peut jalouser Sapho!
Lesbos, où les Phrynés l'une l'autre s'attirent,

Lesbos, terre des nuits chaudes et langoureuses,
Qui font qu'à leurs miroirs stérile volupté!
Les filles aux yeux creux, de leurs corps amoureuses,
Caressent les fruits mûrs de leur nubilité;
Lesbos, terre des nuits chaudes et langoureuses,

Laisse du vieux Platon se froncer l'œil austère;
Tu tires ton pardon de l'excès des baisers,
Reine du doux empire, aimable et noble terre,
Et des raffinements toujours inépuisés.
Laisse du vieux Platon se froncer l'œil austère.

Tu tires ton pardon de l'éternel martyre,
Infligé sans relâche aux cœurs ambitieux,
Qu'attire loin de nous le radieux sourire
Entrevu vaguement au bord des autres cieux!
Tu tires ton pardon de l'éternel martyre!

Qui des Dieux osera, Lesbos, être ton juge!
Et condamner ton front pâli dans les travaux,
Si ses balances d'or n'ont pesé le déluge
De larmes qu'à la mer ont versé tes ruisseaux?
Qui des Dieux osera, Lesbos, être ton juge!

Que nous veulent les lois du juste et de l'injuste?
Vierges au cœur sublime, honneur de l'archipel,
Votre religion comme une autre est auguste,
Et l'amour se rira de l'Enfer et du Ciel!
Que nous veulent les lois du juste et de l'injuste?

Car Lesbos entre tous m'a choisi sur la terre
Pour chanter le secret de ses vierges en fleurs,
Et je fus dès l'enfance admis au noir mystère
Des rires effrénés mêlés aux sombres pleurs;
Car Lesbos entre tous m'a choisi sur la terre.

Et depuis lors je veille au sommet du Leucate,
Comme une sentinelle à l'œil perçant et sûr,
Qui quette nuit et jour brick, tartane ou frégate,
Dont les formes au loin frissonnent dans l'azur;
Et depuis lors je veille au sommet du Leucate,

Pour savoir si la mer est indulgente et bonne,
Et parmi les sanglots dont le roc retentit
Un soir ramènera vers Lesbos, qui pardonne,
Le cadavre adoré de Sapho, qui partit,
Pour savoir si la mer est indulgente et bonne!

De la mâle Sapho, l'amante et le poète,
Plus belle que Vénus par ses mornes pâleurs!
—L'œil d'azur est vaincu par l'œil noir que tachète
Le cercle ténébreux tracé par les douleurs
De la mâle Sapho, l'amante et le poète!

—Plus belle que Vénus se dressant sur le monde
Et versant les trésors de sa sérénité
Et le rayonnement de sa jeunesse blonde
Sur le vieil Océan de sa fille enchanté;
Plus belle que Vénus se dressant sur le monde!

—De Sapho qui mourut le jour de son blasphème,
Quand, insultant le rite et le culte inventé,
Elle fit son beau corps la pâture suprême
D'un brutal dont l'orgueil punit l'impiété
De celle qui mourut le jour de son blasphème.

Et c'est depuis ce temps que Lesbos se lamente,
Et malgré les honneurs que lui rend l'univers,
S'enivre chaque nuit du cri de la tourmente
Que poussent vers les cieux ses rivages déserts!
Et c'est depuis ce temps que Lesbos se lamente!

## LE LÉTHÉ

Viens sur mon cœur, âme cruelle et sourde,
Tigre adoré, monstre aux airs indolents;
Je veux longtemps plonger mes doigts tremblants
Dans l'épaisseur de ta crinière lourde;

Dans des jupons remplis de ton parfum
Ensevelir ma tête endolorie,
Et respirer, comme une fleur flétrie,
Le doux relent de mon amour défunt.

Je veux dormir! dormir plutôt que vivre!
Dans un sommeil aussi doux que la mort,
J'étalerai mes baisers sans remord
Sur ton beau corps poli comme le cuivre.

Pour engloutir mes sanglots apaisés
Rien ne vaut l'abîme de ta couche;
L'oubli puissant habite sur ta bouche,
Et le Léthé coule dans tes baisers.

A mon destin, désormais mon délice,
J'obéirai comme un prédestiné;
Martyr docile, innocent condamné,
Dont la ferveur attise le supplice,

Je sucerai, pour noyer ma rancœur,
Le népenthès et la bonne ciguë
Aux bouts charmants de cette gorge aiguë,
Qui n'a jamais emprisonné de cœur.

## ÉPIGRAPHE
## POUR UN LIVRE CONDAMNÉ

Lecteur paisible et bucolique,
Sobre et naïf homme de bien,
Jette ce livre saturnien,
Orgiaque et mélancolique.

Si tu n'as fait ta rhétorique
Chez Satan, le rusé doyen,
Jette! tu n'y comprendrais rien,
Ou tu me croirais hystérique.

Mais si, sans se laisser charmer,
Ton œil sait plonger dans les gouffres,
Lis-moi, pour apprendre à m'aimer;

Ame curieuse qui souffres
Et vas cherchant ton paradis,
Plains-moi . . . sinon je te maudis!

## RECUEILLEMENT

Sois sage, ô ma Douleur, et tiens-toi plus tranquille.
Tu réclamais le Soir; il descend; le voici:
Une atmosphère obscure enveloppe la ville,
Aux uns portant la paix, aux autres le souci.

Pendant que des mortels la multitude vile,
Sous le fouet du Plaisir, ce bourreau sans merci,
Va cueillir des remords dans la fête servile,
Ma Douleur, donne-moi la main; viens par ici,

Loin d'eux. Vois se pencher les défuntes Années,
Sur les balcons du ciel, en robes surannées;
Surgir du fond des eaux le Regret souriant;

Le Soleil moribond s'endormir sous une arche,
Et, comme un long linceul traînant à l'Orient,
Entends, ma chère, entends la douce Nuit qui marche.

## LE GOUFFRE

Pascal avait son gouffre, avec lui se mouvant.
—Hélas! tout est abîme—action, désir, rêve,
Parole! et sur mon poil qui tout droit se relève
Mainte fois de la Peur je sens passer le vent.

En haut, en bas, partout, la profondeur, la grève,
Le silence, l'espace affreux et captivant. . . .
Sur le fond de mes nuits Dieu de son doigt savant
Dessine un cauchemar multiforme et sans trêve,

J'ai peur du sommeil comme on a peur d'un grand trou,
Tout plein de vague horreur, menant on ne sait où;
Je ne vois qu'infini par toutes les fenêtres,

Et mon esprit, toujours du vertige hanté,
Jalouse du néant l'insensibilité.
—Ah! ne jamais sortir des Nombres et des Êtres!

# Tristan Corbière

### APRÈS LA PLUIE

J'aime la petite pluie
    Qui s'essuie
D'un torchon de bleu troué!
J'aime l'amour et la brise,
    Quand ça frise . . .
Et pas quand c'est secoué.

—Comme un parapluie en flèches,
    Tu te sèches,
O grand soleil! grand ouvert . . .
A bientôt l'ombrelle verte
    Grand'ouverte!
Du printemps—été d'hiver.—

La passion c'est l'averse
    Qui traverse!
Mais la femme n'est qu'un grain:
Grain de beauté, de folie
    Ou de pluie . . .
Grain d'orage—ou de serein.—

Dans un clair rayon de boue,
    Fait la roue,
La roue à grand appareil,
—Plume et queue—une Cocotte
    Qui barbotte;
Vrai déjeuner de soleil!

—"Anne! ou qui que tu sois, chère . . .
    Ou pas chère,
Dont on fait, à l'œil, les yeux . . .
Hum . . . Zoé! Nadjejda! Jane!
    Vois: je flâne,
Doublé d'or comme les cieux!"

"*English spoken?*—Espagnole? . . .
    Batignolle? . . .
Arbore le pavillon
Qui couvre ta marchandise,
    O marquise
D'Amaëgui! . . . Frétillon! . . ."

"Nom de singe ou nom d'Archange?
        Ou mélange? . . .
Petit nom à huit ressorts?
Nom qui ronfle, ou nom qui chante
        Nom d'amante? . . .
Ou nom à coucher dehors? . . .

Veux-tu, d'une amour fidèle,
        Éternelle!
Nous adorer pour ce soir? . . .
Pour tes deux petites bottes
        Que tu crottes,
Prends mon cœur et le trottoir!"

"N'es-tu pas doña Sabine?
        Carabine? . . .
Dis: veux-tu le paradis
De l'Odéon?—traversée
        Insensée! . . .
On emporte des radis"—

C'est alors que se dégaine
        La rengaine:
—"Vous vous trompez . . . quel émoi! . . .
Laissez-moi . . . je suis honnête . . .
        —Pas si bête!
—Pour qui me prends-tu?—Pour moi! . . .

". . . Prendrais-tu pas quelque chose
        Qu'on arrose
Avec n'importe quoi . . . du
Jus de perles dans des coupes
        D'or? . . . Tu coupes!
Mais moi? Mina, me prends-tu?"

"Pourquoi pas? ça va sans dire!"—
        "—O sourire! . . .
Moi, par-dessus le marché! . . .
Hermosa, tu m'as l'air franche
        De la hanche!
Un cuistre en serait fâché!"

—"Mais je me nomme Aloïse . . ."
        "—Héloïse!
Veux-tu, pour l'amour de l'art,
—Abeilard avant la lettre—
        Me permettre
D'être un peu ton Abeilard?"

        .     .     .     .     .     .

Et, comme un grain blanc qui crève,
   Le doux rêve
S'est couché là, sans point noir . . .
"Donne à ma lèvre apaisée
   La rosée
D'un baiser-levant—Bonsoir—

C'est le chant de l'alouette,
   Juliette!
Et c'est le chant du dindon . . .
Je te fais, comme l'aurore
   Qui te dore,
Un rond d'or sur l'édredon."


# INSOMNIE

Insomnie, impalpable Bête!
N'as-tu d'amour que dans la tête?
Pour venir te pâmer à voir,
Sous ton mauvais œil, l'homme mordre
Ses draps, et dans l'ennui se tordre! . . .
Sous ton œil de diamant noir.

Dis: pourquoi, durant la nuit blanche,
Pluvieuse comme un dimanche,
Venir nous lécher comme un chien:
Espérance ou Regret qui veille,
A notre palpitante oreille
Parler bas . . . et ne dire rien?

Pourquoi, sur notre gorge aride,
Toujours pencher ta coupe vide
Et nous laisser le cou tendu,
Tantales, soiffeurs de chimère:
—Philtre amoureux ou lie amère,
Fraîche rosée ou plomb fondu!—

Insomnie, es-tu donc pas belle? . . .
Eh pourquoi, lubrique pucelle,
Nous étreindre entre tes genoux?
Pourquoi râler sur notre bouche,
Pourquoi défaire notre couche,
Et . . . ne pas coucher avec nous?

Pourquoi, Belle-de-nuit impure,
Ce masque noir sur ta figure? . . .
—Pour intriguer les songes d'or?
N'es-tu pas l'amour dans l'espace,
Souffle de Messaline lasse,
Mais pas rassasiée encor!

Insomnie, es-tu l'Hystérie . . .
Es-tu l'orgue de barbarie
Qui moud l'*Hosannah* des Élus? . . .
—Ou n'es-tu pas l'éternel plectre,
Sur les nerfs des damnés-de-lettre,
Raclant leurs vers—qu'eux seuls ont lus?

Insomnie, es-tu l'âne en peine
De Buridan—ou le phalène
De l'enfer?—Ton baiser de feu
Laisse un goût froidi de fer rouge . . .
Oh! viens te poser dans mon bouge! . . .
Nous dormirons ensemble un peu.


## LE CRAPAUD

Un chant dans une nuit sans air . . .
—La lune plaque en métal clair
Les découpures du vert sombre.

Un chant; comme un écho, tout vif
Enterré, là, sous le massif . . .
—Ça se tait: Viens, c'est là, dans l'ombre . . .

—Un crapaud!—Pourquoi cette peur,
Près de moi, ton soldat fidèle?
Vois-le, poète tondu, sans aile,
Rossignol de la boue . . . —Horreur!—

—Il chante.—Horreur!!—Horreur pourquoi?
Vois-tu pas son œil de lumière . . .
Non: il s'en va, froid, sous sa pierre.

          .   .   .   .   .   .   .
Bonsoir—ce crapaud-là, c'est moi.

## HEURES

Aumône au malandrin en chasse!
Mauvais œil à l'œil assassin!
Fer contre fer au spadassin!
—Mon âme n'est pas en état de grâce!—

Je suis le fou de Pampelune,
J'ai peur du rire de la Lune,
Cafarde, avec son crêpe noir . . .
Horreur! tout est donc sous un éteignoir?

J'entends comme un bruit de crécelle . . .
C'est la male heure qui m'appelle.
Dans le creux des nuits tombe: un glas . . . deux glas.

J'ai compté plus de quatorze heures . . .
L'heure est une larme—Tu pleures,
Mon cœur! . . . Chante encor, va—Ne compte pas.


## À MA JUMENT SOURIS

Pas d'éperon ni de cravache,
N'est-ce pas, Maîtresse à poil gris . . .
C'est bon à pousser une vache,
Pas une petite Souris.

Pas de mors à ta pauvre bouche:
Je t'aime, et ma cuisse te touche.
Pas de selle, pas d'étrier:
J'agace du bout de ma botte,
Ta patte d'acier fin qui trotte.
Va: je ne suis pas cavalier . . .

—Hurrah! c'est à nous la poussière!
J'ai la tête dans ta crinière,
Mes deux bras te font un collier.
—Hurrah! c'est à nous le hallier!

—Hurrah! c'est à nous la barrière!
Je suis emballé: tu me tiens—
Hurrah! . . . et le fossé derrière . . .
Et la culbute! . . . —Femme, tiens!!

## RAPSODIE DU SOURD

L'homme de l'art lui dit:—Fort bien, restons-en là.
Le traitement est fait: vous êtes sourd. Voilà
Comme quoi vous avez l'organe bien perdu.—
Et lui comprit trop bien, n'ayant pas entendu.

—Eh bien, merci, Monsieur, vous qui daignez me rendre
　　　La tête comme un bon cercueil.
Désormais, à crédit, je pourrai tout entendre
　　　Avec un légitime orgueil . . .

A *l'œil.*—Mais gare à l'œil jaloux, gardant la place
De l'oreille au clou! . . . —Non.—A quoi sert de braver!
. . . Si j'ai sifflé trop haut le ridicule en face,
En face, et bassement, il pourra me baver! . . .

Moi, mannequin muet, à fil banal!—Demain,
Dans la rue, un ami peut me prendre la main,
En me disant: vieux pot . . ., ou rien, en radouci;
Et je lui répondrai:—Pas mal et vous, merci!—

Si l'un me corne un mot, j'enrage de l'entendre;
Si quelque autre se tait: serait-ce par pitié? . . .
Toujours, comme un *rebus*, je travaille à surprendre
Un mot de travers . . . —Non.—On m'a donc oublié!

—Ou bien—autre guitare—un officieux être
Dont la lippe me fait le mouvement de paître,
Croit me parler . . . Et moi je tire, en me rongeant,
Un sourire idiot—d'un air intelligent!

—Bonnet de laine grise enfoncé sur mon âme!
Et—coup de pied de l'âne . . . Hue!—Une bonne-femme,
Vieille Limonadière, aussi, de la Passion,
Peut venir saliver sa sainte compassion
Dans ma *trompe-d'Eustache*, à pleins cris, à plein cor,
Sans que je puisse au moins lui marcher sur un cor!

—Bête comme une vierge et fier comme un lépreux,
Je suis là, mais absent . . . On dit: Est-ce un gâteux,
Poète muselé, hérisson à rebours? . . . —
Un haussement d'épaule, et ça veut dire: un sourd.

—Hystérique tourment d'un Tantale acoustique!
Je vois voler des mots que je ne puis happer;
Gobe-mouche impuissant, mangé par un moustique,
Tête de turc gratis où chacun peut taper.

O musique céleste: entendre, sur du plâtre,
Gratter un coquillage! un rasoir, un couteau
Grinçant dans un bouchon! . . . un couplet de théâtre!
Un os vivant qu'on scie! un monsieur! un rondeau! . . .

—Rien—Je parle sous moi . . . Des mots qu'à l'air je jette
De chic, et sans savoir si je parle en indou . . .
Ou peut-être en canard, comme la clarinette
D'un aveugle bouché qui se trompe de trou.

—Va donc, balancier, soûl affolé dans ma tête!
Bats en branle ce bon tam-tam, chaudron fêlé
Qui rends la voix de femme ainsi qu'une sonnette,
Qu'un coucou! . . . quelquefois: un moucheron ailé . . .

—Va te coucher, mon cœur! et ne bats plus de l'aile.
Dans la lanterne sourde étouffons la chandelle,
Et tout ce qui vibrait là—je ne sais plus où—
Oubliette où l'on vient de tirer le verrou.

—Soyez muette pour moi, contemplative Idole.
Tous les deux l'un par l'autre, oubliant la parole,
Vous ne me direz mot: je ne répondrai rien . . .
Et lors rien ne pourra dédorer l'entretien.

Le silence est d'or (Saint Jean Chrysostom).


## A L'ETNA

Sicelides Musæ, paulo majora canamus.
VIRGILE.

Etna—j'ai monté le Vésuve . . .
Le Vésuve a beaucoup baissé:
J'étais plus chaud que son effluve,
Plus que sa crête hérissé . . .

—Toi que l'on compare à la femme, . . .
—Pourquoi?—Pour ton âge—? ou ton âme
De caillou cuit? . . . —Ça fait rêver . . .
—Et tu t'en fais rire à crever!—

—Tu ris jaune et tousses: sans doute,
Crachant un vieil amour malsain;
La lave coule sous la croûte
De ton vieux cancer au sein.

—Couchons ensemble, Camarade!
Là—mon flanc sur ton flanc malade:
Nous sommes frères, par Vénus,
Volcan! . . .

      Un peu moins . . . un peu plus . . .


## PAYSAGE MAUVAIS

Sables de vieux os—Le flot râle
Des glas: crevant bruit sur bruit . . .
—Palud pâle, où la lune avale
De gros vers pour passer la nuit.

—Calme de peste, où la fièvre
Cuit . . . Le follet damné languit.
—Herbe puante où le lièvre
Est un sorcier poltron qui fuit . . .

—La Lavandière blanche étale
Des trépassés le linge sale,
Au *soleil des loups* . . . —Les crapauds,

Petits chantres mélancoliques,
Empoisonnent de leurs coliques
Les champignons, leurs escabeaux.


## CRIS D'AVEUGLE

Sur l'air bas-breton: *Ann hini goz*

    L'œil tué n'est pas mort
    Un coin le fend encor
Encloué je suis sans cercueil
On m'a planté le clou dans l'œil
    L'œil cloué n'est pas mort
    Et le coin entre encor

    *Deus misericors*
    *Deus misericors*
Le marteau bat ma tête en bois
Le marteau qui fera la croix
    *Deus misericors*
    *Deus misericors*

Les oiseaux croque-morts
Ont donc peur à mon corps
Mon Golgotha n'est pas fini.
*Lamma lamma sabacthani*
Colombes de la Mort
Soiffez après mon corps


Rouge comme un sabord
La plaie est sur le bord
Comme la gencive bavant
D'une vieille qui rit sans dent
La plaie est sur le bord
Rouge comme un sabord


Je vois des cercles d'or
Le soleil blanc me mord
J'ai deux trous percés par un fer
Rougi dans la forge d'enfer
Je vois un cercle d'or
Le feu d'en haut me mord


Dans la moelle se tord
Une larme qui sort
Je vois dedans le paradis
*Miserere De profundis*
Dans mon crâne se tord
Du soufre en pleur qui sort


Bienheureux le bon mort
Le mort sauvé qui dort
Heureux les martyrs les élus
Avec la Vierge et son Jésus
O bienheureux le mort
Le mort jugé qui dort


Un Chevalier dehors
Repose sans remords
Dans le cimetière bénit
Dans sa sieste de granit
L'homme en pierre dehors
A deux yeux sans remords


Ho je vous sens encor
Landes jaunes d'Armor
Je sens mon rosaire à mes doigts
Et le Christ en os sur le bois
A toi je baye encor
O ciel défunt d'Armor

Pardon de prier fort
Seigneur si c'est le sort
Mes yeux deux bénitiers ardents
Le diable a mis ses doigts dedans
Pardon de crier fort
Seigneur contre le sort

J'entends le vent du nord
Qui bugle comme un cor
C'est l'hallali des trépassés
J'aboie après mon tour assez
J'entends le vent du nord
J'entends le glas du cor


## LETTRE DU MEXIQUE

*La Vera-Cruz, 10 février*

"Vous m'avez confié le petit.—Il est mort.
Et plus d'un camarade avec, pauvre cher être.
L'équipage . . . y en a plus. Il reviendra peut-être
    Quelques-uns de nous.—C'est le sort—

"Rien n'est beau comme ça—Matelot—pour un homme;
Tout le monde en voudrait à terre—C'est bien sûr.
Sans le désagrément. Rien que ça: Voyez comme
    Déjà l'apprentissage est dur!

"Je pleure en marquant ça, moi, vieux *Frère-la-Côte*.
J'aurais donné ma peau joliment sans façon
Pour vous le renvoyer . . . Moi, ce n'est pas ma faute:
    Ce mal-là n'a pas de raison.

"La fièvre est ici comme Mars en carème.
Au cimetière on va toucher sa ration.
Le zouave a nommé ça—Parisien quand-même—
    *Le jardin d'acclimatation.*'

"Consolez-vous. Le monde y crève comme mouches
. . . J'ai trouvé dans son sac des souvenirs de cœur:
Un portrait de fille, et deux petites babouches,
    Et: marqué—*Cadeau pour ma sœur.*—

"Il fait dire à *maman*: qu'il a fait sa prière.
Au père: qu'il serait mieux mort dans un Combat.
Deux anges étaient là sur son heure dernière:
    Un matelot. Un vieux soldat."

## LE MOUSSE

—Mousse: il est donc marin, ton père? . . .
—Pêcheur. Perdu depuis longtemps.
En découchant d'avec ma mère,
Il a couché dans les brisants . . .

Maman lui garde au cimetière
Une tombe—et rien dedans.—
C'est moi son mari sur la terre,
Pour gagner du pain aux enfants.

Deux petits.—Alors, sur la plage,
Rien n'est revenu du naufrage? . . .
—Son garde-pipe et son sabot . . .

La mère pleure, le dimanche,
Pour repos . . . Moi: j'ai ma revanche
Quand je serai grand—matelot!—


## LA FIN

*Oh! combien de marins, combien de capitaines*
*Qui sont partis joyeux pour des courses lointaines*
*Dans ce morne horizon se sont évanouis! . . .*
. . . . . . . . . . . . . . .

*Combien de patrons morts avec leurs équipages!*
*L'Océan de leur vie a pris toutes les pages.*
*Et, d'un souffle, il a tout dispersé sur les flots.*
*Nul ne saura leur fin dans l'abîme plongée . . .*
. . . . . . . . . . . . . . .

*Nul ne saura leurs noms, pas même l'humble pierre,*
*Dans l'étroit cimetière où l'écho nous répond,*
*Pas même un saule vert qui s'effeuille à l'automne,*
*Pas même la chanson plaintive et monotone*
*D'un aveugle qui chante à l'angle d'un vieux pont.*
v. HUGO: Oceano nox.

Eh bien, tous ces marins—matelots, capitaines,
Dans leur grand Océan à jamais engloutis,
Partis insoucieux pour leurs courses lointaines,
Sont morts—absolument comme ils étaient partis.

Allons! c'est leur métier; ils sont morts dans leurs bottes!
Leur *boujaron* au cœur, tout vifs dans leurs capotes . . .
—*Morts* . . . Merci: la *Camarde* a pas le pied marin:—
Qu'elle couche avec vous: c'est votre bonne-femme . . .
—Eux, allons donc: Entiers! enlevés par la lame!
        Ou perdus dans un grain . . .

Un grain . . . est-ce la mort, ça? La basse voilure
Battant à travers l'eau!—Ça se dit *encombrer* . . .
Un coup de mer plombé, puis la haute mâture
Fouettant les flots ras—et ça se dit *sombrer*.

—Sombrer.—Sondez ce mot. Votre *mort* est bien pâle
Et pas grand'chose à bord, sous la lourde rafale . . .
Pas grand'chose devant le grand sourire amer
Du matelot qui lutte.—Allons donc, de la place!—
Vieux fantôme éventé, la Mort change de face:
        La Mer! . . .

Noyés?—Eh allons donc! Les *noyés* sont d'eau douce.
—Coulés! corps et biens! Et, jusqu'au petit mousse,
Le défi dans les yeux, dans les dents le juron!
A l'écume crachant une chique râlée,
Buvant sans hauts-de-cœur *la grand' tasse salée* . . .
      —Comme ils ont bu leur boujaron.—

.   .   .   .   .   .   .   .   .   .

—Pas de fond de six pieds, ni rats de cimetière:
Eux, ils vont aux requins! L'âme d'un matelot,
Au lieu de suinter dans vos pommes de terre,
        Respire à chaque flot.

—Voyez à l'horizon se soulever la houle
        On dirait le ventre amoureux
D'une fille de joie en rut, à moitié soûle . . .
        Ils sont là!—La houle a du creux.—

—Ecoutez, écoutez la tourmente qui beugle! . . .
C'est leur anniversaire.—Il revient bien souvent.—
O poète, gardez pour vous vos chants d'aveugle;
—Eux: le *De profundis* que vous corne le vent.

. . . Qu'ils roulent infinis dans les espaces vierges! . . .
        Qu'ils roulent verts et nus,
Sans clous et sans sapin, sans couvercle, sans cierges! . . .
—Laissez-les donc rouler, *terriens* parvenus!

## PARIS NOCTURNE

*Ce n'est pas une ville, c'est un monde*

—C'est la mer—calme plat.—et la grande marée,
Avec un grondement lointain, s'est retirée . . .
Le flot va revenir, se roulant dans son bruit.
—Entendez-vous gratter les crabes de la nuit . . .

—C'est le Styx asséché: Le chiffonnier Diogène,
La lanterne à la main, s'en vient avec sans-gêne.
Le long du ruisseau noir, les poètes pervers
Pêchent: leur crâne creux leur sert de boîte à vers.

—C'est le champ: Pour glaner les impures charpies
S'abat le vol tournant des hideuses harpies;
Le lapin de gouttière, à l'affût des rongeurs
Fuit les fils de Bondy, nocturnes vendangeurs.

—C'est la mort: La police gît.—En haut, l'amour
Fait sa sieste, en têtant la viande d'un bras lourd
Où le baiser éteint laisse sa plaque rouge . . .
L'heure est seule—Ecoutez . . . pas un rêve ne bouge.

—C'est la vie: Ecoutez: la source vive chante
L'éternelle chanson sur la tête gluante
D'un dieu marin tirant ses membres nus et verts
Sur le lit de la morgue . . . Et les yeux grands ouverts!

## RONDEL

Il fait noir, enfant, voleur d'étincelles!
Il n'est plus de nuits, il n'est plus de jours;
Dors . . . en attendant venir toutes celles
Qui disaient: Jamais! Qui disaient: Toujours!

Entends-tu leurs pas? . . . Ils ne sont pas lourds:
Oh! les pieds légers!—l'Amour a des ailes . . .
Il fait noir, enfant, voleur d'étincelles!

Entends-tu leurs voix? . . . Les caveaux sont sourds.
Dors: Il pèse peu, ton faix d'immortelles:
Ils ne viendront pas, tes amis les ours,
Jeter leur pavé sur tes demoiselles . . .
Il fait noir, enfant, voleur d'étincelles!

## DO, L'ENFANT DO . . .

*Buona vespre!* Dors: Ton bout de cierge,
On l'a posé là, puis on est parti.
Tu n'auras pas peur seul, pauvre petit? . . .
C'est le chandelier de ton lit d'auberge.

Du fesse-cahier ne crains plus la verge,
Val . . . De t'éveiller point n'est si hardi.
*Buona sera!* Dors: Ton bout de cierge . . .

Est mort.—Il n'est plus, ici, de concierge:
Seuls, le vent du nord, le vent du midi
Viendront balancer un fil-de-la-Vierge.
Chut! Pour les pieds-plats, ton sol est maudit.
—*Buona notte!* Dors: Ton bout de cierge . . .


## MIRLITON

Dors d'amour, méchant ferreur de cigales!
Dans le chiendent qui te couvrira
La cigale aussi pour toi chantera,
Joyeuse, avec ses petites cymbales.

La rosée aura des pleurs matinales;
Et le muguet blanc fait un joli drap . . .
Dors d'amour, méchant ferreur de cigales!

Pleureuses en troupeau passeront les rafales . . .

La Muse camarde ici posera.
Sur ta bouche noire encore elle aura
Ces rimes qui vont aux moelles des pâles . . .
Dors d'amour, méchant ferreur de cigales.


## PETIT MORT POUR RIRE

Va vite, léger peigneur de comètes!
Les herbes au vent seront tes cheveux;
De ton œil béant jailliront les feux
Follets, prisonniers dans les pauvres têtes . . .

Les fleurs de tombeau qu'on nomme Amourettes
Foisonneront plein ton rire terreux . . .
Et les myosotis, ces fleurs d'oubliettes . . .

Ne fais pas le lourd: cercueils de poètes
Pour les croque-morts sont de simples jeux,
Boîtes à violon qui sonnent le creux . . .
Ils te croiront mort—les bourgeois sont bêtes—
Va vite, léger peigneur de comètes!

# Paul Verlaine

## MON RÊVE FAMILIER

Je fais souvent ce rêve étrange et pénétrant
D'une femme inconnue, et que j'aime, et qui m'aime,
Et qui n'est, chaque fois, ni tout à fait la même
Ni tout à fait une autre, et m'aime et me comprend.

Car elle me comprend, et mon cœur, transparent
Pour elle seule, hélas! cesse d'être un problème
Pour elle seule, et les moiteurs de mon front blême,
Elle seule les sait refraîchir, en pleurant.

Est-elle brune, blonde ou rousse?—Je l'ignore.
Son nom? Je me souviens qu'il est doux et sonore
Comme ceux des aimés que la Vie exila.

Son regard est pareil au regard des statues,
Et pour sa voix lointaine, et calme, et grave, elle a
L'inflexion des voix chères qui se sont tues.

## L'ANGOISSE

Nature, rien de toi ne m'émeut, ni les champs
Nourriciers, ni l'écho vermeil des pastorales
Siciliennes, ni les pompes aurorales,
Ni la solennité dolente des couchants.

Je ris de l'Art, je ris de l'Homme aussi, des chants,
Des vers, des temples grecs et des tours en spirales
Qu'étirent dans le ciel vide les cathédrales,
Et je vois du même œil les bons et les méchants.

Je ne crois pas en Dieu, j'abjure et je renie
Toute pensée, et quant à la vieille ironie,
L'Amour, je voudrais bien qu'on ne m'en parlât plus.

Lasse de vivre, ayant peur de mourir, pareille
Au brick perdu jouet du flux et du reflux,
Mon âme pour d'affreux naufrages appareille.


## L'HEURE DU BERGER

La lune est rouge au brumeux horizon
Dans un brouillard qui danse, la prairie
S'endort fumeuse, et la grenouille crie
Par les joncs verts où circule un frisson;

Les fleurs des eaux referment leurs corolles;
Des peupliers profilent aux lointains,
Droits et serrés, leurs spectres incertains;
Vers les buissons errent les lucioles;

Les chats-huants s'éveillent, et sans bruit
Rament l'air noir avec leurs ailes lourdes,
Et le zénith s'emplit de lueurs sourdes.
Blanche, Vénus émerge, et c'est la Nuit.


## LE ROSSIGNOL

Comme un vol criard d'oiseaux en émoi,
Tous mes souvenirs s'abattent sur moi,
S'abattent parmi le feuillage jaune
De mon cœur mirant son tronc plié d'aune
Au tain violet de l'eau des Regrets
Qui mélancoliquement coule auprès,
S'abattent, et puis la rumeur mauvaise
Qu'une brise moite en montant apaise,
S'éteint par degrés dans l'arbre, si bien
Qu'au bout d'un instant on n'entend plus rien,
Plus rien que la voix célébrant l'Absente.
Plus rien que la voix—ô si languissante!—
De l'oiseau que fut mon Premier Amour,
Et qui chante encor comme au premier jour;
Et dans la splendeur triste d'une lune
Se levant blafarde et solennelle, une
Nuit mélancolique et lourde d'été,
Pleine de silence et d'obscurité,
Berce sur l'azur qu'un vent doux effleure
L'arbre qui frissonne et l'oiseau qui pleure.

## DANS LES BOIS

D'autres,—des innocents ou bien des lymphatiques,—
Ne trouvent dans les bois que charmes langoureux,
Souffles frais et parfums tièdes. Ils sont heureux!
D'autres s'y sentent pris—rêveurs—d'effrois mystiques.

Ils sont heureux! Pour moi, nerveux, et qu'un remords
Ėpouvantable et vague affole sans relâche,
Par les forêts je tremble à la façon d'un lâche,
Qui craindrait une embûche ou qui verrait des morts.

Ces grands rameaux jamais apaisés, comme l'onde,
D'où tombe un noir silence avec une ombre encor
Plus noire, tout ce morne et sinistre décor
Me remplit d'une horreur triviale et profonde.

Surtout les soirs d'été: la rougeur du couchant
Se fond dans le gris bleu des brumes qu'elle teinte
D'incendie et de sang; et l'angélus qui tinte
Au lointain semble un cri plaintif se rapprochant.

Le vent se lève chaud et lourd, un frisson passe
Et repasse, toujours plus fort, dans l'épaisseur
Toujours plus sombre des hauts chênes, obsesseur,
Et s'éparpille, ainsi qu'un miasme, dans l'espace.

La nuit vient. Le hibou s'envole. C'est l'instant
Où l'on songe aux récits des aïeules naïves . . .
Sous un fourré, là-bas, là-bas, des sources vives
Font un bruit d'assassins postés se concertant.

## CLAIR DE LUNE

Votre âme est un paysage choisi
Que vont charmant masques et bergamasques
Jouant du luth et dansant et quasi
Tristes sous leurs déguisements fantasques.

Tout en chantant sur le mode mineur
L'amour vainqueur et la vie opportune,
Ils n'ont pas l'air de croire à leur bonheur
Et leur chanson se mêle au clair de lune,

Au calme clair de lune triste et beau,
Qui fait rêver les oiseaux dans les arbres
Et sangloter d'extase les jets d'eau,
Les grands jets d'eau sveltes parmi les marbres.


## COLLOQUE SENTIMENTAL

Dans le vieux parc solitaire et glacé,
Deux formes ont tout à l'heure passé.

Leurs yeux sont morts et leurs lèvres sont molles,
Et l'on entend à peine leurs paroles.

Dans le vieux parc solitaire et glacé,
Deux spectres ont évoqué le passé.

—Te souvient-il de notre extase ancienne?
—Pourquoi voulez-vous donc qu'il m'en souvienne?

—Ton cœur bat-il toujours à mon seul nom?
Toujours vois-tu mon âme en rêve?—Non.

—Ah! les beaux jours de bonheur indicible
Où nous joignions nos bouches!—C'est possible.

—Qu'il était bleu, le ciel, et grand, l'espoir!
—L'espoir a fui, vaincu, vers le ciel noir.

Tels ils marchaient dans les avoines folles,
Et la nuit seule entendit leurs paroles.


## LA LUNE BLANCHE

La lune blanche
Luit dans les bois;
De chaque branche
Part une voix
Sous la ramée . . .

O bien-aimée.

L'étang reflète,
Profond miroir,
La silhouette
Du saule noir
Où le vent pleure . . .

Rêvons, c'est l'heure.

Un vaste et tendre
Apaisement
Semble descendre
Du firmament
Que l'astre irise . . .

C'est l'heure exquise.


## LE BRUIT DES CABARETS . . .

Le bruit des cabarets, la fange des trottoirs,
Les platanes déchus s'effeuillant dans l'air noir,
L'omnibus, ouragan de ferraille et de boues,
Qui grince, mal assis entre ses quatre roues,
Et roule ses yeux verts et rouges lentement,
Les ouvriers allant au club, tout enfumant
Le brûle-gueule au nez des agents de police,
Toits qui dégouttent, murs suintant, pavé qui glisse,
Bitume défoncé, ruisseaux comblant l'égout,
Voilà ma route—avec le paradis au bout.


## IL PLEURE DANS MON COEUR . . .

*Il pleut doucement sur la ville.*
ARTHUR RIMBAUD

Il pleure dans mon cœur
Comme il pleut sur la ville,
Quelle est cette langueur
Qui pénètre mon cœur?

O bruit doux de la pluie
Par terre et sur les toits!
Pour un cœur qui s'ennuie
O le chant de la pluie!

Il pleure sans raison
Dans ce cœur qui s'écœure.
Quoi! nulle trahison?
Ce deuil est sans raison.

C'est bien la pire peine
De ne savoir pourquoi,
Sans amour et sans haine,
Mon cœur a tant de peine.


## O TRISTE, TRISTE ETAIT MON ÂME . . .

O triste, triste était mon âme
A cause, à cause d'une femme.

Je ne me suis pas consolé
Bien que mon cœur s'en soit allé,

Bien que mon cœur, bien que mon âme
Eussent fui loin de cette femme.

Je ne me suis pas consolé,
Bien que mon cœur s'en soit allé.

Et mon cœur, mon cœur trop sensible
Dit à mon âme: Est-il possible,

Est-il possible,—le fût-il—
Ce fier exil, ce triste exil?

Mon âme dit à mon cœur: Sais-je
Moi-même, que nous veut ce piège

D'être présents bien qu'exilés,
Encore que loin en allés?


## DANS L'INTERMINABLE ENNUI . . .

Dans l'interminable
Ennui de la plaine,
La neige incertaine
Luit comme du sable.

Le ciel est de cuivre
Sans lueur aucune.
On croirait voir vivre
Et mourir la lune.

Comme des nuées
Flottent gris les chênes
Des forêts prochaines
Parmi les buées.

Le ciel est de cuivre
Sans lueur aucune.
On croirait voir vivre
Et mourir la lune.

Corneille poussive
Et vous, les loups maigres,
Par ces bises aigres
Quoi donc vous arrive?

Dans l'interminable
Ennui de la plaine,
La neige incertaine
Luit comme du sable.

## ÉCOUTEZ LA CHANSON BIEN DOUCE . . .

Écoutez la chanson bien douce
Qui ne pleure que pour vous plaire.
Elle est discrète, elle est légère:
Un frisson d'eau sur de la mousse!

La voix vous fut connue (et chère?),
Mais à présent elle est voilée
Comme une veuve désolée,
Pourtant comme elle encore fière,

Et dans les longs plis de son voile
Qui palpite aux brises d'automne,
Cache et montre au cœur qui s'étonne
La vérité comme une étoile.

Elle dit, la voix reconnue,
Que la bonté c'est notre vie,
Que de la haine et de l'envie
Rien ne reste, la mort venue.

Elle parle aussi de la gloire
D'être simple sans plus attendre,
Et de noces d'or et du tendre
Bonheur d'une paix sans victoire.

Accueillez la voix qui persiste
Dans son naïf épithalame.
Allez, rien n'est meilleur à l'âme
Que de faire une âme moins triste!

Elle est "en peine" et "de passage,"
L'âme qui souffre sans colère,
Et comme sa morale est claire! . . .
Écoutez la chanson bien sage.


## ET J'AI REVU L'ENFANT UNIQUE . . .

Et j'ai revu l'enfant unique: il m'a semblé
Que s'ouvrait dans mon cœur la dernière blessure,
Celle dont la douleur plus exquise m'assure
D'une mort désirable en un jour consolé.

La bonne flèche aiguë et sa fraîcheur qui dure!
En ces instants choisis elles ont éveillé
Les rêves un peu lourds du scrupule ennuyé,
Et tout mon sang chrétien chanta la Chanson pure.

J'entends encor, je vois encor. Loi du devoir
Si douce! Enfin, je sais ce qu'est entendre et voir,
J'entends, je vois toujours! Voix des bonnes pensées,

Innocence, avenir! Sage et silencieux,
Que je vais vous aimer, vous un instant pressées,
Belles petites mains qui fermerez nos yeux!


## MON DIEU M'A DIT . . .

Mon Dieu m'a dit:—Mon fils, il faut m'aimer. Tu vois
Mon flanc percé, mon cœur qui rayonne et qui saigne,
Et mes pieds offensés que Madeleine baigne
De larmes, et mes bras douloureux sous le poids

De tes péchés, et mes mains! Et tu vois la croix,
Tu vois les clous, le fiel, l'éponge, et tout t'enseigne
A n'aimer, en ce monde amer où la chair règne,
Que ma Chair et mon Sang, ma parole et ma voix.

Ne t'ai-je pas aimé jusqu'à la mort moi-même,
O mon frère en mon Père, ô mon fils en l'Esprit.
Et n'ai-je pas souffert, comme c'était écrit?

N'ai-je pas sangloté ton angoisse suprême
Et n'ai-pe pas sué la sueur de tes nuits,
Lamentable ami qui me cherches où je suis?


## UN GRAND SOMMEIL NOIR . . .

Un grand sommeil noir
Tombe sur ma vie:
Dormez, tout espoir,
Dormez, toute envie!

Je ne vois plus rien,
Je perds la mémoire
Du mal et du bien . . .
O la triste histoire!

Je suis un berceau
Qu'une main balance
Au creux d'un caveau:
Silence, silence!


## LE CIEL EST, PAR-DESSUS LE TOIT . . .

Le ciel est, par-dessus le toit,
Si bleu, si calme!
Un arbre, par-dessus le toit,
Berce sa palme.

La cloche dans le ciel qu'on voit
Doucement tinte.
Un oiseau sur l'arbre qu'on voit
Chante sa plainte.

Mon Dieu, mon Dieu, la vie est là,
   Simple et tranquille.
Cette paisible rumeur-là
   Vient de la ville.

—Qu'as-tu fait, ô toi que voilà
   Pleurant sans cesse,
Dis, qu'as-tu fait, toi que voilà,
   De ta jeunesse?

## JE NE SAIS POURQUOI . . .

   Je ne sais pourquoi
   Mon esprit amer
D'une aile inquiète et folle vole sur la mer,
   Tout ce qui m'est cher,
   D'une aile d'effroi
Mon amour le couve au ras des flots. Pourquoi, pourquoi?

   Mouette à l'essor mélancolique,
   Elle suit la vague, ma pensée,
   A tous les vents du ciel balancée
   Et biaisant quand la marée oblique,
   Mouette à l'essor mélancolique.

   Ivre de soleil
   Et de liberté,
Un instinct la guide à travers cette immensité.
   La brise d'été
   Sur le flot vermeil
Doucement la porte en un tiède demi-sommeil.

   Parfois si tristement elle crie
   Qu'elle alarme au lointain le pilote,
   Puis au gré du vent se livre et flotte
   Et plonge, et l'aile toute meurtrie
   Revole, et puis si tristement crie!

   Je ne sais pourquoi
   Mon esprit amer
D'une aile inquiète et folle vole sur la mer.
   Tout ce qui m'est cher,
   D'une aile d'effroi
Mon amour le couve au ras des flots. Pourquoi, pourquoi?

## ART POÉTIQUE

*A Charles Morice*

De la musique avant toute chose,
Et pour cela préfère l'Impair
Plus vague et plus soluble dans l'air,
Sans rien en lui qui pèse ou qui pose.

Il faut aussi que tu n'ailles point
Choisir tes mots sans quelque méprise:
Rien de plus cher que la chanson grise
Où l'Indécis au Précis se joint.

C'est des beaux yeux derrière des voiles,
C'est le grand jour tremblant de midi,
C'est, par un ciel d'automne attiédi,
Le bleu fouillis des claires étoiles!

Car nous voulons la Nuance encor,
Pas la Couleur, rien que la nuance!
Oh! la nuance seule fiance
Le rêve au rêve et la flûte au cor!

Fuis du plus loin la Pointe assassine,
L'Esprit cruel et le Rire impur,
Qui font pleurer les yeux de l'Azur,
Et tout cet ail de basse cuisine!

Prends l'éloquence et tords-lui son cou!
Tu feras bien, en train d'énergie,
De rendre un peu la Rime assagie,
Si l'on n'y veille, elle ira jusqu'où?

Oh! qui dira les torts de la Rime?
Quel enfant sourd ou quel nègre fou
Nous a forgé ce bijou d'un sou
Qui sonne creux et faux sous la lime?

De la musique encore et toujours!
Que ton vers soit la chose envolée
Qu'on sent qui fuit d'une âme en allée
Vers d'autres cieux à d'autres amours.

Que ton vers soit la bonne aventure
Éparse au vent crispé du matin
Qui va fleurant la menthe et le thym . . .
Et tout le reste est littérature.

## LANGUEUR

Je suis l'Empire à la fin de la décadence,
Qui regarde passer les grands Barbares blancs
En composant des acrostiches indolents
D'un style d'or où la langueur du soleil danse.

L'âme seulette a mal au cœur d'un ennui dense.
Là-bas on dit qu'il est de longs combats sanglants.
O n'y pouvoir, étant si faible aux vœux si lents,
O n'y vouloir fleurir un peu cette existence!

O n'y vouloir, ô n'y pouvoir mourir un peu!
Ah! tout est bu! Bathylle, as-tu fini de rire?
Ah! tout est bu, tout est mangé! Plus rien à dire!

Seul, un poème un peu niais qu'on jette au feu,
Seul, un esclave un peu coureur qui vous néglige,
Seul, un ennui d'on ne sait quoi qui vous afflige!

# Arthur Rimbaud

## OPHÉLIE

### I

Sur l'onde calme et noire où dorment les étoiles
La blanche Ophélia flotte comme un grand lys,
Flotte très lentement, couchée en ses longs voiles . . .
—On entend dans les bois lointains des hallalis.

Voici plus de mille ans que la triste Ophélie
Passe, fantôme blanc, sur le long fleuve noir.
Voici plus de mille ans que sa douce folie
Murmure sa romance à la brise du soir.

Le vent baise ses seins, et déploie en corolle
Ses grands voiles bercés mollement par les eaux;
Les saules frisonnants pleurent sur son épaule,
Sur son grand front rêveur s'inclinent les roseaux.

Les nénuphars froissés soupirent autour d'elle;
Elle éveille parfois, dans un aune qui dort,
Quelque nid, d'où s'échappe un petit frisson d'aile:
—Un chant mystérieux tombe des astres d'or.

## II

O pâle Ophélia! belle comme la neige!
Oui, tu mourus, enfant, par un fleuve emporté!
—C'est que les vents tombant des grands monts de Norwège
T'avaient parlé tout bas de l'âpre liberté;

C'est qu'un souffle, tordant ta grande chevelure,
A ton esprit rêveur portait d'étranges bruits;
Que ton cœur écoutait le chant de la Nature
Dans les plaintes de l'arbre et les soupirs des nuits;

C'est que la voix des mers folles, immense râle,
Brisait ton sein d'enfant, trop humain et trop doux;
C'est qu'un matin d'avril, un beau cavalier pâle,
Un pauvre fou, s'assit muet à tes genoux!

Ciel! Amour! Liberté! Quel rêve, ô pauvre Folle!
Tu te fondais à lui comme une neige au feu:
Tes grandes visions étranglaient ta parole
—Et l'Infini terrible effara ton œil bleu!

## III

—Et le Poète dit qu'aux rayons des étoiles
Tu viens chercher, la nuit, les fleurs que tu cueillis,
Et qu'il a vu sur l'eau, couchée en ses longs voiles,
La blanche Ophélia flotter, comme un grand lys.

## MA BOHÈME

Je m'en allais, les poings dans mes poches crevées;
Mon paletot aussi devenait idéal;
J'allais sous le ciel, Muse! et j'étais féal;
Oh! là là! que d'amours splendides j'ai rêvées!

Mon unique culotte avait un large trou.
—Petit-Poucet rêveur, j'égrenais dans ma course
Des rimes. Mon auberge était à la Grande-Ourse.
—Mes étoiles au ciel avaient un doux frou-frou

Et je les écoutais, assis au bord des routes,
Ces bons soirs de septembre où je sentais des gouttes
De rosée à mon front, comme un vin de vigueur;

Où, rimant au milieu des ombres fantastiques,
Comme des lyres, je tirais les élastiques
De mes souliers blessés, un pied près de mon cœur!


## LES POÈTES DE SEPT ANS

Et la Mère, fermant le livre du devoir,
S'en allait satisfaite et très fière, sans voir,
Dans les yeux bleus et sous le front plein d'éminences,
L'âme de son enfant livrée aux répugnances.


Tout le jour il suait d'obéissance; très
Intelligent; pourtant des tics noirs, quelques traits
Semblaient prouver en lui d'âcres hypocrisies.
Dans l'ombre des couloirs aux tentures moisies,
En passant il tirait la langue, les deux poings
A l'aine, et dans ses yeux fermés voyait des points.
Une porte s'ouvrait sur le soir: à la lampe
On le voyait, là-haut, qui râlait sur la rampe,
Sous un golfe de jour pendant du toit. L'été
Surtout, vaincu, stupide, il était entêté
A se renfermer dans la fraîcheur des latrines:
Il pensait là, tranquille et livrant ses narines.


Quand, lavé des odeurs du jour, le jardinet,
Derrière la maison, en hiver, s'illunait:
Gisant au pied d'un mur, enterré dans la marne
Et pour des visions écrasant son œil darne,
Il écoutait grouiller les galeux espaliers.
Pitié! Ces enfants seuls étaient ses familiers
Qui, chétifs, fronts nus, œil déteignant sur la joue,
Cachant de maigres doigts jaunes et noirs de boue
Sous des habits puant la foire et tout vieillots,
Conversaient avec la douceur des idiots!
Et si, l'ayant surpris à des pitiés immondes,
Sa mère s'effrayait, les tendresses profondes,
De l'enfant se jetaient sur cet étonnement.
C'était bon. Elle avait le bleu regard,—qui ment!

A sept ans, il faisait des romans sur la vie
Du grand désert, où luit la Liberté ravie,
Forêts, soleils, rives, savanes!—Il s'aidait
De journaux illustrés où, rouge, il regardait
Des Espagnoles rire et des Italiennes.
Quand venait, l'œil brun, folle, en robe d'indiennes,
—Huit ans,—la fille des ouvriers d'à côté,
La petite brutale, et qu'elle avait sauté,
Dans un coin, sur son dos, en secouant ses tresses,
Et qu'il était sous elle, il lui mordait les fesses,
Car elle ne portait jamais de pantalons;
—Et, par elle meurtri des poings et des talons,
Remportait les saveurs de sa peau dans sa chambre.

Il craignait les blafards dimanches de décembre,
Où, pommadé, sur un guéridon d'acajou,
Il lisait une Bible à la tranche vert-chou;
Des rêves l'oppressaient chaque nuit dans l'alcôve.
Il n'aimait pas Dieu; mais les hommes, qu'au soir fauve,
Noirs, en blouse, il voyait rentrer dans le faubourg
Où les crieurs, en trois roulements de tambour,
Font autour des édits rire et gronder les foules.
—Il rêvait la prairie amoureuse, où des houles
Lumineuses, parfums sains, pubescences d'or,
Font leur remuement calme et prennent leur essor!

Et comme il savourait surtout les sombres choses,
Quand, dans la chambre nue aux persiennes closes,
Haute et bleue, âcrement prise d'humidité,
Il lisait son roman sans cesse médité,
Plein de lourds ciels ocreux et de forêts noyées,
De fleurs de chair au bois sidérals deployées,
Vertige, écroulements, déroutes et pitié!
—Tandis que se faisait la rumeur du quartier,
En bas,—seul, et couché sur des pièces de toile
Écrue et pressentant violemment la voile!

## LES CHERCHEUSES DE POUX

Quand le front de l'enfant, plein de rouges tourmentes,
Implore l'essaim blanc des rêves indistincts,
Il vient près de son lit deux grandes sœurs charmantes
Avec de frêles doigts aux ongles argentins.

Elles assoient l'enfant auprès d'une croisée
Grande ouverte où l'air bleu baigne un fouillis de fleurs,
Et dans ses lourds cheveux où tombe la rosée
Promènent leurs doigts fins, terribles et charmeurs.

Il écoute chanter leurs haleines craintives
Qui fleurent de longs miels végétaux et rosés,
Et qu'interrompt parfois un sifflement, salives
Reprises sur la lèvre ou désires de baisers.

Il entend leurs cils noirs battant sous les silences
Parfumés; et leurs doigts électriques et doux
Font crépiter parmi ses grises indolences
Sous leurs ongles royaux la mort des petits poux.

Voilà que monte en lui le vin de la Paresse,
Soupir d'harmonica qui pourrait délirer;
L'enfant se sent, selon la lenteur des caresses,
Sourdre et mourir sans cesse un désir de pleurer.


## LE BATEAU IVRE

Comme je descendais des Fleuves impassibles,
Je ne me sentis plus guidé par les haleurs:
Des Peaux-Rouges criards les avaient pris pour cibles,
Les ayant cloués nus aux poteaux de couleurs.

J'étais insoucieux de tous les équipages,
Porteur de blés flamands ou de cotons anglais
Quand avec mes haleurs ont fini ces tapages,
Les Fleuves m'ont laissé descendre où je voulais.

Dans les clapotements furieux des marées,
Moi, l'autre hiver, plus sourd que les cerveaux d'enfants,
Je courus! Et les Péninsules démarrées
N'ont pas subi tohu-bohus plus triomphants.

La tempête a béni mes éveils maritimes.
Plus léger qu'un bouchon j'ai dansé sur les flots
Qu'on appelle rouleurs éternels de victimes,
Dix nuits, sans regretter l'œil niais des falots!

Plus douce qu'aux enfants la chair des pommes sures,
L'eau verte pénétra ma coque de sapin
Et des taches de vins bleus et des vomissures
Me lava, dispersant gouvernail et grappin.

Et dès lors, je me suis baigné dans le Poème
De la Mer, infusé d'astres, et lactescent,
Dévorant les azurs verts; où, flottaison blême
Et ravie, un noyé pensif parfois descend;

Où, teignant tout à coup les bleuités, délires
Et rhythmes lents sous les rutilements du jour,
Plus fortes que l'alcool, plus vastes que nos lyres,
Fermentent les rousseurs amères de l'amour!

Je sais les cieux crevant en éclairs, et les trombes
Et les ressacs et les courants: je sais le soir,
L'aube exaltée ainsi qu'un peuple de colombes,
Et j'ai vu quelquefois ce que l'homme a cru voir!

J'ai vu le soleil bas, taché d'horreurs mystiques,
Illuminant de longs figements violets,
Pareils à des acteurs de drames très-antiques,
Les flots roulant au loin leurs frissons de volets!

J'ai rêvé la nuit verte aux neiges éblouies,
Baiser montant aux yeux des mers avec lenteurs,
La circulation des sèves inouïes,
Et l'éveil jaune et bleu des phosphores chanteurs!

J'ai suivi, des mois pleins, pareille aux vacheries
Hystériques, la houle à l'assaut des récifs,
Sans songer que les pieds lumineux des Maries
Pussent forcer le mufle aux Océans poussifs!

J'ai heurté, savez-vous, d'incroyables Florides
Mêlant aux fleurs des yeux de panthères à peaux
D'hommes! Des arcs-en-ciel tendus comme des brides
Sous l'horizon des mers, à de glauques troupeaux!

J'ai vu fermenter les marais énormes, nasses
Où pourrit dans les joncs tout un Léviathan!
Des écroulements d'eaux au milieu des bonaces,
Et les lointains vers les gouffres cataractant!

Glaciers, soleils d'argent, flots nacreux, cieux de braises,
Échouages hideux au fond des golfes bruns
Où les serpents géants dévorés des punaises
Choient, des arbres tordus, avec de noirs parfums!

J'aurais voulu montrer aux enfants ces dorades
Du flot bleu, ces poissons d'or, ces poissons chantants.
—Des écumes de fleurs ont béni mes dérades,
Et d'ineffables vents m'ont ailé par instants.

Parfois, martyr lassé des pôles et des zones,
La mer dont le sanglot faisait mon roulis doux
Montait vers moi ses fleurs d'ombre aux ventouses jaunes
Et je restais, ainsi qu'une femme à genoux . . .

Presqu'île, ballottant sur mes bords les querelles
Et les fientes d'oiseaux clabaudeurs aux yeux blonds.
Et je voguais, lorsqu'à travers mes liens frêles
Des noyés descendaient dormir, à reculons! . . .

Or moi, bateau perdu sous les cheveux des anses,
Jeté par l'ouragan dans l'éther sans oiseau,
Moi dont les Monitors et les voiliers des Hanses
N'auraient pas repêché la carcasse ivre d'eau;

Libre, fumant, monté de brumes violettes,
Moi qui trouais le ciel rougeoyant comme un mur
Qui portes, confiture exquise aux bons poètes,
Les lichens de soleil et des morves d'azur;

Qui courais, taché de lunules électriques,
Planche folle, escorté des hippocampes noirs,
Quand les juillets faisaient crouler à coups de triques
Les cieux ultramarins aux ardents entonnoirs;

Moi qui tremblais, sentant geindre à cinquante lieues
Le rut des Béhémots et les Maelstroms épais,
Fileur éternel des immobilités bleues,
Je regrette l'Europe aux anciens parapets!

J'ai vu des archipels sidéraux! et des îles
Dont les cieux délirants sont ouverts au vogueur:
—Est-ce en ces nuits sans fond que tu dors et t'exiles,
Million d'oiseaux d'or, ô future Vigueur?

Mais, vrai, j'ai trop pleuré! Les Aubes sont navrantes.
Toute lune est atroce et tout soleil amer:
L'âcre amour m'a gonflé de torpeurs enivrantes.
O que ma quille éclate! O que j'aille à la mer!

Si je désire une eau d'Europe, c'est la flache
Noire et froide où vers le crépuscule embaumé
Un enfant accroupi plein de tristesses, lâche
Un bateau frêle comme un papillon de mai.

Je ne puis plus, baigné de vos langueurs, ô lames,
Enlever leur sillage aux porteurs de cotons,
Ni traverser l'orgueil des drapeaux et des flammes,
Ni nager sous les yeux horribles des pontons.

## VOYELLES

A noir, E blanc, I rouge, U vert, O bleu: voyelles,
Je dirai quelque jour vos naissances latentes:
A, noir corset velu des mouches éclatantes
Qui bombinent autour des puanteurs cruelles,

Golfes d'ombre; E, candeurs des vapeurs et des tentes,
Lances des glaciers fiers, rois blancs, frissons d'ombrelles;
I, pourpres, sang craché, rire des lèvres belles
Dans la colère ou les ivresses pénitentes;

U, cycles, vibrements divins des mers virides,
Paix des pâtis semés d'animaux, paix des rides
Que l'alchimie imprime aux grands fronts studieux;

O, suprême Clairon plein de strideurs étranges,
Silences traversés des Mondes et des Anges:
—O l'Oméga, rayon violet de Ses Yeux!

## MÉMOIRE

### I

L'eau claire; comme le sel des larmes d'enfance,
l'assaut au soleil des blancheurs des corps de femme;
la soie, en foule et de lys pur, des oriflammes
sous les murs dont quelque pucelle eut la défense;

l'ébat des anges;—Non . . . le courant d'or en marche,
meut ses bras, noirs et lourds, et frais surtout, d'herbe. Elle,
sombre, ayant le Ciel bleu pour ciel-de-lit, appelle
pour rideaux l'ombre de la colline et de l'arche.

II

Eh! l'humide carreau tend ses bouillons limpides!
l'eau meuble d'or pâle et sans fond les couches prêtes.
Les robes vertes et déteintes des fillettes
font les saules, d'où sautent les oiseaux sans brides.

Plus jaune qu'un louis, pure et chaude paupière,
le souci d'eau—ta foi conjugale, ô l'Épouse!—
au midi prompt, de son terne miroir, jalouse
au ciel gris de chaleur la Sphère rose et chère.

III

Madame se tient trop debout dans la prairie
prochaine où neigent les fils du travail; l'ombrelle
aux doigts; foulant l'ombelle, trop fière pour elle;
des enfants lisant dans la verdure fleurie

leur livre de maroquin rouge! Hélas, Lui, comme
mille anges blancs qui se séparent sur la route,
s'éloigne par delà la montagne! Elle, toute
froide, et noire, court! après le départ de l'homme!

IV

Regret des bras épais et jeunes d'herbe pure!
Or des lunes d'avril au cœur du saint lit! Joie
des chantiers riverains à l'abandon, en proie
aux soirs d'août qui faisaient germer ces pourritures!

Qu'elle pleure à présent sous les remparts! l'haleine
des peupliers d'en haut est pour la seule brise.
Puis, c'est la nappe, sans reflets, sans source, grise:
un vieux, dragueur, dans sa barque immobile, peine.

V

Jouet de cet œil d'eau morne, je n'y puis prendre,
ô canot immobile! oh! bras trop courts! ni l'une
ni l'autre fleur: ni la jaune qui m'importune,
là; ni la bleue, amie à l'eau couleur de cendre.

Ah! la poudre des saules qu'une aile secoue!
Les roses des roseaux dès longtemps dévorées!
Mon canot, toujours fixe et sa chaîne tirée
Au fond de cet œil d'eau sans bords,—à quelle boue?


## QU'EST-CE POUR NOUS, MON CŒUR . . .

Qu'est-ce pour nous, mon cœur, que les nappes de sang
Et de braise, et mille meurtres, et les longs cris
De rage, sanglots de tout enfer renversant
Tout ordre; et l'Aquilon encor sur les débris;


Et toute vengeance? Rien! . . . —Mais si, toute encor,
Nous la voulons! Industriels, princes, sénats:
Périssez! Puissance, justice, histoire: à bas!
Ça nous est dû. Le sang! le sang! la flamme d'or!


Tout à la guerre, à la vengeance, à la terreur,
Mon esprit! Tournons dans la morsure: Ah! passez,
Républiques de ce monde! Des empereurs,
Des régiments, des colons, des peuples, assez!


Qui remuerait les tourbillons de feu furieux,
Que nous et ceux que nous nous imaginons frères?
À nous, romanesques amis: ça va nous plaire.
Jamais nous ne travaillerons, ô flots de feux!


Europe, Asie, Amérique, disparaissez.
Notre marche vengeresse a tout occupé,
Cités et campagnes! —Nous serons écrasés!
Les volcans sauteront! Et l'Océan frappé . . .


Oh! mes amis! —Mon cœur, c'est sûr, ils sont des frères:
Noirs inconnus, si nous allions! Allons! allons!
O malheur! je me sens frémir, la vieille terre,
Sur moi de plus en plus à vous! la terre fond.


*Ce n'est rien: j'y suis; j'y suis toujours.*

## MICHEL ET CHRISTINE

Zut alors, si le soleil quitte ces bords!
Puis, clair déluge! Voici l'ombre des routes.
Dans les saules, dans la vieille cour d'honneur,
L'orage d'abord jette ses larges gouttes.

O cent agneaux, de l'idylle soldats blonds,
Des aqueducs, des bruyères amaigries,
Fuyez! plaine, déserts, prairie, horizons
Sont à la toilette rouge de l'orage!

Chien noir, brun pasteur dont le manteau s'engouffre,
Fuyez l'heure des éclairs supérieurs;
Blond troupeau, quand voici nager ombre et soufre,
Tâchez de descendre à des retraits meilleurs.

Mais moi, Seigneur! voici que mon esprit vole,
Après les cieux glacés de rouge, sous les
Nuages céleste qui courent et volent
Sur cent Solognes longues comme un railway.

Voilà mille loups, mille graines sauvages
Qu'emporte, non sans aimer les liserons,
Cette religieuse après-midi d'orage
Sur l'Europe ancienne où cent hordes iront!

Après, le clair de lune! partout la lande,
Rougis et leurs fronts aux cieux noirs, les guerriers
Chevauchent lentement leurs pâles coursiers!
Les cailloux sonnent sous cette fière bande!

—Et verrai-je le bois jaune et le val clair,
L'Épouse aux yeux bleus, l'homme au front rouge, ô Gaule,
Et le blanc Agneau Pascal, à leurs pieds chers,
—Michel et Christine,—et Christ!—fin de l'Idylle.


## LARME

Loin des oiseaux, des troupeaux, des villageoises,
Je buvais, accroupi dans quelque bruyère
Entourée de tendres bois de noisetiers,
Par un brouillard d'après-midi tiède et vert.

Que pouvais-je boire dans cette jeune Oise,
Ormeaux sans voix, gazon sans fleurs, ciel couvert.
Que tirais-je à la gourde de colocase?
Quelque liqueur d'or, fade et qui fait suer.

Tel, j'eusse été mauvaise enseigne d'auberge.
Puis l'orage changea le ciel, jusqu'au soir.
Ce furent des pays noirs, des lacs, des perches,
Des colonnades sous la nuit bleue, des gares.

L'eau des bois se perdait sur des sables vierges.
Le vent, du ciel, jetait des glaçons aux mares . . .
Or! tel qu'un pêcheur d'or ou de coquillages,
Dire que je n'ai pas eu souci de boire!


## CHANSON DE LA PLUS HAUTE TOUR

Oisive jeunesse
A tout asservie,
Par délicatesse
J'ai perdu ma vie.
Ah! Que le temps vienne
Où les cœurs s'éprennent.

Je me suis dit: laisse,
Et qu'on ne te voie:
Et sans la promesse
De plus hautes joies.
Que rien ne t'arrête,
Auguste retraite.

J'ai tant fait patience
Qu'à jamais j'oublie;
Craintes et souffrances
Aux cieux sont parties.
Et la soif malsaine
Obscurcit mes veines.

Ainsi la prairie
A l'oubli livrée,
Grandie, et fleurie
D'encens et d'ivraies
Au bourdon farouche
De cent sales mouches.

Ah! Mille veuvages
De la si pauvre âme
Qui n'a que l'image
De la Notre-Dame!
Est-ce que l'on prie
La Vierge Marie?

Oisive jeunesse
A tout asservie,
Par délicatesse
J'ai perdu ma vie.
Ah! Que le temps vienne
Où les cœurs s'éprennent!

## L'ÉTERNITE

Elle est retrouvée.
Quoi?—L'Éternité,
C'est la mer allée
Avec le soleil.

Ame sentinelle,
Murmurons l'aveu
De la nuit si nulle
Et du jour en feu.

Des humains suffrages,
Des communs élans
Là tu te dégages
Et voles selon.

Puisque de vous seules,
Braises de satin,
Le Devoir s'exhale
Sans qu'on dise: enfin.

Là pas d'espérance,
Nul orietur.
Science avec patience,
Le supplice est sûr.

Elle est retrouvée.
Quoi?—L'Éternité.
C'est la mer allée
Avec le soleil.

## JEUNE MENAGE

La chambre est ouverte au ciel bleu-tourquin;
Pas de place: des coffrets et des huches!
Dehors le mur est plein d'aristoloches
Où vibrent les gencives des lutins.

Que ce sont bien intrigues de génies
Cette dépense et ces désordres vains!
C'est la fée africaine qui fournit
La mûre, et les résilles dans les coins.

Plusieurs entrent, marraines mécontentes,
En pans de lumière dans les buffets,
Puis y restent! le ménage s'absente
Peu sérieusement, et rien ne se fait.

La marié a le vent qui le floue
Pendant son absence, ici, tout le temps.
Même des esprits des eaux, malfaisants
Entrent vaguer aux sphères de l'alcôve.

La nuit, l'amie oh! la lune de miel
Cueillera leur sourire et remplira
De mille bandeaux de cuivre le ciel.
Puis ils auront affaire au malin rat.

—S'il n'arrive pas un feu follet blême,
Comme un coup de fusil, après des vêpres.
—O Spectres saints et blancs de Bethléem,
Charmez plutôt le bleu de leur fenêtre!


## BRUXELLES

*Juillet*                                *Boulevard du Regent*

Plates-bandes d'amarantes jusqu'à
L'agréable palais de Jupiter.
—Je sais que c'est Toi qui, dans ces lieux,
Mêles ton Bleu presque de Sahara!

Puis, comme rose et sapin du soleil
Et liane ont ici leurs jeux enclos,
Cage de la petite veuve! . . .
                                    Quelles
Troupes d'oiseaux, ô ia io, ia io! . . .

—Calmes maisons, anciennes passions!
Kiosque de la Folle par affection.
Après les fesses des rosiers, balcon
Ombreux et très bas de la Juliette.

—La Juliette, ça rappelle l'Henriette,
Charmante station du chemin de fer,
Au cœur d'un mont, comme au fond d'un verger
Où mille diables bleus dansent dans l'air!

Banc vert où chante au paradis d'orage,
Sur la guitare, la blanche Irlandaise.
Puis, de la salle à manger guyanaise,
Bavardage des enfants et des cages.

Fenêtre du duc qui fais que je pense
Au poison des escargots et du buis
Qui dort ici-bas au soleil.
                          Et puis
C'est trop beau! trop! Gardons notre silence.

—Boulevard sans mouvement ni commerce,
Muet, tout drame et toute comédie,
Réunion des scènes infinie,
Je te connais et t'admire en silence.


## HONTE

Tant que la lame n'aura
Pas coupé cette cervelle,
Ce paquet blanc, vert et gras,
A vapeur jamais nouvelle,

(Ah! Lui, devrait couper son
Nez, sa lèvre, ses oreilles,
Son ventre! et faire abandon
De ses jambes! ô merveille!)

Mais, non; vrai, je crois que tant
Que pour sa tête la lame,
Que les cailloux pour son flanc,
Que pour ses boyaux la flamme,

N'auront pas agi, l'enfant
Gêneur, la si sotte bête,
Ne doit cesser un instant
De ruser et d'être traître,

Comme un chat des Monts-Rocheux,
D'empuantir toutes sphères!
Qu'à sa mort, pourtant, ô mon Dieu!
S'élève quelque prière!


## MARINE

Les chars d'argent et de cuivre—
Les proues d'acier et d'argent—
Battent l'écume—
Soulèvent les souches des ronces.
Les courants de la lande,
Et les ornières immenses du reflux,
Filent circulairement vers l'est,
Vers les piliers de la forêt,
Vers les fûts de la jetée,
Dont l'angle est heurté par des tourbillons de lumière.


## *Stéphane Mallarmé*

### APPARITION

La lune s'attristait. Des séraphins en pleurs
Rêvant, l'archet aux doigts, dans le calme des fleurs
Vaporeuses, tiraient de mourantes violes
De blancs sanglots glissant sur l'azur des corolles.
—C'était le jour béni de ton premier baiser.
Ma songerie aimant à me martyriser
S'enivrait savamment du parfum de tristesse
Que même sans regret et sans déboire laisse
La cueillaison d'un Rêve au cœur qui l'a cueilli.
J'errais donc, l'œil rivé sur le pavé vieilli
Quand avec du soleil aux cheveux, dans la rue
Et dans le soir, tu m'es en riant apparue
Et j'ai cru voir la fée au chapeau de clarté
Qui jadis sur mes beaux sommeils d'enfant gâté
Passait, laissant toujour de ses mains mal fermées
Neiger de blancs bouquets d'étoiles parfumées.

## LES FENÊTRES

Las du triste hôpital, et de l'encens fétide
Qui monte en la blancheur banale des rideaux
Vers le grand crucifix ennuyé du mur vide,
Le moribond sournois y redresse un vieux dos,

Se traîne et va moins pour chauffer sa pourriture
Que pour voir du soleil sur les pierres, coller
Les poils blancs et les os de la maigre figure
Aux fenêtres qu'un beau rayon clair veut hâler,

Et la bouche, fiévreuse et d'azur bleu vorace,
Telle, jeune, elle alla respirer son trésor,
Une peau virginale et de jadis! encrasse
D'un long baiser amer les tièdes carreaux d'or.

Ivre, il vit, oubliant l'horreur des saintes huiles,
Les tisanes, l'horloge et le lit infligé,
La toux; et quand le soir saigne parmi les tuiles,
Son œil, à l'horizon de lumière gorgé,

Voit des galères d'or, belles comme des cygnes,
Sur un fleuve de pourpre et de parfums dormir
En berçant l'éclair fauve et riche de leurs lignes
Dans un grand nonchaloir chargé de souvenir!

Ainsi, pris du dégoût de l'homme à l'âme dure
Vautré dans le bonheur, où ses seuls appétits
Mangent, et qui s'entête à chercher cette ordure
Pour l'offrir à la femme allaitant ses petits,

Je fuis et je m'accroche à toutes les croisées
D'où l'on tourne l'épaule à la vie, et, béni,
Dans leur verre, lavé d'éternelles rosées,
Que dore le matin chaste de l'Infini

Je me mire et me vois ange! et je meure, et j'aime
—Que la vitre soit l'art, soit la mysticité—
A renaître, portant mon rêve en diadème,
Au ciel antérieur où fleurit la Beauté!

Mais, hélas! Ici-bas est maître: sa hantise
Vient m'écœurer parfois jusqu'en cet abri sûr,
Et le vomissement impur de la Bêtise
Me force à me boucher le nez devant l'azur.

Est-il moyen, ô Moi qui connais l'amertume,
D'enfoncer le cristal par le monstre insulté
Et de m'enfuir, avec mes deux ailes sans plume
—Au risque de tomber pendant l'éternité?

## ANGOISSE

Je ne viens pas ce soir vaincre ton corps, ô bête
En qui vont les péchés d'un peuple, ni creuser
Dans tes cheveux impurs une triste tempête
Sous l'incurable ennui que verse mon baiser:

Je demande à ton lit le lourd sommeil sans songes
Planant sous les rideaux inconnus du remords,
Et que tu peux goûter après tes noirs mensonges,
Toi qui sur le néant en sais plus que les morts.

Car le Vice, rongeant ma native noblesse
M'a comme toi marqué de sa stérilité,
Mais tandis que ton sein de pierre est habité

Par un cœur que la dent d'aucun crime ne blesse,
Je fuis, pâle, défait, hanté par mon linceul,
Ayant peur de mourir lorsque je couche seul.

## SOUPIR

Mon âme vers ton front où rêve, ô calme sœur,
Un automne jonché de taches de rousseur
Et vers le ciel errant de ton œil angélique
Monte, comme dans un jardin mélancholique,
Fidèle, un blanc jet d'eau soupire vers l'Azur!
—Vers l'Azur attendri d'Octobre pâle et pur
Qui mire aux grands bassins sa langueur infinie
Et laisse, sur l'eau morte où la fauve agonie
Des feuilles erre au vent et creuse un froid sillon,
Se traîner le soleil jaune d'un long rayon.

## LAS DE L'AMER REPOS . . .

Las de l'amer repos où ma paresse offense
Une gloire pour qui jadis j'ai fui l'enfance
Adorable des bois de roses sous l'azur
Naturel, et plus las sept fois du pacte dur
De creuser par veillée une fosse nouvelle
Dans le terrain avare et froid de ma cervelle,
Fossoyeur sans pitié pour la stérilité,
—Que dire à cette Aurore, ô Rêves, visité
Par les roses, quand, peur de ses roses livides,
Le vaste cimetière unira les trous vides?—

Je veux délaisser l'Art vorace d'un pays
Cruel, et, souriant aux reproches vieillis
Que me font mes amis, le passé, le génie,
Et ma lampe qui sait pourtant mon agonie,
Imiter le Chinois au cœur limpide et fin
De qui l'extase pure est de peindre la fin
Sur ses tasses de neige à la lune ravie
D'une bizarre fleur qui parfume sa vie
Transparente, la fleur qu'il a sentie, enfant,
Au filigrane bleu de l'âme se greffant.
Et, la mort telle avec le seul rêve du sage,
Serein, je vais choisir un jeune paysage
Que je peindrais encor sur les tasses, distrait.
Une ligne d'azur mince et pâle serait
Un lac, parmi le ciel de porcelaine nue,
Un clair croissant perdu par une blanche nue
Trempe sa corne calme en la glace des eaux,
Non loin de trois grands cils d'émeraude, roseaux.

## L'AZUR

De l'éternel azur la sereine ironie
Accable, belle indolemment comme les fleurs,
Le poète impuissant qui maudit son gènie
A travers un désert stérile de Douleurs.

Fuyant, les yeux fermés, je le sens qui regarde
Avec l'intensité d'un remords atterrant,
Mon âme vide. Où fuir? Et quelle nuit hagarde
Jeter, lambeaux, jeter sur ce mépris navrant?

Brouillards, montez! versez vos cendres monotones
Avec de longs haillons de brume dans les cieux
Qui noiera le marais livide des automnes
Et bâtissez un grand plafond silencieux!

Et toi, sors des étangs léthéens et ramasse
En t'en venant la vase et les pâles roseaux,
Cher Ennui, pour boucher d'une main jamais lasse
Les grands trous bleus que font méchamment les oiseaux.

Encor! que sans répit les tristes cheminées
Fument, et que de suie une errante prison
Éteigne dans l'horreur de ses noires traînées
Le soleil se mourant jaunâtre à l'horizon!

—Le Ciel est mort. —Vers toi, j'accours! donne, ô matière,
L'oubli de l'Idéal cruel et du Péché
A ce martyr qui vient partager la litière
Où le bétail heureux des hommes est couché,

Car j'y veux, puisque enfin ma cervelle, vidée
Comme le pot de fard gisant au pied d'un mur,
N'a plus l'art d'attifer la sanglotante idée,
Lugubrement bâiller vers un trépas obscur . . .

En vain! l'Azur triomphe, et je l'entends qui chante
Dans les cloches. Mon âme, il se fait voix pour plus
Nous faire peur avec sa victoire méchante,
Et du métal vivant sort en bleus angélus!

Il roule par la brume, ancien et traverse
Ta native agonie ainsi qu'un glaive sûr;
Où fuir dans la révolte inutile et perverse?
*Je suis hanté.* L'Azur! l'Azur! l'Azur! l'Azur!


## DON DU POÈME

Je t'apporte l'enfant d'une nuit d'Idumée!
Noire, à l'aile saignante et pâle, déplumée,
Par le verre brûlé d'aromates et d'or,
Par les carreaux glacés, hélas! mornes encor,
L'aurore se jeta sur la lampe angélique.

Palmes! et quand elle a montré cette relique
A ce père essayant un sourire ennemi,
La solitude bleue et stérile a frémi.
O la berceuse, avec ta fille et l'innocence
De vos pieds froids, accueille une horrible naissance:
Et ta voix rappelant viole et clavecin,
Avec le doigt fané presseras-tu le sein
Par qui coule en blancheur sibylline la femme
Pour les lèvres que l'air du vierge azur affame?

## BRISE MARINE

La chair est triste, hélas! et j'ai lu tous les livres.
Fuir! là-bas fuir! Je sens que des oiseaux sont ivres
D'être parmi l'écume inconnue et les cieux!
Rien, ni les vieux jardins reflétés par les yeux
Ne retiendra ce cœur qui dans la mer se trempe
O nuits! ni la clarté déserte de ma lampe
Sur le vide papier que la blancheur défend
Et ni la jeune femme allaitant son enfant.
Je partirai! Steamer balançant ta mâture,
Lève l'ancre pour une exotique nature!

Un Ennui, désolé par les cruels espoirs,
Croit encore à l'adieu suprême des mouchoirs!
Et, peut-être, les mâts, invitant les orages
Sont-ils de ceux qu'un vent penche sur les naufrages
Perdus, sans mâts, sans mâts ni fertiles îlots . . .
Mais, ô mon cœur, entends le chant des matelots!

## HÉRODIADE

### FRAGMENT

NOURRICE:                  . . . pour qui, dévorée
          D'angoisses, gardez-vous la splendeur ignorée
          Et le mystère vain de votre être?
HÉRODIADE:                                  Pour moi.
NOURRICE:  Triste fleur qui croît seule et n'a pas d'autre émoi
          Que son ombre dans l'eau vue avec atonie.
HÉRODIADE: Va, garde ta pitié comme ton ironie.
NOURRICE:  Toutefois expliquez: oh! non, naïve enfant,
          Décroîtra, quelque jour, ce dédain triomphant.
HÉRODIADE: Mais qui me toucherait, des lions respectée?

Du reste, je ne veux rien d'humain et, sculptée,
Si tu me vois les yeux perdus au paradis,
C'est quand je me souviens de ton lait bu jadis.

NOURRICE: Victime lamentable à son destin offerte!

HÉRODIADE: Oui, c'est pour moi, pour moi, que je fleuris,
déserte!
Vous le savez, jardins d'améthyste enfouis
Sans fin dans de savants abîmes éblouis,
Ors ignorés, gardant votre antique lumière
Sous le sombre sommeil d'une terre première,
Vous, pierres où mes yeux comme de purs bijoux
Empruntent leur clarté mélodieuse, et vous
Métaux qui donnez à ma jeune chevelure
Une splendeur fatale et sa massive allure!
Quant à toi, femme née en des siècles malins
Pour la méchanceté des antres sibyllins,
Qui parles d'un mortel! selon qui, des calices
De mes robes, arome aux farouches délices,
Sortirait le frisson blanc de ma nudité,
Prophétise que si le tiède azur d'été,
Vers lui nativement la femme se dévoile,
Me voit dans ma pudeur grelottante d'étoile,
Je meurs!
            J'aime l'horreur d'être vierge et je veux
Vivre parmi l'effroi que me font mes cheveux
Pour, le soir, retirée en ma couche, reptile
Inviolé sentir en la chair inutile
Le froid scintillement de ta pâle clarté
Toi qui te meurs, toi qui brûles de chasteté,
Nuit blanche de glaçons et de neige cruelle!
Et ta sœur solitaire, ô ma sœur éternelle
Mon rêve montera vers toi: telle déjà,
Rare limpidité d'un cœur qui le songea,
Je me crois seule en ma monotone patrie
Et tout, autour de moi, vit dans l'idolâtrie
D'un miroir qui reflète en son calme dormant
Hérodiade au clair regard de diamant . . .
O charme dernier, oui! je le sens, je suis seule.

NOURRICE: Madame, allez-vous donc mourir?

HÉRODIADE:                    Non, pauvre aïeule,
Sois calme et, t'éloignant, pardonne à ce cœur dur,
Mais avant, si tu veux, clos les volets, l'azur
Séraphique sourit dans les vitres profondes,
Et je déteste, moi, le bel azur!
                                Des ondes
Se bercent et, là-bas, sais-tu pas un pays
Où le sinistre ciel ait les regards haïs
De Vénus qui, le soir, brûle dans le feuillage:

J'y partirais.

                Allume encore, enfantillage
Dis-tu, ces flambeaux où la cire au feu léger
Pleure parmi l'or vain quelque pleur étranger
Et . . .

NOURRICE:        Maintenant?
HÉRODIADE:             Adieu.

                      Vous mentez, ô fleur nue
De mes lèvres.

                J'attends une chose inconnue
Ou peut-être, ignorant le mystère et vos cris,
Jetez-vous les sanglots suprêmes et meurtris
D'une enfance sentant parmi les rêveries
Se séparer enfin ses froides pierreries.


## SAINTE

A la fenêtre recélant
Le santal vieux qui se dédore
De sa viole étincelant
Jadis avec flûte ou mandore,


Est la Sainte pâle, étalant
Le livre vieux qui se déplie
Du Magnificat ruisselant
Jadis selon vêpre et complie:


A ce vitrage d'ostensoir
Que frôle une harpe par l'Ange
Formée avec son vol du soir
Pour la délicate phalange


Du doigt que, sans le vieux santal
Ni le vieux livre, elle balance
Sur le plumage instrumental,
Musicienne du silence.

# L'APRÈS-MIDI D'UN FAUNE

ÉGLOGUE

*Le Faune*

Ces nymphes, je les veux perpétuer.
　　　　　　　　　　　Si clair,
Leur incarnat léger, qu'il voltige dans l'air
Assoupi de sommeils touffus.

　　　　　　　　　　Aimai-je un rêve?
Mon doute, amas de nuit ancienne, s'achève
En maint rameau subtil, qui, demeuré les vrais
Bois mêmes, prouve, hélas! que bien seul je m'offrais
Pour triomphe la faute idéale de roses.
Réfléchissons . . .

　　　　　　　　ou si les femmes dont tu gloses
Figurent un souhait de tes sens fabuleux!
Faune, l'illusion s'échappe des yeux bleus
Et froids, comme une source en pleurs, de la plus chaste:
Mais, l'autre tout soupirs, dis-tu qu'elle contraste
Comme brise du jour chaude dans ta toison?
Que non! par l'immobile et lasse pâmoison
Suffoquant de chaleurs le matin frais s'il lutte,
Ne murmure point d'eau que ne verse ma flûte
Au bosquet arrosé d'accords; et le seul vent
Hors des deux tuyaux prompt à s'exhaler avant
Qu'il disperse le son dans une pluie aride,
C'est, à l'horizon pas remué d'une ride,
Le visible et serein souffle artificiel
De l'inspiration, qui regagne le ciel.

O bords siciliens d'un calme marécage
Qu'à l'envi de soleils ma vanité saccage,
Tacite sous les fleurs d'étincelles, CONTEZ
*"Que je coupais ici les creux roseaux domptés*
　*Par le talent; quand, sur l'or glauque de lointaines*
*Verdures dédiant leur vigne à des fontaines,*
*Ondoie une blancheur animale au repos:*
　*Et qu'au prélude lent où naissent les pipeaux,*
*Ce vol de cygnes, non! de naïades se sauve*
*Ou plonge . . ."*

　　　　　　　　Inerte, tout brûle dans l'heure fauve

Sans marquer par quel art ensemble détala
Trop d'hymen souhaité de qui cherche le *la*:
Alors m'éveillerai-je à la ferveur première,
Droit et seul, sous un flot antique de lumière,
Lys! et l'un de vous tous pour l'ingénuité.

Autre que ce doux rien par leur lèvre ébruité,
Le baiser, qui tout bas des perfides assure,
Mon sein, vierge de preuve, atteste une morsure
Mystérieuse, due à quelque auguste dent;
Mais, bast! arcane tel élut pour confident
Le jonc vaste et jumeau dont sous l'azur on joue:
Qui, détournant à soi le trouble de la joue
Rêve, dans un solo long, que nous amusions
La beauté d'alentour par des confusions
Fausses entre elle-même et notre chant crédule;
Et de faire aussi haut que l'amour se module
Évanouir du songe ordinaire de dos
Ou de flanc pur suivis avec mes regards clos,
Une sonore, vaine et monotone ligne.

Tâche donc, instrument des fuites, ô maligne
Syrinx, de refleurir aux lacs où tu m'attends!
Moi, de ma rumeur fier, je vais parler longtemps
Des déesses; et par d'idolâtres peintures,
A leur ombre enlever encore des ceintures:
Ainsi, quand des raisins j'ai sucé la clarté,
Pour bannir un regret par ma feinte écarté,
Rieur, j'élève au ciel d'été la grappe vide
Et, soufflant dans ses peaux lumineuses, avide
D'ivresse, jusqu'au soir je regarde au travers.

O nymphes, regonflons des SOUVENIRS divers.
  *"Mon œil, trouant les joncs, dardait chaque encolure*
  *Immortelle, qui noie en l'onde sa brûlure*
  *Avec un cri de rage au ciel de la forêt;*
  *Et le splendide bain de cheveux disparaît*
  *Dans les clartés et les frissons, ô pierreries!*
  *J'accours; quand, à mes pieds, s'entrejoignent (meurtries*
  *De la langueur goûtée à ce mal d'être deux)*
  *Des dormeuses parmi leurs seuls bras hasardeux;*
  *Je les ravis, sans les désenlacer, et vole*
  *A ce massif, haï par l'ombrage frivole,*
  *De roses tarissant tout parfum au soleil,*
  *Où notre ébat au jour consumé soit pareil."*
Je t'adore, courroux des vierges, ô délice
Farouche du sacré fardeau nu qui se glisse
Pour fuir ma lèvre en feu buvant, comme un éclair

Tressaille! la frayeur secrète de la chair:
Des pieds de l'inhumaine au cœur de la timide
Que délaisse à la fois une innocence, humide
De larmes folles ou de moins tristes vapeurs.
*"Mon crime, c'est d'avoir, gai de vaincre ces peurs*
*Traîtresses, divisé la touffe échevelée*
*De baisers que les dieux gardaient si bien mêlée;*
*Car, à peine j'allais cacher un rire ardent*
*Sous les replis heureux d'une seule (gardant*
*Par un doigt simple, afin que sa candeur de plume*
*Se teignît à l'émoi de sa sœur qui s'allume,*
*La petite, naïve et ne rougissant pas:)*
*Que de mes bras, défaits par de vagues trépas,*
*Cette proie, à jamais ingrate, se délivre*
*Sans pitié du sanglot dont j'étais encore ivre."*

Tant pis! vers le bonheur d'autres m'entraîneront
Par leur tresse nouée aux cornes de mon front:
Tu sais, ma passion, que, pourpre et déjà mûre,
Chaque grenade éclate et d'abeilles murmure;
Et notre sang, épris de qui le va saisir,
Coule pour tout l'essaim éternelle du désir
A l'heure où ce bois d'or et de cendres se teinte
Une fête s'exalte en la feuillée éteinte:
Etna! c'est parmi toi visité de Vénus
Sur ta lave posant ses talons ingénus,
Quand tonne un somme triste ou s'épuise la flamme.
Je tiens la reine!

       O sûr châtiment . . .

                     Non, mais l'âme
De paroles vacante et ce corps alourdi
Tard succombent au fier silence de midi:
Sans plus il fait dormir en l'oubli du blasphème,
Sur le sable altéré gisant et comme j'aime
Ouvrir ma bouche à l'astre efficace des vins!

Couple, adieu; je vais voir l'ombre que tu devins.


## LE TOMBEAU D'EDGAR POE

Tel qu'en Lui-même enfin l'éternité le change,
Le Poète suscite avec un glaive nu
Son siècle épouvanté de n'avoir pas connu
Que la mort triomphait dans cette voix étrange!

Eux, comme un vil sursaut d'hydre oyant jadis l'ange
Donner un sens plus pur aux mots de la tribu
Proclamèrent très haut le sortilège bu
Dans le flot sans honneur de quelque noir mélange.

Du sol et de la nue hostiles, ô grief!
Si notre idée avec ne sculpte un bas-relief
Dont la tombe de Poe éblouissante s'orne

Calme bloc ici-bas chu d'un désastre obscur
Que ce granit du moins montre à jamais sa borne
Aux noirs vols du Blasphème épars dans le futur.

## SUR LES BOIS OUBLIÉS . . .

"—Sur les bois oubliés quand passe l'hiver sombre
Tu te plains, ô captif solitaire du seuil,
Que ce sépulcre à deux qui fera notre orgueil
Hélas! du manque seul des lourds bouquets s'encombre.

Sans écouter Minuit qui jeta son vain nombre,
Une veille t'exalte à ne pas fermer l'œil
Avant que dans les bras de l'ancien fauteuil
Le suprême tison n'ait éclairé mon Ombre.

Qui veut souvent avoir la Visite ne doit
Par trop de fleurs charger la pierre que mon doigt
Soulève avec l'ennui d'une force défunte.

Ame au si clair foyer tremblante de m'asseoir,
Pour revivre il suffit qu'à tes lèvres j'emprunte
Le souffle de mon nom murmuré tout un soir."

## AUTRE ÉVENTAIL

*de Mademoiselle Mallarmé*

O rêveuse, pour que je plonge
Au pur délice sans chemin,
Sache, par un subtil mensonge,
Garder mon aile dans ta main.

Une fraîcheur de crépuscule
Te vient à chaque battement
Dont le coup prisonnier recule
L'horizon délicatement.

Vertige! voici que frissonne
L'espace comme un grand baiser
Qui, fou de naître pour personne
Ne peut jaillir ni s'apaiser.

Sens-tu le paradis farouche
Ainsi qu'un rire enseveli
Se couler du coin de ta bouche
Au fond de l'unanime pli!

Le sceptre des rivages roses
Stagnants sur les soirs d'or, ce l'est,
Ce blanc vol fermé que tu poses
Contre le feu d'un bracelet.

## LE VIERGE, LE VIVACE ET LE BEL AUJOURD'HUI . . .

Le vierge, le vivace et le bel aujourd'hui
Va-t-il nous déchirer avec un coup d'aile ivre,
Ce lac dur oublié que hante sous le givre
Le transparent glacier des vols qui n'ont pas fui!

Un cygne d'autrefois se souvient que c'est lui
Magnifique mais qui sans espoir se délivre
Pour n'avoir pas chanté la région où vivre
Quand du stérile hiver a resplendi l'ennui.

Tout son col secouera cette blanche agonie
Par l'espace infligée à l'oiseau qui le nie,
Mais non l'horreur du sol où le plumage est pris.

Fantôme qu'à ce lieu son pur éclat assigne,
Il s'immobilise au songe froid de mépris
Que vêt parmi l'exil inutile le Cygne.

## M'INTRODUIRE DANS TON HISTOIRE . . .

M'introduire dans ton histoire
C'est en héros effarouché
S'il a du talon nu touché
Quelque gazon de territoire

A des glaciers attentatoire
Je ne sais le naïf péché
Que tu n'auras pas empêché
De rire très haut sa victoire

Dis si je ne suis pas joyeux
Tonnerre et rubis aux moyeux
De voir en l'air que ce feu troue

Avec des royaumes épars
Comme mourir pourpre la roue
Du seul vespéral de mes chars.

## MES BOUQUINS REFERMÉS . . .

Mes bouquins refermés sur le nom de Paphos,
Il m'amuse d'élire avec le seul génie
Une ruine, par mille écumes bénie
Sous l'hyacinthe, au loin, de ses jours triomphaux.

Coure le froid avec ses silences de faux,
Je n'y hululerai pas de vide nénie
Si ce très blanc ébat au ras du sol dénie
A tout site l'honneur du paysage faux.

Ma faim qui d'aucuns fruits ici ne se régale
Trouve en leur docte manque une saveur égale:
Qu'un éclate de chair humain et parfumant!

Le pied sur quelque guivre où notre amour tisonne,
Je pense plus longtemps peut-être éperdument
A l'autre, au sein brûlé d'une antique amazone.

## LE PITRE CHÂTIÉ

Yeux, lacs avec ma simple ivresse de renaître
Autre que l'histrion qui du geste évoquais
Comme plume la suie ignoble des quinquets
J'ai troué dans le mur de toile une fenêtre.

De ma jambe et des bras limpide nageur traître,
A bonds multipliés, reniant les mauvais
Hamlet! c'est comme si dans l'onde j'innovais
Mille sépulcres pour y vierge disparaître.

Hilare or de cymbale à des poings irrité,
Tout à coup le soleil frappe la nudité
Qui pure s'exhala de ma fraîcheur de nacre,

Rance nuit de la peau quand sur moi vous passiez,
Ne sachant pas, ingrat! que c'était tout mon sacre,
Ce fard noyé dans l'eau perfide des glaciers.

## LA MARCHANDE D'HABITS

Le vif œil dont tu regardes
Jusques à leur contenu
Me sépare de mes hardes
Et comme un dieu je vais nu.

## SALUT

Rien, cette écume, vierge vers
A ne désigner que la coupe;
Telle loin se noie une troupe
De sirènes mainte à l'envers.

Nous naviguons, ô mes divers
Amis, moi déjà sur la poupe
Vous l'avant fastueux qui coupe
Le flot de foudres et d'hivers;

Une ivresse belle m'engage
Sans craindre même son tangage
De porter debout ce salut

Solitude, récif, étoile
A n'importe ce qui valut
Le blanc souci de notre toile.

## PETIT AIR

### I

Quelconque une solitude
Sans le cygne ni le quai
Mire sa désuétude
Au regard que j'abdiquai

Ici de la gloriole
Haute à ne la pas toucher
Dont maint ciel se bariole
Avec les ors de coucher

Mais langoureusement longe
Comme de blanc linge ôté
Tel fugace oiseau si plonge
Exultatrice à côté

Dans l'onde toi devenue
Ta jubilation nue.

### II

Indomptablement a dû
Comme mon espoir s'y lance
Éclater là-haut perdu
Avec furie et silence,

Voix étrangère au bosquet
Ou par nul écho suivie,
L'oiseau qu'on n'ouït jamais
Une autre fois en la vie.

Le hagard musicien,
Cela dans le doute expire
Si de mon sein pas du sien
A jailli le sanglot pire

Déchiré va-t-il entier
Rester sur quelque sentier!

## LE TOMBEAU DE CHARLES BAUDELAIRE

Le temple enseveli divulgue par la bouche
Sépulcrale d'égout bavant boue et rubis
Abominablement quelque idole Anubis
Tout le museau flambé comme un aboi farouche.

Ou que le gaz récent torde la mèche louche
Essuyeuse on le sait des opprobres subis
Il allume hagard un immortel pubis
Dont le vol selon le réverbère découche

Quel feuillage séché dans les cités sans soir
Votif pourra bénir comme elle se rasseoir
Contre le marbre vainement de Baudelaire

Au voile qui la ceint absente avec frissons
Celle son Ombre même un poison tutélaire
Toujours à respirer si nous en périssons.

## À LA NUE ACCABLANTE TU . . .

A la nue accablante tu
Basse de basalte et de laves
A même les échos esclaves
Par une trompe sans vertu

Quel sépulcral naufrage (tu
Le sais, écume, mais y baves)
Suprême une entre les épaves
Abolit le mât dévêtu

Ou cela que furibond faute
De quelque perdition haute
Tout l'abîme vain éployé

Dans le si blanc cheveu qui traîne
Avarement aura noyé
Le flanc enfant d'une sirène.

## TOMBEAU [DE PAUL VERLAINE]

*Anniversaire—Janvier 1897*

Le noir roc courroucé que la bise le roule
Ne s'arrêtera ni sous de pieuses mains
Tâtant sa ressemblance avec les maux humains
Comme pour en bénir quelque funeste moule.

Ici presque toujours si le ramier roucoule
Cet immatériel deuil opprime de maints
Nubiles plis l'astre mûri des lendemains
Dont un scintillement argentera la foule.

Qui cherche, parcourant le solitaire bond
Tantôt extérieur de notre vagabond—
Verlaine? Il est caché parmi l'herbe, Verlaine

A ne surprendre que naïvement d'accord
La lèvre sans y boire ou tarir son haleine
Un peu profond ruisseau calomnié la mort.

## O SI CHÈRE DE LOIN ET PROCHE ET BLANCHE . . .

O si chère de loin et proche et blanche, si
Délicieusement toi, Mary, que je songe
A quelque baume rare émané par mensonge
Sur aucun bouquetier de cristal obscurci

Le sais-tu, oui! pour moi voici des ans, voici
Toujours que ton sourire éblouissant prolonge
La même rose avec son bel été qui plonge
Dans autrefois et puis dans le futur aussi.

Mon cœur qui dans les nuits parfois cherche à s'entendre
Ou de quel dernier mot t'appeler le plus tendre
S'exalte en celui rien que chuchoté de sœur

N'était, très grand trésor et tête si petite,
Que tu m'enseignes bien toute une autre douceur
Tout bas par le baiser seul dans tes cheveux dite.

# Jules Laforgue

## COMPLAINTE
## DE L'ORGANISTE DE NOTRE-DAME DE NICE

Voici que les corbeaux hivernaux
Ont psalmodié parmi nos cloches,
Les averses d'automne sont proches,
Adieu les bosquets des casinos.

Hier, elle était encor plus blême,
Et son corps frissonnait tout transi,
Cette église est glaciale aussi!
Ah! nul ici-bas que moi ne l'aime.

Moi! Je m'entaillerai bien le cœur,
Pour un sourire si triste d'elle!
Et je lui en resterai fidèle
A jamais, dans ce monde vainqueur.

Le jour qu'elle quittera ce monde,
Je vais jouer un *Miserere*
Si cosmiquement désespéré
Qu'il faudra bien que Dieu me réponde!

Non, je resterai seul, ici-bas,
Tout à la chère morte phtisique,
Berçant mon cœur trop hyptertrophique
Aux éternelles fugues de Bach.


Et tous les ans, à l'anniversaire,
Pour nous, sans qu'on se doute de rien,
Je déchaînerai ce *Requiem*
Que j'ai fait pour la mort de la Terre!


## LA CHANSON DU PETIT HYPERTROPHIQUE

C'est d'un' maladie d'cœur
Qu'est mort', m'a dit l'docteur,
   Tir-lan-laire!
    Ma pauv'mère;
Et que j'irai là-bas,
Fair' dodo z'avec elle.
J'entends mon cœur qui bat,
C'est maman qui m'appelle!


On rit d'moi dans les rues,
De mes min's incongrues
   La-i-tou!
    D'enfant saoul;
Ah! Dieu! C'est qu'à chaqu' pas
J'étouff', moi, je chancelle!
J'entends mon cœur qui bat,
C'est maman qui m'appelle!


Aussi j' vais par les champs
Sangloter aux couchants,
   La-ri-rette!
    C'est bien bête.
Mais le soleil, j' sais pas,
M' semble un cœur qui ruisselle!
J'entends mon cœur qui bat,
C'est maman qui m'appelle!

Ah! si la p'tite Gen'viève
Voulait d' mon cœur qui s' crève.
   Pi-lou-i!
    Ah, oui!
J' suis jaune et triste, hélas!
Elle est ros', gaie et belle!
J'entends mon cœur qui bat,
C'est maman qui m'appelle!


Non, tout l' monde est méchant,
Hors le cœur des couchants,
   Tir-lan-laire!
    Et ma mère,
Et j' veux aller là-bas
Fair' dodo z'avec elle . . .
Mon cœur bat, bat, bat . . .
Dis, Maman, tu m'appelles?


## APOTHÉOSE

En tous sens, à jamais, le silence fourmille
De grappes d'astres d'or mêlant leurs tournoiements.
On dirait des jardins sablés de diamants,
Mais, chacun, morne et très solitaire, scintille.


Or, là-bas, dans ce coin inconnu, qui pétille
D'un sillon de rubis mélancoliquement,
Tremblote une étincelle au doux clignotement:
Patriarche éclaireur conduisant sa famille.


Sa famille: un essaim de globes lourds fleuris.
Et sur l'un, c'est la terre, un point jaune, Paris,
Où, pendue, une lampe, un pauvre fou qui veille:


Dans l'ordre universel, frêle, unique merveille.
Il en est le miroir d'un jour et le connaît.
Il y rêve longtemps, puis en fait un sonnet.

## POUR LE LIVRE D'AMOUR

Je puis mourir demain et je n'ai pas aimé.
Mes lèvres n'ont jamais touché lèvres de femme,
Nulle ne m'a donné dans un regard son âme,
Nulle ne m'a tenu contre son cœur pâmé.

Je n'ai fait que souffrir, pour toute la nature,
Pour les êtres, le vent, les fleurs, le firmament,
Souffrir par tous mes nerfs, minutieusement
Souffrir de n'avoir pas d'âme encore assez pure.

J'ai craché sur l'amour et j'ai tué la chair!
Fou d'orgueil, je me suis roidi contre la vie!
Et seul sur cette Terre à l'Instinct asservie
Je défiais l'Instinct avec un rire amer.

Partout, dans les salons, au théâtre, à l'église,
Devant ces hommes froids, les plus grands, les plus fins,
Et ces femmes aux yeux doux, jaloux ou hautains
Dont on redorerait chastement l'âme exquise,

Je songeais: tous en sont venus là! J'entendais
Les râles de l'immonde accouplement des brutes!
Tant de fanges pour un accès de trois minutes!
Hommes, soyez corrects! ô femmes, minaudez!

## COUCHANT D'HIVER

Quel couchant douloureux nous avons eu ce soir!
Dans les arbres pleurait un vent de désespoir,
Abattant du bois mort dans les feuilles rouillées.
A travers le lacis des branches dépouillées
Dont l'eau-forte sabrait le ciel bleu-clair et froid,
Solitaire et navrant, descendait l'astre-roi.
O Soleil! l'autre été, magnifique en ta gloire,
Tu sombrais, radieux comme un grand Saint-Ciboire,
Incendiant l'azur! A présent, nous voyons
Un disque safrané, malade, sans rayons,
Qui meurt à l'horizon balayé de cinabre,
Tout seul, dans un décor poitrinaire et macabre,
Colorant faiblement les nuages frileux
En blanc morne et livide, en verdâtre fielleux,

Vieil or, rose-fané, gris de plomb, lilas pâle.
Oh! c'est fini, fini! longuement le vent râle,
Tout est jaune et poussif; les jours sont révolus,
La Terre a fait son temps; ses reins n'en peuvent plus.
Et ses pauvres enfants, grêles, chauves et blêmes
D'avoir trop médité les éternels problèmes,
Grelottants et voûtés sous le poids des foulards
Au gaz jaune et mourant des brumeux boulevards,
D'un œil vide et muet contemplent leurs absinthes,
Riant amèrement, quand des femmes enceintes
Defilent, étalant leurs ventres et leurs seins,
Dans l'orgueil bestial des esclaves divins . . .

Ouragans inconnus des débâcles finales,
Accourez! déchaînez vos trombes de rafales!
Prenez ce globe immonde et poussif! balayez
Sa lèpre de cités et ses fils ennuyés!
Et jetez ses débris sans nom au noir immense!
Et qu'on ne sache rien dans la grande innocence
Des soleils éternels, des étoiles d'amour,
De ce Cerveau pourri qui fut la Terre, un jour!


## NOËL SCEPTIQUE

Noël! Noël? j'entends les cloches dans la nuit . . .
Et j'ai, sur ces feuillets sans foi, posé ma plume:
O souvenirs, chantez! tout mon orgueil s'enfuit,
Et je me sens repris de ma grande amertume.

Ah! ces voix dans la nuit chantant Noël! Noël!
M'apportent de la nef qui, là-bas, s'illumine,
Un si tendre, un si doux reproche maternel
Que mon cœur trop gonflé crève dans ma poitrine . . .

Et j'écoute longtemps les cloches, dans la nuit . . .
Je suis le paria de la famille humaine,
A qui le vent apporte en son sale réduit
La poignante remeur d'une fête lointaine.


## L'IMPOSSIBLE

Je puis mourir ce soir! Averses, vents, soleil
Distribueront partout mon cœur, mes nerfs, mes moelles.
Tout sera dit pour moi! Ni rêve, ni réveil.
Je n'aurai pas été là-bas, dans les étoiles!

En tous sens, je le sais, sur ces mondes lointains,
Pèlerins comme nous des pâles solitudes,
Dans la douceur des nuits tendant vers nous les mains,
Des Humanités sœurs rêvent par multitudes!


Oui! des frères partout! (Je le sais, je la sais!)
Ils sont seuls comme nous. —Palpitants de tristesse,
La nuit, ils nous font signe! Ah! n'irons-nous, jamais?
On se consolerait dans la grande détresse!


Les astres, c'est certain, un jour s'aborderont!
Peut-être alors luira l'Aurore universelle
Que nous chantent ces gueux qui vont, l'Idée au front!
Ce sera contre Dieu la clameur fraternelle!


Hélas! avant ces temps, averses, vents, soleil
Auront au loin perdu mon cœur, mes nerfs, mes moelles,
Tout se fera sans moi! Ni rêve, ni réveil!
Je n'aurai pas été dans les douces étoiles!


## ECLAIR DE GOUFFRE

J'étais sur une tour au milieu des étoiles.

Soudain, coup de vertige! un éclair où, sans voiles,
Je sondais, grelottant d'effarement, de peur,
L'énigme du Cosmos dans toute sa stupeur!
Tout est-il seul? Où suis-je? Où va ce bloc qui roule
Et m'emporte?—Et je puis mourir! mourir! partir,
Sans rien savoir! Parlez! O rage! et le temps coule
Sans retour! Arrêtez, arrêtez! Et jouir?
Car j'ignore tout, moi! mon heure est là peut-être?
Je ne sais pas! J'étais dans la nuit, puis je nais,
Pourquoi? D'où l'univers? Où va-t-il? Car le prêtre
N'est qu'un homme. On ne sait rien! Montre-toi, parais,
Dieu, témoin éternel! Parle, pourquoi la vie?
Tout se tait! Oh! l'espace est sans cœur! Un moment!
Astres! je ne veux pas mourir! J'ai du génie!
Ah! redevenir rien irrévocablement!

## LA PREMIÈRE NUIT

Voici venir le Soir, doux au vieillard lubrique.
Mon chat Mürr accroupi comme un sphinx héraldique
Contemple, inquiet, de sa prunelle fantastique
Marcher à l'horizon la lune chlorotique.

C'est l'heure où l'enfant prie, où Paris-lupanar
Jette sur le pavé de chaque boulevard
Ses filles aux seins froids qui, sous le gaz blafard
Voguent, flairant de l'œil un mâle de hasard.

Mais, près de mon chat Mürr, je rêve à ma fenêtre.
Je songe aux enfants qui partout viennent de naître.
Je songe à tous les morts enterrés d'aujourd'hui.

Et je me figure être au fond du cimetière,
Et me mets à la place, en entrant dans leur bière,
De ceux qui vont passer là leur première nuit.


## COMPLAINTE DE CETTE BONNE LUNE

*On entend les Etoiles:*

> Dans l'giron
> Du Patron,
> On y danse, on y danse
> Dans l'giron
> Du Patron
> On y danse tous en rond.

—Là, voyons, mam'zell' la Lune,
Ne gardons pas ainsi rancune;
Entrez en danse, et vous aurez
Un collier de soleils dorés.

—Mon Dieu, c'est à vous bien honnête,
Pour une pauvre Cendrillon;
Mais, me suffit le médaillon
Que m'a donné ma sœur planète.

—Fi! votre Terre est un suppôt
De la Pensée! Entrez en fête;
Pour sûr vous tournerez la tête
Aux astres les plus comme il faut.

—Merci, merci, je n'ai que ma mie,
Juste que je l'entends gémir!
—Vous vous trompez, c'est le soupir
Des universelles chimies!

—Mauvaises langues, taisez-vous!
Je dois veiller. Tas de traînées,
Allez courir vos guilledous!

—Va donc, rosière enfarinée!
Hé! Notre-Dame des gens saouls,
Des filous et des loups-garous!
Metteuse en rut des vieux matous!
    Coucou!

*Exeunt les étoiles. Silence et Lune. On entend:*

   Sous l'plafond
    Sans fond,
 On y danse, on y danse
   Sous l'plafond
    Sans fond,
 On y danse tous en rond.


## COMPLAINTE DES PIANOS
## QU'ON ENTEND DANS LES QUARTIERS AISÉS

Menez l'âme que les Lettres ont bien nourrie,
Les pianos, les pianos, dans les quartiers aisés.
Premiers soirs, sans pardessus, chaste flânerie,
Aux complainte des nerfs incompris ou brisés,

  Ces enfants, à quoi rêvent-elles,
  Dans les ennuis des ritournelles?

   —"Préaux des soirs,
   Christs des dortoirs!

  "Tu t'en vas et tu nous laisses,
  Tu nous laiss's et tu t'en vas,
  Défaire et refaire ses tresses,
  Broder d'eternels canevas."

Jolie ou vague? triste ou sage? encore pure?
O jours, tout m'est égal? ou, monde, moi je veux?
Et si vierge, du moins, de la bonne blessure,
Sachant quels gras couchants ont les plus blancs aveux?

Mon Dieu, a quoi donc rêvent-elles?
A des Roland, à des dentelles?

—"Cœurs en prison,
Lentes saisons!

"Tu t'en vas et tu nous quittes,
Tu nous quitt's et tu t'en vas!
Couvents gris, chœurs de Sulamites,
Sur nos seins nuls croisons nos bras."

Fatales clés de l'être un beau jour apparues;
    Psitt! aux hérédités en ponctuels ferments,
Dans le bal incessant de nos étranges rues;
Ah! pensionnats, théâtres, journaux, romans!

Allez, stériles ritournelles,
La vie est vraie et criminelle.

—"Rideaux tirés,
Peut-on entrer?

"Tu t'en vas et tu nous laisses,
Tu nous laiss's et tu t'en vas,
La source des frais rosiers baisse,
Vraiment! Et lui qui ne vient pas . . ."

Il viendra! Vous serez les pauvres cœurs en faute,
Fiancés au remords comme aux essais sans fond
Et les suffisants cœurs cossus, n'ayant d'autre hôte
Qu'un train-train pavoisé d'estime et de chiffons.

Mourir? peut-être brodent-elles
Pour un oncle à dot, des bretelles?

—"Jamais! Jamais!
Si tu savais!

"Tu t'en vas et tu nous quittes,
Tu nous quitt's et tu t'en vas,
Mais tu nous reviendras bien vite
Guérir mon beau mal, n'est-ce pas?"

Et c'est vrai! l'Idéal les fait divaguer toutes,
Vigne bohême, même en ces quartiers aisés.
La vie est là; le pur flacon des vives gouttes
Sera, *comme il convient*, d'eau propre baptisé.

Aussi, bientôt, se joueront-elles
De plus exactes ritournelles.


"—Seul oreiller!
Mur familier!


"Tu t'en vas et tu nous laisses,
Tu nous laiss's et tu t'en vas.
Que ne suis-je morte à la messe!
Ô mois, ô linges, ô repas."



## AUTRE COMPLAINTE DE LORD PIERROT

Celle qui doit me mettre au courant de la Femme!
Nous lui dirons d'abord, de mon air le moins froid:
"La somme des angles d'un triangle, chèr âme,
    "Est égale à deux droits."


Et si ce cri lui part: "Dieu de Dieu! que je t'aime!"
—"Dieu reconnaîtra les siens." Ou piquée au vif:
—"Mes claviers ont du cœur, tu seras mon seul thème."
    Moi: "Tout est relatif."


De tous ses yeux, alors! se sentant trop banale:
"Ah! tu ne m'aimes pas; tant d'autres sont jaloux!"
Et moi, d'un œil qui vers l'Inconscient s'emballe:
    "Merci, pas mal; et vous?"


—"Jouons au plus fidèle!" —"A quoi bon, ô Nature!"
"Autant à qui perd gagne!" Alors, autre couplet:
—"Ah! tu te lasseras le premier, j'en suis sure . . ."
    —"Après vous, s'il vous plaît."


Enfin, si, par un soir, elle meurt dans mes livres,
Douce; feignant de n'en pas croire encor mes yeux,
J'aurai un: "Ah ça, mais, nous avions De Quoi vivre!
    "C'était donc sérieux?"

## COMPLAINTE DU ROI DE THULÉ

Il était un roi de Thulé,
　　Immaculé,
Qui loin des jupes et des choses,
Pleurait sur la métempsychose
　　Des lys en roses,
　　Et quel palais!

Ses fleurs dormant, il s'en allait,
　　Traînant des clés,
Broder aux seuls yeux des étoiles,
Sur une tour, un certain Voile.
　　De vive toile,
　　Aux nuits de lait!

Quand le voile fut bien ourlé,
　　Loin de Thulé,
Il rama fort sur les mers grises,
Vers le soleil qui s'agonise,
　　Féerique Église!
　　Il ululait:

"Soleil-crevant, encore un jour,
Vous avez tendu votre phare
Aux holocaustes vivipares,
Du culte qu'ils nomment l'Amour.

"Et comme, devant la nuit fauve,
Vous vous sentez défaillir,
D'un dernier flot d'un sang martyr
Vous lavez le seuil le l'Alcôve!

"Soleil! Soleil! moi je descends
Vers vos navrants palais polaires,
Dorloter dans ce Saint-Suaire
　　Votre cœur bien en sang,
　　En le berçant!"

Il dit, et, le Voile étendu,
　　Tout éperdu,
Vers les coraux et les naufrages,
Le roi raillé des doux corsages
　　Beau comme un Mage
　　Est descendu!

Braves amants! aux nuits de lait,
    Tournez vos clés!
Une ombre, d'amour pur transie,
Viendrait vous gémir cette scie:
"Il était un roi de Thulé
    Immaculé . . ."


## COMPLAINTE DE L'OUBLI DES MORTS

Mesdames et Messieurs,
Vous dont la mère est morte.
C'est le bon fossoyeux
Qui gratte à votre porte.

    Les morts,
    C'est sous terre;
    Ça n'en sort
      Guère.

Vous fumez dans vos bocks,
Vous soldez quelque idylle,
Là-bas chante le coq,
Pauvres morts hors des villes!

Grand-papa se penchait,
Là, le doigt sur la tempe,
Sœur faisait du crochet,
Mère montait la lampe.

    Les morts
    C'est discret,
      Ça dort
    Trop au frais.

Vous avez bien dîné,
Comment va cette affaire?
Ah! les petits mort-nés
Ne se dorlotent guère!

Notez, d'un trait égal,
Au livre de la caisse,
Entre deux frais de bal:
Entretien tombe et messe.

C'est gai,
Cette vie;
Hein, ma mie,
O gué?


Mesdames et Messieurs,
Vous dont la sœur est morte,
Ouvrez au fossoyeux
Qui claque à votre porte;


Si vous n'avez pitié,
Il viendra (sans rancune)
Vous tirer par les pieds,
Une nuit de grand'lune!


Importun
Vent qui rage!
Les défunts?
Ça voyage.


## PIERROTS (ON A DES PRINCIPES)

Elle disait, de son air vain fondamental:
"Je t'aime pour toi seul!" —Oh! là, là, grêle histoire;
Oui, comme l'art! Du calme, ô salaire illusoire
    Du capitaliste Idéal!


Elle faisait: "J'attends, me voici, je sais pas. . . ."
Le regard pris de ces larges candeurs des lunes;
—Oh! là, là, ce n'est pas peut-être pour des prunes,
    Qu'on a fait ses classes ici-bas?


Mais voici qu'un beau soir, infortunée à point,
Elle meurt! —Oh! là, là; bon, changement de thème!
On sait que tu dois ressusciter le troisième
    Jour, sinon en personne, du moins


Dans l'odeur, les verdures, les eaux des beaux mois!
Et tu iras, levant encore bien plus de dupes
Vers le Zaïmph de la Joconde, vers la Jupe!
    Il se pourra même que j'en sois.

## J'ENTENDS BATTRE MON SACRÉ-CŒUR . . .

J'entends battre mon Sacré-Cœur
Dans le crépuscule de l'heure,
Comme il est méconnu, sans sœur,
Et sans destin, et sans demeure!

J'entends battre ma jeune chair
Equivoquant par mes artères,
Entre les Edens de mes vers
Et la province de mes pères.

Et j'entends la flûte de Pan
Qui chante: "Bats, bats la campagne!
"Meurs, quand tout vit à tes dépens;
"Mais entre nous, va, qui perd gagne!"

## ROMANCE

HAMLET: *To a nunnery, go*

J'ai mille oiseaux de mer d'un gris pâle,
Qui nichent au haut de ma belle âme,
Ils en emplissent les tristes salles
De rythmes pris aux plus fines lames . . .

Or, ils salissent tout de charognes,
Et aussi de coraux, de coquilles;
Puis volent en ronds fous, et se cognent
A mes probes lambris de famille . . .

Oiseaux pâles, oiseaux des sillages!
Quand la fiancée ouvrira la porte,
Faites un collier de coquillages
Et que l'odeur de charogn's soit forte! . . .

Qu'Elle dise: "Cette âme est bien forte
Pour mon petit nez . . . —je me r'habille.
Mais ce beau collier? hein, je l'emporte?
Il ne lui sert de rien, pauvre fille. . . ."

## L'HIVER QUI VIENT

Blocus sentimental! Messageries du Levant! . . .
Oh! tombée de la pluie! Oh! tombée de la nuit,
Oh! le vent! . . .
La Toussaint, la Noël, et la Nouvelle Année,
Oh, dans les bruines, toutes mes cheminées! . . .
D'usines . . .


On ne peut plus s'asseoir, tous le bancs sont mouillés;
Crois-moi, c'est bien fini jusqu'à l'année prochaine,
Tous les bancs sont mouillés, tant les bois sont rouillés,
Et tant les cors ont fait ton ton, ont fait ton taine! . . .


Ah! nuées accourues des côtes de la Manche,
Vous nous avez gâté notre dernier dimanche.


Il bruine;
Dans la forêt mouillée, les toiles d'araignées
Ploient sous les gouttes d'eau, et c'est leur ruine.
Soleils plénipotentiaires des travaux en blonds Pactoles
Des spectacles agricoles,
Où êtes-vous ensevelis?
Ce soir un soleil fichu gît au haut du coteau,
Gît sur le flanc, dans les genêts, sur son manteau.
Un soleil blanc comme un crachat d'estaminet
Sur une litière de jaunes genêts,
De jaunes genêts d'automne.
Et les cors lui sonnent!
Qu'il revienne . . .
Qu'il revienne à lui!
Taïaut! Taïaut! et hallali!
O triste antienne, as-tu fini! . . .
Et font les fous! . . .
Et il gît là, comme une glande arrachée dans un cou,
Et il frissonne, sans personne! . . .


Allons, allons, et hallali!
C'est l'Hiver bien connu qui s'amène;
Oh! les tournants des grandes routes,
Et sans petit Chaperon Rouge qui chemine! . . .
Oh! leurs ornières des chars de l'autre mois,
Montant en don quichottesques rails
Vers les patrouilles des nuées en déroute
Que le vent malmène vers les transatlantiques bercails! . . .

Accélérons, accélérons, c'est la saison bien connue, cette fois
Et le vent, cette nuit, il en a fait de belles!
O dégâts, ô nids, ô modestes jardinets!
Mon cœur et mon sommeil: ô échos des cognées! . . .


Tous ces rameaux avaient encor leurs feuilles vertes,
Les sous-bois ne sont plus qu'un fumier de feuilles mortes;
Feuilles, folioles, qu'un bon vent vous emporte
Vers les étangs par ribambelles,
Ou pour le feu du garde-chasse,
Ou les sommiers des ambulances
Pour les soldats loin de la France.


C'est la saison, c'est la saison, la rouille envahit les masses,
La rouille ronge en leurs spleens kilométriques
Les fils télégraphiques des grandes routes où nul ne passe.


Les cors, les cors, les cors—mélancoliques! . . .
Mélancoliques! . . .
S'en vont, changeant de ton,
Changeant de ton et de musique,
Ton ton, ton taine, ton ton! . . .
Les cors, les cors, les cors! . . .
S'en sont allés au vent du Nord.


Je ne puis quitter ce ton: que d'échos! . . .
C'est la saison, c'est la saison, adieu vendanges! . . .
Voici venir les pluies d'une patience d'ange,
Adieu vendanges, et adieu tous les paniers,
Tous les paniers Watteau des bourrées sous les marronniers,
C'est la toux dans les dortoirs du lycée qui rentre,
C'est la tisane sans le foyer
La phtisie pulmonaire attristant le quartier,
Et toute la misère des grands centres.


Mais, lainages, caoutchoucs, pharmacie, rêve,
Rideaux écartés du haut des balcons des grèves
Devant l'ocean de toitures des faubourgs,
Lampes, estampes, thé, petits-fours,
Serez-vous pas mes seules amours! . . .
(Oh! et puis, est-ce que tu connais, outre les pianos,
Le sobre et vespéral mystère hebdomadaire
Des statistiques sanitaires
Dans les journaux?)

Non, non! c'est la saison et la planète falote!
Que l'autan, que l'autan
Effiloche les savates que le Temps se tricote!
C'est la saison, oh déchirements! c'est la saison!
Tous les ans, tous les ans,
J'essaierai en chœur d'en donner la note.


## SOLO DE LUNE


Je fume, étalé face au ciel,
Sur l'impériale de la diligence,
Ma carcasse est cahotée, mon âme danse
Comme un Ariel;
Sans miel, sans fiel, ma belle âme danse
O routes, coteaux, ô fumées, ô vallons,
Ma belle âme, ah! récapitulons.

Nous nous aimions comme deux fous,
On s'est quitté sans en parler,
Un spleen me tenait exilé,
Et ce spleen me venait de tout. Bon.

Ses yeux disaient: "Comprenez-vous?
Pourquoi ne comprenez-vous pas?"
Mais nul n'a voulu faire le premier pas,
Voulant trop tomber *ensemble* à genoux.
(Comprenez-vous?)

Où est-elle à cette heure?
Peut-être qu'elle pleure . . .
Où est-elle à cette heure?
Oh! du moins, soigne-toi, je t'en conjure!

O fraîcheur des bois le long de la route,
O châle de mélancholie, tout âme est un peu aux écoutes
Que ma vie
Fait envie!
Cette impériale de diligence tient de la magie.

Accumulons l'irréparable!
Renchérissons sur notre sort!
Les étoiles sont plus nombreuses que le sable
Des mers où d'autres ont vu se baigner son corps;
Tout n'en va pas moins à la Mort.
Y a pas de port.

Des ans vont passer là-dessus,
On s'endurcira chacun pour soi,
Et bien souvent et déjà je m'y vois,
On se dira: "Si j'avais su . . ."
Mais mariés de même, ne se fût-on pas dit
"Si j'avais su, si j'avais su! . . ."
Ah! rendez-vous maudit!
Ah! mon cœur sans issue! . . .
Je me suis mal conduit.


Maniaques de bonheur,
Donc, que ferons-nous? Moi de mon âme,
Elle de sa faillible jeunesse?
O vieillissante pécheresse,
Oh! que de soirs je vais me rendre infâme
En ton honneur!


Ses yeux clignaient: "Comprenez-vous?
Pourquoi ne comprenez-vous pas?"
Mais nul n'a fait le premier pas
Pour tomber ensemble à genoux. Ah! . . .


La Lune se lève,
O route en grand rêve! . . .
On a dépassé les filatures, les scieries,
Plus que les bornes kilométriques,
De petits nuages d'un rose de confiserie,
Cependant qu'un fin croissant de lune se lève,
O route de rêve, ô nulle musique . . .
Dans ces bois de pins où depuis
Le commencement du monde
Il fait toujours nuit,
Que de chambres propres et profondes!
Oh! pour un soir d'enlèvement!
Et je les peuple et je m'y vois,
Et c'est un beau couple d'amants,
Qui gesticulent hors la loi.


Et je passe et les abandonne,
Et me recouche face au ciel.
La route tourne, je suis Ariel,
Nul ne m'attend, je ne vais chez personne.
Je n'ai que l'amitié des chambres d'hôtel.

La lune se lève,
O route en grand rêve,
O route sans terme.
Voici le relais,
Où l'on allume les lanternes,
Où l'on boit un verre de lait,
Et fouette postillon,
Dans le chant des grillons,
Sous les étoiles de juillet.


O clair de Lune,
Noce de feux de Bengale noyant mon infortune,
Les ombres des peupliers sur la route . . .
Le gave qui s'écoute . . .
Qui s'écoute chanter . . .
Dans ces inondations du fleuve du Léthé . . .


O Solo de lune,
Vous défiez ma plume,
Oh! cette nuit sur la route;
O Étoiles, vous êtes à faire peur,
Vous y êtes toutes! toutes!
O fugacité de cette heure . . .
Oh! qu'il y eût moyen
De m'en garder l'âme pour l'automne qui vient! . . .


Voici qu'il fait très, très frais,
Oh! si à la même heure,
Elle va de même le long des forêts,
Noyer son infortune
Dans les noces du clair de lune! . . .
(Elle aime tant errer tard!)
Elle aura oublié son foulard,
Elle va prendre mal, vu la beauté de l'heure!
Oh! soigne-toi, je t'en conjure!
Oh! je ne veux plus entendre cette toux!


Ah! que ne suis-je tombé à tes genoux!
Ah! que n'as-tu défailli à mes genoux!
J'eusse été le modèle des époux!
Comme le frou-frou de ta robe est le modèle des frou-frou.

# *Guillaume Apollinaire*

## ZONE

A la fin tu es las de ce monde ancien

Bergère ô tour Eiffel le troupeau des ponts bêle ce matin

Tu en as assez de vivre dans l'antiquité grecque et romaine

Ici même les automobiles ont l'air d'être anciennes
La religion seule est restée toute neuve la religion
Est restée simple comme les hangars de Port-Aviation

Seul en Europe tu n'es pas antique ô Christianisme
L'Européen le plus moderne c'est vous Pape Pie X
Et toi que les fenêtres observent la honte te retient
D'entrer dans une église et de t'y confesser ce matin
Tu lis les prospectus les catalogues les affiches qui chantent
    tout haut
Voilà la poésie ce matin et pour la prose il y a les journaux
Il y a les livraisons à 25 centimes pleines d'aventures policières
Portraits des grands hommes et mille titres divers

J'ai vu ce matin une jolie rue dont j'ai oublié le nom
Neuve et propre du soleil elle était le clairon
Les directeurs les ouvriers et les belles sténo-dactylographes
Du lundi matin au samedi soir quatre fois par jour y passent
Le matin par trois fois la sirène y gémit
Une cloche rageuse y aboie vers midi
Les inscriptions des enseignes et des murailles
Les plaques les avis à la façon des perroquets criaillent
J'aime la grâce de cette rue industrielle
Située à Paris entre la rue Aumont-Thiéville et l'avenue des
    Ternes

Voilà la jeune rue et tu n'es encore qu'un petit enfant
Ta mère ne t'habille que de bleu et de blanc
Tu es très pieux et avec le plus ancien de tes camarades René
    Dalize
Vous n'aimez rien tant que les pompes de l'Église
Il est neuf heures le gaz est baissé tout bleu vous sortez du
    dortoir en cachette
Vous priez toute la nuit dans la chapelle du collège
Tandis qu'éternelle et adorable profondeur améthyste
Tourne à jamais la flamboyante gloire du Christ
C'est le beau lys que tous nous cultivons

C'est la torche aux cheveux roux que n'éteint pas le vent
C'est le fils pâle et vermeil de la douloureuse mère
C'est l'arbre toujours touffu de toutes les prières
C'est la double potence de l'honneur et de l'éternité
C'est l'étoile à six branches
C'est Dieu qui meurt le vendredi et ressuscite le dimanche
C'est le Christ qui monte au ciel mieux que les aviateurs
Il détient le record du monde pour la hauteur

Pupille Christ de l'œil
Vingtième pupille des siècles il sait y faire
Et changé en oiseau ce siècle comme Jésus monte dans l'air
Les diables dans les abîmes lèvant la tête pour le regarder
Ils disent qu'il imite Simon Mage en Judée
Ils crient s'il sait voler qu'on l'appelle voleur
Les anges voltigent autour du joli voltigeur
Icare Énoch Élie Apollonius de Thyane
Flottent autour du premier aéroplane
Ils s'écartent parfois pour laisser passer ceux que transporte la
    Sainte-Eucharistie
Ces prêtres qui montent éternellement en élevant l'hostie
L'avion se pose enfin sans refermer les ailes
Le ciel s'emplit alors de millions d'hirondelles
A tire d'aile viennent les corbeaux les faucons les hiboux
D'Afrique arrivent les ibis les flamants les marabouts
L'oiseau Roc célébré par les conteurs et les poètes
Plane tenant dans les serres le crâne d'Adam la première tête
L'aigle fond de l'horizon en poussant un grand cri
Et d'Amérique vient le petit colibri
De Chine sont venus les pihis longs et souples
Qui n'ont qu'une seule aile et qui volent par couples
Puis voici la colombe esprit immaculé
Qu'escortent l'oiseau-lyre et le paon ocellé
Le phénix ce bûcher qui soi-même s'engendre
Un instant voile tout de son ardente cendre
Les sirènes laissant les périlleux détroits
Arrivent en chantant bellement toutes trois
Et tous aigle phénix et pihis de la Chine
Fraternisent avec la volante machine

Maintenant tu marches dans Paris tout seul parmi la foule
Des troupeaux d'autobus mugissants près de toi roulent
L'angoisse de l'amour te serre le gosier
Comme si tu ne devais jamais plus être aimé
Si tu vivais dans l'ancien temps tu entrerais dans un monastère
Vous avez honte quand vous vous surprenez à dire une prière
Tu te moques de toi et comme le feu de l'Enfer ton rire pétille
Les étincelles de ton rire dorent le fond de ta vie

C'est un tableau pendu dans un sombre musée
Et quelquefois tu vas le regarder de près

Aujourd'hui tu marches dans Paris les femmes sont ensanglantées
C'était et je voudrais ne pas m'en souvenir c'était au déclin de
la beauté

Entourée de flammes fervents Notre-Dame m'a regardé à
Chartres
Le sang de votre Sacré-Cœur m'a inondé à Montmartre
Je suis malade d'ouïr les paroles bienheureuses
L'amour dont je souffre est une maladie honteuse
Et l'image qui te possède te fait survivre dans l'insomnie et
dans l'angoisse
C'est toujours près de toi cette image qui passe

Maintenant tu es au bord de la Méditerranée
Sous les citronniers qui sont en fleur toute l'année
Avec tes amis tu te promènes en barque
L'un est Nissard il y a un Mentonasque et deux Turbiasques
Nous regardons avec effroi les poulpes des profondeurs
Et parmi les algues nagent les poissons images du Sauveur

Tu es dans le jardin d'une auberge aux environs de Prague
Tu te sens tout heureux une rose est sur la table
Et tu observes au lieu d'écrire ton conte en prose
La cétoine qui dort dans le cœur de la rose

Épouvanté tu te vois dessiné dans les agates de Saint-Vit
Tu étais triste à mourir le jour où tu t'y vis
Tu ressembles au Lazare affolé par le jour
Les aiguilles de l'horloge du quartier juif vont à rebours
Et tu recules aussi dans ta vie lentement
En montant au Hradchin et le soir en écoutant
Dans les tavernes chanter des chansons tchèques

Te voici à Marseille au milieu des pastèques

Te voici à Coblence à l'hôtel du Géant

Te voici à Rome assis sous un néflier du Japon

Te voici à Amsterdam avec une jeune fille que tu trouves belle
et qui est laide
Elle doit se marier avec un étudiant de Leyde
On y loue des chambres en latin Cubicula locanda
Je m'en souviens j'y ai passé trois jours et autant à Gouda

Tu es à Paris chez le juge d'instruction
Comme un criminel on te met en état d'arrestation

Tu as fait de douloureux et de joyeux voyages
Avant de t'apercevoir du mensonge et de l'âge
Tu as souffert de l'amour à vingt et à trente ans
J'ai vécu comme un fou et j'ai perdu mon temps
Tu n'oses plus regarder tes mains et à tous moments je vou-
    drais sangloter
Sur toi sur celle que j'aime sur tout ce qui t'a épouvanté

Tu regardes les yeux pleins de larmes ces pauvres émigrants
Ils croient en Dieu ils prient les femmes allaitent des enfants
Ils emplissent de leur odeur le hall de la gare Saint-Lazare
Ils ont foi dans leur étoile comme les rois-mages
Ils espèrent gagner de l'argent dans l'Argentine
Et revenir dans leur pays après avoir fait fortune
Une famille transporte un édredon rouge comme vous trans-
    portez votre cœur
Cet édredon et nos rêves sont aussi irréels
Quelques-uns de ces émigrants restent ici et se logent
Rue des Rosiers ou rue des Écouffes dans des bouges
Je les ai vus souvent le soir ils prennent l'air dans la rue
Et se déplacent rarement comme les pièces aux échecs
Il y a surtout des Juifs leurs femmes portent perruque
Elles restent assises exsangues au fond des boutiques

Tu es debout devant le zinc d'un bar crapuleux
Tu prends un café à deux sous parmi les malheureux

Tu es la nuit dans un grand restaurant

Ces femmes ne sont pas méchantes elles ont des soucis cepen-
    dant
Toutes même la plus laide a fait souffrir son amant
Elle est la fille d'un sergent de ville de Jersey

Ses mains que je n'avais pas vues sont dures et gercées

J'ai une pitié immense pour les coutures de son ventre

J'humilie maintenant à une pauvre fille au rire horrible ma
    bouche

Tu es seul le matin va venir
Les laitiers font tinter leurs bidons dans les rues

La nuit s'éloigne ainsi qu'une belle Métive
C'est Ferdine la fausse ou Léa l'attentive

Et tu bois cet alcool brûlant comme ta vie
Ta vie que tu bois comme une eau-de-vie

Tu marches vers Auteuil tu veux aller chez toi à pied
Dormir parmi tes fétiches d'Océanie et de Guinée
Ils sont des Christ d'une autre forme et d'une autre croyance
Ce sont les Christ inférieurs des obscures espérances

Adieu Adieu

Soleil cou coupé

## LE PONT MIRABEAU

Sous le pont Mirabeau coule la Seine
            Et nos amours
        Faut-il qu'il m'en souvienne
La joie venait toujours après la peine

            Vienne la nuit sonne l'heure
            Les jours s'en vont je demeure

Les mains dans les mains restons face à face
            Tandis que sous
        Le pont de nos bras passe
Des éterneles regards l'onde si lasse

            Vienne la nuit sonne l'heure
            Les jours s'en vont je demeure

L'amour s'en va comme cette eau courante
            L'amour s'en va
        Comme la vie est lente
Et comme l'Espérance est violente

            Vienne la nuit sonne l'heure
            Les jours s'en vont je demeure

Passent les jours et passent les semaines
            Ni temps passé
        Ni les amours reviennent
Sous le pont Mirabeau coule la Seine

            Vienne la nuit sonne l'heure
            Les jours s'en vont je demeure

## LA CHANSON DU MAL-AIMÉ

*A Paul Léautaud*

*Et je chantais cette romance*
*En 1903 sans savoir*
*Que mon amour à la semblance*
*Du beau Phénix s'il meurt un soir*
*Le matin voit sa renaissance*

*Un soir de demi-brume à Londres*
*Un voyou qui ressemblait à*
*Mon amour vint à ma rencontre*
*Et le regard qu'il me jeta*
*Me fit baisser les yeux de honte*

*Je suivis ce mauvais garçon*
*Qui sifflotait mains dans les poches*
*Nous semblions entre les maisons*
*Onde ouverte de la mer Rouge*
*Lui les Hébreux moi Pharaon*

*Que tombent ces vagues de briques*
*Si tu ne fus pas bien aimée*
*Je suis le souverain d'Égypte*
*Sa sœur-épouse son armée*
*Si tu n'es pas l'amour unique*

*Au tournant d'une rue brûlant*
*De tous les feux de ses façades*
*Plaies du brouillard sanguinolent*
*Où se lamentaient les façades*
*Une femme lui ressemblant*

*C'était son regard d'inhumaine*
*La cicatrice à son cou nu*
*Sortit saoule d'une taverne*
*Au moment où je reconnus*
*La fausseté de l'amour même*

*Lorsqu'il fut de retour enfin*
*Dans sa patrie le sage Ulysse*
*Son vieux chien de lui se souvint*
*Près d'un tapis de haute lisse*
*Sa femme attendait qu'il revînt*

L'époux royal de Sacontale
Las de vaincre se réjouit
Quand il la retrouva plus pâle
D'attente et d'amour yeux pâlis
Caressant sa gazelle mâle

J'ai pensé à ces rois heureux
Lorsque le faux amour et celle
Dont je suis encore amoureux
Heurtant leurs ombres infidèles
Me rendirent si malheureux

Regrets sur quoi l'enfer se fonde
Qu'un ciel d'oubli s'ouvre à mes vœux
Pour son baiser les rois du monde
Seraient morts les pauvres fameux
Pour elle eussent vendu leur ombre

J'ai hiverné dans mon passé
Revienne le soleil de Pâques
Pour chauffer un cœur plus glacé
Que les quarante de Sébaste
Moins que ma vie martyrisés

Mon beau navire ô ma mémoire
Avons-nous assez navigué
Dans une onde mauvaise à boire
Avons-nous assez divagué
De la belle aube au triste soir

Adieu faux amour confondu
Avec la femme qui s'éloigne
Avec celle que j'ai perdue
L'année dernière en Allemagne
Et que je ne reverrai plus

Voie lactée ô sœur lumineuse
Des blancs ruisseaux de Chanaan
Et des corps blancs des amoureuses
Nageurs morts suivrons-nous d'ahan
Ton cours vers d'autres nébuleuses

Je me souviens d'une autre année
C'était l'aube d'un jour d'avril
J'ai chanté ma joie bien-aimée
Chanté l'amour à voix virile
Au moment d'amour de l'année

C'est le printemps viens-t'en Pâquette
Te promener au bois joli
Les poules dans la cour caquètent
L'aube au ciel fait de roses plis
L'amour chemine à ta conquête

Mars et Vénus sont revenus
Ils s'embrassent à bouches folles
Devant des sites ingénus
Où sous les roses qui feuillolent
De beaux dieux roses dansent nus

Viens ma tendresse est la régente
De la floraison qui paraît
La nature est belle et touchante
Pan sifflote dans la forêt
Les grenouilles humides chantent

*Beaucoup de ces dieux out péri*
*C'est sur eux que pleurent les saules*
*Le grand Pan l'amour Jésus-Christ*
*Sont bien morts et les chats miaulent*
*Dans la cour je pleure à Paris*

*Moi qui sais des lais pour les reines*
*Les complaintes de mes années*
*Des hymnes d'esclave aux murènes*
*La romance du mal-aimé*
*Et des chansons pour les sirènes*

*L'amour est mort j'en suis tremblant*
*J'adore de belles idoles*
*Les souvenirs lui ressemblant*
*Comme la femme de Mausole*
*Je reste fidèle et dolent*

*Je suis fidèle comme un dogue*
*Au maître le lierre au tronc*
*Et les Cosaques Zaporogues*
*Ivrognes pieux et larrons*
*Aux steppes et au décalogue*

*Portez comme un joug le Croissant*
*Qu'interrogent les astrologues*
*Je suis le Sultan tout-puissant*
*O mes Cosaques Zaporogues*
*Votre Seigneur éblouissant*

*Devenez mes sujets fidèles*
*Leur avait écrit le Sultan*
*Ils rirent à cette nouvelle*
*Et répondirent à l'instant*
*A la lueur d'une chandelle*

Plus criminel que Barrabas
Cornu comme les mauvais anges
Quel Belzébuth es-tu là-bas
Nourri d'immondice et de fange
Nous n'irons pas à tes sabbats

RÉPONSE DES CO-
SAQUES ZAPORO-
GUES AU SULTAN DE
CONSTANTINOPLE

Poisson pourri de Salonique
Long collier des sommeils affreux
D'yeux arrachés à coup de pique
Ta mère fit un pet foireux
Et tu naquis de sa colique

Bourreau de Podolie Amant
Des plaies des ulcères des croûtes
Groin de cochon cul de jument
Tes richesses garde-les toutes
Pour payer tes médicaments

*Voie lactée ô sœur lumineuse*
*Des blancs ruisseaux de Chanaan*
*Et des corps blancs des amoureuses*
*Nageurs morts suivrons-nous d'ahan*
*Ton cours vers d'autres nébuleuses*

*Regret des yeux de la putain*
*Et belle comme une panthère*
*Amour vos baisers florentins*
*Avaient une saveur amère*
*Qui a rebuté nos destins*

*Ses regards laissaient une traîne*
*D'étoiles dans les soirs tremblants*
*Dans ses yeux nageaient les sirènes*
*Et nos baisers mordus sanglants*
*Faisaient pleurer nos fées marraines*

*Mais en vérité je l'attends*
*Avec mon cœur avec mon âme*
*Et sur le pont des Reviens-t'en*
*Si jamais revient cette femme*
*Je lui dirai Je suis content*

*Mon cœur et ma tête se vident*
*Tout le ciel s'écoule par eux*
*O mes tonneaux des Danaïdes*
*Comment faire pour être heureux*
*Comme un petit enfant candide*

*Je ne veux jamais l'oublier*
*Ma colombe ma blanche rade*
*O marguerite exfoliée*
*Mon île au loin ma Désirade*
*Ma rose mon giroflier*

*Les satyres et les pyraustes*
*Les égypans les feux follets*
*Et les destins damnés ou faustes*
*La corde au cou comme à Calais*
*Sur ma douleur quel holocauste*

*Douleur qui doubles les destins*
*La licorne et le capricorne*
*Mon âme et mon corps incertain*
*Te fuient ô bûcher divin qu'ornent*
*Des astres des fleurs du matin*

*Malheur dieu pâle aux yeux d'ivoire*
*Tes prêtres fous t'ont-ils paré*
*Tes victimes en robe noire*
*Ont-elles vainement pleuré*
*Malheur dieu qu'il ne faut pas croire*

*Et toi qui me suis en rampant*
*Dieu de mes dieux morts en automne*
*Tu mesures combien d'empans*
*J'ai droit que la terre me donne*
*O mon ombre ô mon vieux serpent*

*Au soleil parce que tu l'aimes*
*Je t'ai menée souviens-t'en bien*
*Ténébreuse épouse que j'aime*
*Tu es à moi en n'étant rien*
*O mon ombre en deuil de moi-même*

*L'hiver est mort tout enneigé*
*On a brûlé les ruches blanches*
*Dans les jardins et les vergers*
*Les oiseaux chantent sur les branches*
*Le printemps clair l'avril léger*

*Mort d'immortels argyraspides*
*La neige aux boucliers d'argent*
*Fuit les dandrophores livides*
*Du printemps cher aux pauvres gens*
*Qui resourient les yeux humides*

*Et moi j'ai le cœur aussi gros*
*Qu'un cul de dame damascène*
*Ô mon amour je t'aimais trop*
*Et maintenant j'ai trop de peine*
*Les sept épées hors du fourreau*

*Sept épées de mélancolie*
*Sans morfil ô claires douleurs*
*Sont dans mon cœur et la folie*
*Veut raisonner pour mon malheur*
*Comment voulez-vous que j'oublie*

LES SEPT
ÉPÉES

La première est toute d'argent
Et son nom tremblant c'est Pâline
Sa lame un ciel d'hiver neigeant
Son destin sanglant gibeline
Vulcain mourut en la forgeant

La seconde nommée Noubosse
Est un bel arc-en-ciel joyeux
Les dieux s'en servent à leurs noces
Elle a tué trente Bé-Rieux
Et fut douée par Carabosse

La troisième bleu féminin
N'en est pas moins un chibriape
Appelé Lul de Faltenin
Et que porte sur une nappe
L'Hermès Ernest devenu nain

La quatrième Malourène
Est un fleuve vert et doré
C'est le soir quand les riveraines
Y baignent leurs corps adorés
Et des chants de rameurs s'y traînent

La cinquième Sainte-Fabeau
C'est la plus belle des quenouilles
C'est un cyprès sur un tombeau
Où les quatre vents s'agenouillent
Et chaque nuit c'est un flambeau

La sixième métal de gloire
C'est l'ami aux si douces mains
Dont chaque matin nous sépare
Adieu voilà votre chemin
Les coqs s'épuisaient en fanfares

Et la septième s'exténue
Une femme une rose morte
Merci que le dernier venu
Sur mon amour ferme la porte
Je ne vous ai jamais connue

*Voie lactée ô sœur lumineuse*
*Des blancs ruisseaux de Chanaan*
*Et des corps blancs des amoureuses*
*Nageurs morts suivrons-nous d'ahan*
*Ton cours vers d'autres nébuleuses*

*Les démons du hasard selon*
*Le chant du firmament nous mènent*
*A sons perdus leurs violons*
*Font danser notre race humaine*
*Sur la descente à reculons*

*Destins destins impénétrables*
*Rois secoués par la folie*
*Et ces grelottantes étoiles*
*De fausses femmes dans vos lits*
*Aux déserts que l'histoire accable*

*Luitpold le vieux prince régent*
*Tuteur de deux royautés folles*
*Sanglote-t-il en y songeant*
*Quand vacillent les lucioles*
*Mouches dorées de la Saint-Jean*

*Près d'un château sans châtelaine*
*La barque aux barcarols chantants*
*Sur un lac blanc et sous l'haleine*
*Des vents qui tremblent au printemps*
*Voguait cygne mourant sirène*

*Un jour le roi dans l'eau d'argent*
*Se noya puis la bouche ouverte*
*Il s'en revint en surnageant*
*Sur la rive dormir inerte*
*Face tournée au ciel changeant*

Juin ton soleil ardente lyre
Brûle mes doigts endoloris
Triste et mélodieux délire
J'erre à travers mon beau Paris
Sans avoir le cœur d'y mourir

Les dimanches s'y éternisent
Et les orgues de Barbarie
Y sanglotent dans les cours grises
Les fleurs aux balcons de Paris
Penchent comme la tour de Pise

Soirs de Paris ivres du gin
Flambant de l'électricité
Les tramways feux verts sur l'échine
Musiquent au long des portées
De rails leur folie de machines

Les cafés gonflés de fumée
Crient tout l'amour de leurs tziganes
De tous leurs siphons enrhumés
De leurs garçons vêtus d'un pagne
Vers toi toi que j'ai tant aimée

Moi qui sais des lais pour les reines
Les complaintes de mes années
Des hymnes d'esclave aux murènes
La romance du mal-aimé
Et des chansons pour les sirènes

## CRÉPUSCULE

*A Mademoiselle Marie Laurencin*

Frôlée par les ombres des morts
Sur l'herbe où le jour s'exténue
L'arlequine s'est mise nue
Et dans l'étang mire son corps

Un charlatan crépusculaire
Vante les tours que l'on va faire
Le ciel sans teinte est constellé
D'astres pâles comme du lait

Sur les tréteaux l'arlequin blême
Salue d'abord les spectateurs
Des sorciers venus de Bohème
Quelques fées et les enchanteurs

Ayant décroché une étoile
Il la manie à bras tendu
Tandis que des pieds un pendu
Sonne en mesure les cymbales

L'aveugle berce un bel enfant
La biche passe avec ses faons
Le nain regarde d'un air triste
Grandir l'arlequin trismégiste

## ANNIE

Sur la côte du Texas
Entre Mobile et Galveston il y a
Un grand jardin tout plein de roses
Il contient aussi une villa
Qui est une grande rose

Une femme se promène souvent
Dans le jardin toute seule
Et quand je passe sur la route bordée de tilleuls
Nous nous regardons

Comme cette femme est mennonite
Ses rosiers et ses vêtements n'ont pas de boutons
Il en manque deux à mon veston
La dame et moi suivons presque le même rite

## MARIZIBILL

Dans la Haute-Rue à Cologne
Elle allait et venait le soir
Offerte à tous en tout mignonne
Puis buvait lasse des trottoirs
Très tard dans les brasseries borgnes

Elle se mettait sur la paille
Pour un maquereau roux et rose
C'était un juif il sentait l'ail
Et l'avait venant de Formose
Tirée d'un bordel de Changaï

Je connais gens de toutes sortes
Ils n'égalent pas leurs destins
Indécis comme feuilles mortes
Leurs yeux sont des feux mal éteints
Leurs cœurs bougent comme leurs portes

## LA BLANCHE NEIGE

Les anges les anges dans le ciel
L'un est vêtu en officier
L'un est vêtu en cuisinier
Et les autres chantent

Bel officier couleur du ciel
Le doux printemps longtemps après Noël
Te médaillera d'un beau soleil
    D'un beau soleil

Le cuisinier plume les oies
    Ah! tombe neige
    Tombe et que n'ai-je
Ma bien-aimée entre mes bras

## SALOMÉ

Pour que sourie encore une fois Jean-Baptiste
Sire je danserais mieux que les séraphins
Ma mère dites-moi pourquoi vous êtes triste
En robe de comtesse à côté du Dauphin

Mon cœur battait battait très fort à sa parole
Quand je dansais dans le fenouil en écoutant
Et je brodais des lys sur une banderole
Destinée à flotter au bout de son bâton

Et pour qui voulez-vous qu'à présent je la brode
Son bâton refleurit sur les bords du Jourdain
Et tous les lys quand vos soldats ô roi Hérode
L'emmenèrent se sont flétris dans mon jardin

Venez tous avec moi là-bas sous les quinconces
    Ne pleure pas ô joli fou du roi
Prends cette tête au lieu de ta marotte et danse
N'y touchez pas son front ma mère est déjà froid

Sire marchez devant trabants marchez derrière
Nous creuserons un trou et l'y enterrerons
Nous planterons des fleurs et danserons en rond
Jusqu'à l'heure où j'aurai perdu ma jarretière
        Le roi sa tabatière
        L'infante son rosaire
        Le curé son bréviaire


## AUTOMNE

Dans le brouillard s'en vont un paysan cagneux
Et son bœuf lentement dans le brouillard d'automne
Qui cache les hameaux pauvres et vergogneux

Et s'en allant là-bas le paysan chantonne
Une chanson d'amour et d'infidélité
Qui parle d'une bague et d'un cœur que l'on brise

Oh! l'automne l'automne a fait mourir l'été
Dans le brouillard s'en vont deux silhouettes grises


## RHÉNANE D'AUTOMNE

*A Toussaint Luca*

Les enfants des morts vont jouer
Dans le cimetière
Martin Gertrude Hans et Henri
Nul coq n'a chanté aujourd-hui
Kikiriki

Les vieilles femmes
Tout en pleurant cheminent
Et les bons ânes
Braillent hi han et se mettent à brouter les fleurs
Des couronnes mortuaires

C'est le jour des morts et de toutes leurs âmes
Les enfants et les vieilles femmes
Allument des bougies et des cierges
Sur chaque tombe catholique
Les voiles des vieilles
Les nuages du ciel
Sont comme des barbes de biques

L'air tremble de flammes et de prières

Le cimetière est un beau jardin
Plein de saules gris et de romarins
Il vous vient souvent des amis qu'on enterre
Ah! que vous êtes bien dans le beau cimetière
Vous mendiants morts saouls de bière
Vous les aveugles comme le destin
Et vous petits enfants morts en prière

Ah! que vous êtes bien dans le beau cimetière
Vous bourgmestres vous bateliers
Et vous conseillers de régence
Vous aussi tziganes sans papiers
La vie vous pourrit dans la panse
La croix nous pousse entre les pieds

Le vent du Rhin ulule avec tous les hiboux
Il éteint les cierges que toujours les enfants rallument
Et les feuilles mortes
Viennent couvrir les morts

Des enfants morts parlent parfois avec leur mère
Et des mortes parfois voudraient bien revenir

Oh! je ne veux pas que tu sortes
L'automne est plein de mains coupées
Non non ce sont des feuilles mortes
Ce sont les mains des chères mortes
Ce sont tes mains coupées

Nous avons tant pleuré aujourd'hui
Avec ces morts leurs enfants et les vieilles femmes
Sous le ciel sans soleil
Au cemetière plein de flammes

Puis dans le vent nous nous en retournâmes

A nos pieds roulaient des châtaignes
Dont les bogues étaient
Comme le cœur blessé de la madone
Dont on doute si elle eut la peau
Couleur des châtaignes d'automne


## J'AI EU LE COURAGE . . .

J'ai eu le courage de regarder en arrière
Les cadavres de mes jours
Marquent ma route et je les pleure
Les uns pourrissent dans les églises italiennes
Ou bien dans de petits bois de citronniers
Qui fleurissent et fructifient
En même temps et en toute saison
D'autres jours ont pleuré avant de mourir dans des tavernes
Où d'ardents bouquets rouaient
Aux yeux d'une mulâtresse qui inventait la poésie
Et les roses de l'électricité s'ouvrent encore
Dans le jardin de ma mémoire


## CORS DE CHASSE

Notre histoire est noble et tragique
Comme le masque d'un tyran
Nul drame hasardeux ou magique
Aucun détail indifférent
Ne rend notre amour pathétique

Et Thomas de Quincey buvant
L'opium poison doux et chaste
A sa pauvre Anne allait rêvant
Passons passons puisque tout passe
Je me retournerai souvent

Les souvenirs sont cors de chasse
Dont meurt le bruit parmi le vent

## VENDÉMIAIRE

Hommes de l'avenir souvenez-vous de moi
Je vivais à l'époque où finissaient les rois
Tour à tour ils mouraient silencieux et tristes
Et trois fois courageux devenaient trismégistes

Que Paris était beau à la fin de septembre
Chaque nuit devenait une vigne où les pampres
Répandaient leur clarté sur la ville et là-haut
Astres mûrs becquetés par les ivres oiseaux
De ma gloire attendaient la vendange de l'aube

Un soir passant le long des quais déserts et sombres
En rentrant à Auteuil l'entendis une voix
Qui chantait gravement se taisant quelquefois
Pour que parvînt aussi sur les bords de la Seine
La plainte d'autres voix limpides et lointaines

Et j'écoutai longtemps tous ces chants et ces cris
Qu'éveillait dans la nuit la chanson de Paris

J'ai soif villes de France et d'Europe et du monde
Venez toutes couler dans ma gorge profonde

Je vis alors que déjà ivre dans la vigne Paris
Vendangeait le raisin le plus doux de la terre
Ces grains miraculeux qui aux treilles chantèrent

Et Rennes répondit avec Quimper et Vannes
Nous voici ô Paris Nos maisons nos habitants
Ces grappes de nos sens qu'enfanta le soleil
Se sacrifient pour te désaltérer trop avide merveille
Nous t'apportons tous les cerveaux les cimetières les murailles
Ces berceaux pleins de cris que tu n'entendras pas
Et d'amont en aval nos pensées ô rivières
Les oreilles des écoles et nos mains rapprochées
Aux doigts allongés nos mains les clochers
Et nous t'apportons aussi cette souple raison
Que le mystère clôt comme une porte la maison
Ce mystère courtois de la galanterie
Ce mystère fatal fatal d'une autre vie
Double raison qui est au delà de la beauté
Et que la Grèce n'a pas connue ni l'Orient
Double raison de la Bretagne où lame à lame
L'océan châtre peu à peu l'ancien continent

Et les villes du Nord répondirent gaîment

O Paris nous voici boissons vivantes
Les viriles cités où dégoisent et chantent
Les métalliques saints de nos saintes usines
Nos cheminées à ciel ouvert engrossent les nuées
Comme fit autrefois l'Ixion mécanique
Et nos mains innombrables
Usines manufactures fabriques mains
Où les ouvriers nus semblables à nos doigts
Fabriquent du réel à tant par heure
Nous te donnons tout cela

Et Lyon répondit tandis que les anges de Fourvières
Tissaient un ciel nouveau avec la soie des prières

Désaltère-toi Paris avec les divines paroles
Que mes lèvres le Rhône et la Saône murmurent
Toujours le même culte de sa mort renaissant
Divise ici les saints et fait pleuvoir le sang
Heureuse pluie ô gouttes tièdes ô douleur
Un enfant regarde les fenêtres s'ouvrir
Et des grappes de têtes à d'ivres oiseaux s'offrir

Les villes du Midi répondirent alors

Noble Paris seule raison qui vis encore
Qui fixes notre humeur selon ta destinée
Et toi qui te retires Méditerranée
Partagez-vous nos corps comme on rompt des hosties
Ces très hautes amours et leur danse orpheline
Deviendront ô Paris le vin pur que tu aimes

Et un râle infini qui venait de Sicile
Signifiait en battement d'ailes ces paroles

Les raisins de nos vignes on les a vendangés
Et ces grappes de morts dont les grains allongés
Ont la saveur du sang de la terre et du sel
Les voici pour ta soif ô Paris sous le ciel
Obscurci de nuées faméliques
Que caresse Ixion le créateur oblique
Et où naissent sur la mer tous les corbeaux d'Afrique
O raisins Et ces yeux ternes et en famille
L'avenir et la vie dans ces treilles s'ennuyent

Mais où est le regard lumineux des sirènes
Il trompa les marins qu'aimaient ces oiseaux-là
Il ne tournera plus sur l'écueil de Scylla
Où chantaient les trois voix suaves et sereines


Le détroit tout à coup avait changé de face
Visages de la chair de l'onde de tout
Ce que l'on peut imaginer
Vous n'êtes que des masques sur des faces masquées


Il souriait jeune nageur entre les rives
Et les noyés flottant sur son onde nouvelle
Fuyaient en le suivant les chanteuses plaintives


Elles dirent adieu au gouffre et à l'écueil
A leurs pâles époux couchés sur les terrasses
Puis ayant pris leur vol vers le brûlant soleil
Les suivirent dans l'onde où s'enfoncent les astres


Lorsque la nuit revint couverte d'yeux ouverts
Errer au site où l'hydre a sifflé cet hiver
Et j'entendis soudain ta voix impérieuse
O Rome
Maudire d'un seul coup mes anciennes pensées
Et le ciel où l'amour guide les destinées


Les feuillards repoussés sur l'arbre de la croix
Et même la fleur de lys qui meurt au Vatican
Macèrent dans le vin que je t'offre et qui a
La saveur du sang pur de celui qui connaît
Une autre liberté végétale dont tu
Ne sais pas que c'est elle la suprême vertu


Une couronne de trirègne est tombée sur les dalles
Les hiérarques la foulent sous leurs sandales
O splendeur démocratique qui pâlit
Vienne la nuit royale où l'on tuera les bêtes
La louve avec l'agneau l'aigle avec la colombe
Une foule de rois ennemis et cruels
Ayant soif comme toi dans la vigne éternelle
Sortiront de la terre et viendront dans les airs
Pour boire de mon vin par deux fois millénaire

La Moselle et le Rhin se joignent en silence
C'est l'Europe qui prie nuit et jour à Coblence
Et moi qui m'attardais sur le quai à Auteuil
Quand les heures tombaient parfois comme les feuilles
Du cep lorsqu'il est temps j'entendis la prière
Qui joignait la limpidité de ces rivières


O Paris le vin de ton pays est meilleur que celui
Qui pousse sur nos bords mais aux pampres du nord
Tous les grains ont mûri pour cette soif terrible
Mes grappes d'hommes forts saignent dans le pressoir
Tu boiras à longs traits tout le sang de l'Europe
Parce que tu es beau et que seul tu es noble
Parce que c'est dans toi que Dieu peut devenir
Et tous mes vignerons dans ces belles maisons
Qui reflètent le soir leurs feux dans nos deux eaux
Dans ces belles maisons nettement blanches et noires
Sans savoir que tu es la réalité chantent ta gloire
Mais nous liquides mains jointes pour la prière
Nous menons vers le sel des eaux aventurières
Et la ville entre nous comme entre des ciseaux
Ne reflète en dormant nul feu dans ses deux eaux
Dont quelque sifflement lointain parfois s'élance
Troublant dans leur sommeil les filles de Coblence


Les villes répondaient maintenant par centaines
Je ne distinguais plus leurs paroles lointaines
Et Trèves la ville ancienne
A leur voix mêlait la sienne
L'univers tout entier concentré dans ce vin
Qui contenait les mers les animaux les plantes
Les cités les destins et les astres qui chantent
Les hommes à genoux sur la rive du ciel
Et le docile fer notre bon compagnon
Le feu qu'il faut aimer comme on s'aime soi-même
Tous les fiers trépassés qui sont un sous mon front
L'éclair qui luit ainsi qu'une pensée naissante
Tous les noms six par six les nombres un à un
Des kilos de papier tordus comme des flammes
Et ceux-là qui sauront blanchir nos ossements
Les bons vers immortels qui s'ennuient patiemment      1
Des armées rangées en bataille
Des forêts de crucifix et mes demeures lacustres
Au bord des yeux de celle que j'aime tant
Les fleurs qui s'écrient hors de bouches
Et tout ce que je ne sais pas dire

Tout ce que je ne connaîtrai jamais
Tout cela tout cela changé en ce vin pur
Dont Paris avait soif
Me fut alors présenté

Actions belles journées sommeils terribles
Végétation Accouplements musiques éternelles
Mouvements Adorations douleur divine
Mondes qui vous ressemblez et qui nous ressemblez
Je vous ai bu et ne fus pas désaltéré

Mais je connus dès lors quelle saveur a l'univers

Je suis ivre d'avoir bu tout l'univers
Sur le quai d'où je voyais l'onde couler et dormir les bélandres

Écoutez-moi je suis le gosier de Paris
Et je boirai encore s'il me plaît l'univers

Écoutez mes chants d'universelle ivrognerie

Et la nuit de septembre s'achevait lentement
Les feux rouges des ponts s'éteignaient dans la Seine
Les étoiles mouraient le jour naissait à peine


## ÉTOILE

Je songe à Gaspard ce n'est certainement pas
Son vrai nom il voyage il a quitté la ville
Bleue Lanchi où tant d'enfants l'appelaient papa
Au fond du golfe calme en face des sept îles
Gaspard marche et regrette et le riz et le thé
            La voie lactée
La nuit car naturellement il ne marche
Que la nuit attire souvent ses regards
            Mais Gaspard
Sait bien qu'il ne faut pas la suivre


## LES COLLINES

Au-dessus de Paris un jour
Combattaient deux grands avions
L'un était rouge et l'autre noir
Tandis qu'au zénith flamboyait
L'éternel avion solaire

L'un était toute ma jeunesse
Et l'autre c'était l'avenir
Ils se combattaient avec rage
Ainsi fit contre Lucifer
L'Archange aux ailes radieuses

Ainsi le calcul au problème
Ainsi la nuit contre le jour
Ainsi attaque ce que j'aime
Mon amour ainsi l'ouragan
Déracine l'arbre qui crie

Mais vois quelle douceur partout
Paris comme une jeune fille
S'éveille langoureusement
Secoue sa longue chevelure
Et chante sa belle chanson

Où donc est tombée ma jeunesse
Tu vois que flambe l'avenir
Sache que je parle aujourd'hui
Pour annoncer au monde entier
Qu'enfin est né l'art de prédire

Certains hommes sont des collines
Qui s'élèvent d'entre les hommes
Et voient au loin tout l'avenir
Mieux que s'il était le présent
Plus net que s'il était passé

Ornement des temps et des routes
Passe et dure sans t'arrêter
Laissons sibiler les serpents
En vain contre le vent du sud
Les Psylles et l'onde ont péri

Ordre des temps si les machines
Se prenaient enfin à penser
Sur les plages de pierreries
Des vagues d'or se briseraient
L'écume serait mère encore

Moins haut que l'homme vont les aigles
C'est lui qui fait la joie des mers
Comme il dissipe dans les airs
L'ombre et les spleens vertigineux
Par où l'esprit rejoint le songe

Voici le temps de la magie
Il s'en revient attendez-vous
A des milliards de prodiges
Qui n'ont fait naître aucune fable
Nul les ayant imaginés

Profondeurs de la conscience
On vous explorera demain
Et qui sait quels êtres vivants
Seront tirés de ces abîmes
Avec des univers entiers

Voici s'élever des prophètes
Comme au loin des collines bleues
Ils sauront des choses précises
Comme croient savoir les savants
Et nous transporteront partout

La grande force est le désir
Et viens que je te baise au front
O légère comme une flamme
Dont tu as toute la souffrance
Toute l'ardeur et tout l'éclat

L'âge en vient on étudiera
Toute ce que c'est que de souffrir
Ce ne sera pas du courage
Ni même du renoncement
Ni tout ce que nous pouvons faire

On cherchera dans l'homme même
Beaucoup plus qu'on n'y a cherché
On scrutera sa volonté
Et quelle force naîtra d'elle
Sans machine et sans instrument

Les secourables même errent
Se compénétrant parmi nous
Depuis les temps qui nous rejoignent
Rien n'y finit rien n'y commence
Regarde la bague à ton doigt

Temps des déserts des carrefours
Temps des places et des collines
Je viens ici faire des tours
Où joue son rôle un talisman
Mort et plus subtil que la vie

Je me suis enfin détaché
De toutes choses naturelles
Je peux mourir mais non pécher
Et ce qu'on n'a jamais touché
Je l'ai touché je l'ai palpé

Et j'ai scruté tout ce que nul
Ne peut en rien imaginer
Et j'ai soupesé maintes fois
Même la vie impondérable
Je peux mourir en souriant

Bien souvent j'ai plané si haut
Si haut qu'adieu toutes les choses
Les étrangetés les fantômes
Et je ne veux plus admirer
Ce garçon qui mime l'effroi

Jeunesse adieu jasmin du temps
J'ai respiré ton frais parfum
A Rome sur les chars fleuris
Chargés de masques de guirlandes
Et des grelots du carnaval

Adieu jeunesse blanc Noël
Quand la vie n'était qu'une étoile
Dont je contemplais le reflet
Dans la mer Méditerranée
Plus nacrée que les météores

Duvetée comme un nid d'archanges
Où la guirlande des nuages
Et plus lustrée que les halos
Emanations et splendeurs
Unique douceur harmonies

Je m'arrête pour regarder
Sur la pelouse incandescente
Un serpent erre c'est moi-mème
Qui suis la flûte dont je joue
Et le fouet qui châtie les autres

Il vient un temps pour la souffrance
Il vient un temps pour la bonté
Jeunesse adieu voici le temps
Où l'on connaîtra l'avenir
Sans mourir de sa connaissance

C'est le temps de la grâce ardente
La volonté seule agira
Sept ans d'incroyables épreuves
L'homme se divinisera
Plus pur plus vif et plus savant

Il découvrira d'autres mondes
L'esprit languit comme les fleurs
Dont naissent les fruits savoureux
Que nous regarderons mûrir
Sur la colline ensoleillée

Je dis ce qu'est au vrai la vie
Seul je pouvais chanter ainsi
Mes chants tombent comme des graines
Taisez-vous tous vous qui chantez
Ne mêlez pas l'ivraie au blé

Un vaisseau s'en vint dans le port
Un grand navire pavoisé
Mais nous n'y trouvâmes personne
Qu'une femme belle et vermeille
Elle y gisait assassinée

Une autre fois je mendiais
L'on ne me donna qu'une flamme
Dont je fus brûlé jusqu'aux lèvres
Et je ne pus dire merci
Torche que rien ne peut éteindre

Où donc es-tu ô mon ami
Qui rentrais si bien en toi-même
Qu'un abîme seul est resté
Où je me suis jeté moi-même
Jusqu'aux profondeurs incolores

Et j'entends revenir mes pas
Le long des sentiers que personne
N'a parcourus j'entends mes pas
A toute heure ils passent là-bas
Lents ou pressés ils vont ou viennent

Hiver toi qui te fais la barbe
Il neige et je suis malheureux
J'ai traversé le ciel splendide
Où la vie est une musique
Le sol est trop blanc pour mes yeux

Habituez-vous comme moi
A ces prodiges que j'annonce
A la bonté qui va régner
A la souffrance que j'endure
Et vous connaîtrez l'avenir

C'est de souffrance et de bonté
Que sera faite la beauté
Plus parfaite que n'était celle
Qui venait des proportions
Il neige et je brûle et je tremble

Maintenant je suis à ma table
J'écris ce que j'ai ressenti
Et ce que j'ai chanté là-haut
Un arbre élancé que balance
Le vent dont les cheveux s'envolent

Un chapeau haut de forme est sur
Une table chargée de fruits
Les gants sont morts près d'une pomme
Une dame se tord le cou
Auprès d'un monsieur qui s'avale

Le bal tournoie au fond du temps
J'ai tué le beau chef d'orchestre
Et je pèle pour mes amis
L'orange dont la saveur est
Un merveilleux feu d'artifice

Tous sont morts le maitre d'hôtel
Leur verse un champagne irréel
Qui mousse comme un escargot
Ou comme un cerveau de poète
Tandis que chantait une rose

L'esclave tient une épée nue
Semblable aux sources et aux fleuves
Et chaque fois quelle s'abaisse
Un univers est éventré
Dont il sort des mondes nouveaux

Le chauffeur se tient au volant
Et chaque fois que sur la route
Il corne en passant le tournant
Il paraît à perte de vue
Un univers encore vierge

Et le tiers nombre c'est la dame
Elle monte dans l'ascenseur
Elle monte monte toujours
Et la lumière se déploie
Et ces clartés la transfigurent

Mais ce sont de petits secrets
Il en est d'autres plus profonds
Qui se dévoileront bientôt
Et feront de vous cent morceaux
A la pensée toujours unique

Mais pleure pleure et repleurons
Et soit que la lune soit pleine
Ou soit qu'elle n'ait qu'un croissant
Ah! pleure pleure et repleurons
Nous avons tant ri au soleil

Des bras d'or supportent la vie
Pénétrez le secret doré
Tout n'est qu'une flamme rapide
Que fleurit la rose adorable
Et d'où monte un parfum exquis

## TOUJOURS

*A Madame Faure-Favier*

Toujours
Nous irons plus loin sans avancer jamais

Et de planète en planète
De nébuleuse en nébuleuse
Le Don Juan des mille et trois comètes
Même sans bouger de la terre
Cherche les forces neuves
Et prend au sérieux les fantômes

Et tant d'univers s'oublient
Quels sont les grands oublieurs
Qui donc saura nous faire oublier telle
    ou telle partie du monde
Où est le Christophe Colomb à qui l'on
    devra l'oubli d'un continent

Perdre
Mais perdre vraiment
Pour laisser place à la trouvaille
Perdre
La vie pour trouver la Victoire


## CHEF DE SECTION

Ma bouche aura des ardeurs de géhenne
Ma bouche te sera un enfer de douceur et de séduction
Les anges de ma bouche trôneront dans ton cœur
Les soldats de ma bouche te prendront d'assaut
Les prêtres de ma bouche encenseront ta beauté
Ton âme s'agitera comme une région pendant un tremblement
    de terre
Tes yeux seront alors chargés de tout l'amour qui s'est amassé
    dans les regards de l'humanité depuis qu'elle existe
Ma bouche sera une armée contre toi une armée pleine de dis-
    parates
Variée comme un enchanteur qui sait varier ses métamorphoses
L'orchestre et les chœurs de ma bouche te diront mon amour
Elle te le murmure de loin
Tandis que les yeux fixés sur la montre j'attends la minute pre-
    scrite pour l'assaut


## LA JOLIE ROUSSE

Me voici devant tous un homme plein de sens
Connaissant la vie et de la mort ce qu'un vivant peut connaître
Ayant éprouvé les douleurs et les joies de l'amour
Ayant su quelquefois imposer ses idées
Connaissant plusieurs langages
Ayant pas mal voyagé
Ayant vu la guerre dans l'Artillerie et l'Infanterie
Blessé à la tête trépané sous le chloroforme
Ayant perdu ses meilleurs amis dans l'effroyable lutte
Je sais d'ancien et de nouveau autant qu'un homme seul pour-
    rait des deux savoir
Et sans m'inquiéter aujourd'hui de cette guerre
Entre nous et pour nous mes amis
Je juge cette longue querelle de la tradition et de l'invention
            De l'Ordre et de l'Aventure

Vous dont la bouche est faite à l'image de celle de Dieu
Bouche qui est l'ordre même
Soyez indulgents quand vous nous comparez
A ceux qui furent la perfection de l'ordre
Nous qui quêtons partout l'aventure

Nous ne sommes pas vos ennemies
Nous voulons vous donner de vastes et d'étranges domaines
Où le mystère en fleurs s'offre à qui veut le cueillir
Il y a là des feux nouveaux des couleurs jamais vues
Mille phantasmes impondérables
Auxquels il faut donner de la réalité
Nous voulons explorer la bonté contrée énorme où tout se tait
Il y a aussi le temps qu'on peut chasser ou faire revenir
Pitié pour nous qui combattons toujours aux frontières
De l'illimité et de l'avenir
Pitié pour nos erreurs pitié pour nos péchés

Voici que vient l'été la saison violente
Et ma jeunesse est morte ainsi que le printemps
O Soleil c'est le temps de la Raison ardente
             Et j'attends
Pour la suivre toujours la forme noble et douce
Qu'elle prend afin que je l'aime seulement
Elle vient et m'attire ainsi qu'un fer l'aimant
             Elle a l'aspect charmant
             D'une adorable rousse

Ses cheveux sont d'or on dirait
Un bel éclair qui durerait
Ou ces flammes qui se pavanent
Dans les roses-thé qui se fanent

Mais riez riez de moi
Hommes de partout surtout gens d'ici
Car il y a tant de choses que je n'ose vous dire
Tant de choses que vous ne me laisseriez pas dire
Ayez pitié de moi

# *Paul Valéry*

## HÉLÈNE

Azur! c'est moi . . . Je viens des grottes de la mort
Entendre l'onde se rompre aux degrés sonores,
Et je revois les galères dans les aurores
Ressusciter de l'ombre au fil des rames d'or.

Mes solitaires mains appellent les monarques
Dont la barbe de sel amusait mes doigts purs;
Je pleurais. Ils chantaient leurs triomphes obscurs
Et les golfes enfuis des poupes de leurs barques,

J'entends les conques profondes et les clairons
Militaires rythmer le vol des avirons;
Le chant clair des rameurs enchaîne le tumulte,

Et les Dieux, à la proue héroïque exaltés
Dans leur sourire antique et que l'écume insulte
Tendent vers moi leurs bras indulgents et sculptés.

## LE BOIS AMICAL

Nous avons pensé des choses pures
Côte à côte, le long des chemins,
Nous nous sommes tenus par les mains
Sans dire . . . parmi les fleurs obscures;

Nous marchions comme des fiancés
Seuls, dans la nuit verte des prairies;
Nous partagions ce fruit de féeries
La lune amicale aux insensés

Et puis, nous sommes morts sur la mousse,
Très loin, tout seuls parmi l'ombre douce
De ce bois intime et murmurant;

Et là-haut, dans la lumière immense,
Nous nous sommes trouvés en pleurant
O mon cher compagnon de silence!

## LE CIMETIÈRE MARIN

Μή, φίλα ψυχά, βίον ἀθάνατον
σπεῦδε, ταν δ'ἔμπρακτον ἄντλεῖ
μαχάνάν.

PINDARE *Pythiques III*

Ce toit tranquille, où marchent des colombes,
Entre les pins palpite, entre les tombes;
Midi le juste y compose de feux
La mer, la mer, toujours recommencée!
O récompense après une pensée
Qu'un long regard sur le calme des dieux!

Quel pur travail de fins éclairs consume
Maint diamant d'imperceptible écume,
Et quelle paix semble se concevoir!
Quand sur l'abîme un soleil se repose,
Ouvrages purs d'une éternelle cause,
Le Temps scintille et le Songe est savoir.

Stable trésor, temple simple à Minerve,
Masse de calme, et visible réserve,
Eau sourcilleuse, Œil qui gardes en toi
Tant de sommeil sous un voile de flamme,
O mon silence! . . . Édifice dans l'âme,
Mais comble d'or aux mille tuiles, Toit!

Temple du Temps, qu'un seul soupir résume,
A ce point pur je monte et m'accoutume,
Tout entouré de mon regard marin;
Et comme aux dieux mon offrande suprême,
La scintillation sereine sème
Sur l'altitude un dédain souverain.

Comme le fruit se fond en jouissance,
Comme en délice il change son absence
Dans une bouche où sa forme se meurt,
Je hume ici ma future fumée,
Et le ciel chante à l'âme consumée
Le changement des rives en rumeur.

Beau ciel, vrai ciel, regarde-moi qui change!
Après tant d'orgueil, après tant d'étrange
Oisiveté, mais pleine de pouvoir,
Je m'abandonne à ce brillant espace,
Sur les maisons des morts mon ombre passe
Qui m'apprivoise à son frêle mouvoir.

L'âme exposée aux torches du solstice,
Je te soutiens, admirable justice
De la lumière aux armes sans pitié!
Je te rends pure à ta place première:
Regarde-toi! . . . Mais rendre la lumière
Suppose d'ombre une morne moitié.

O pour moi seul, à moi seul, en moi-même,
Auprès d'un cœur, aux sources du poème,
Entre le vide et l'événement pur,
J'attends l'écho de ma grandeur interne,
Amère, sombre et sonore citerne,
Sonnant dans l'âme un creux toujours futur!

Sais-tu, fausse captive des feuillages,
Golfe mangeur de ces maigres grillages,
Sur mes yeux clos, secrets éblouissants,
Quel corps me traîne à sa fin paresseuse,
Quel front l'attire à cette terre osseuse?
Une étincelle y pense à mes absents.

Fermé, sacré, plein d'un feu sans matière,
Fragment terrestre offert à la lumière,
Ce lieu me plaît, dominé de flambeaux,
Composé d'or, de pierre et d'arbres sombres,
Où tant de marbre est tremblant sur tant d'ombres;
La mer fidèle y dort sur mes tombeaux!

Chienne splendide, écarte l'idolâtre!
Quand solitaire au sourire de pâtre,
Je pais longtemps, moutons mystérieux,
Le blanc troupeau de mes tranquilles tombes,
Éloignes-en les prudentes colombes,
Les songes vains, les anges curieux!

Ici venu, l'avenir est paresse.
L'insecte net gratte la sécheresse;
Tout est brûlé, défait, reçu dans l'air
A je ne sais quelle sévère essence . . .
La vie est vaste, étant ivre d'absence,
Et l'amertume est douce, et l'esprit clair.

Les morts cachés sont bien dans cette terre
Qui les réchauffe et sèche leur mystère.
Midi là-haut, Midi sans mouvement
En soi se pense et convient à soi-même . . .
Tête complète et parfait diadème,
Je suis en toi le secret changement.

Tu n'as que moi pour contenir tes craintes!
Mes repentirs, mes doutes, mes contraintes
Sont le défaut de ton grand diamant . . .
Mais dans leur nuit toute lourde de marbres,
Un peuple vague aux racines des arbres
A pris déjà ton parti lentement.

Ils ont fondu dans une absence épaisse,
L'argile rouge a bu la blanche espèce,
Le don de vivre a passé dans les fleurs!
Où sont des morts les phrases familières,
L'art personnel, les âmes singulières?
La larve file où se formaient des pleurs.

Les cris aigus des filles chatouillées,
Les yeux, les dents, les paupières mouillées,
Le sein charmant qui joue avec le feu,
Le sang qui brille aux lèvres qui se rendent,
Les derniers dons, les doigts qui les défendent,
Tout va sous terre et rentre dans le jeu!

Et vous, grande âme, espérez-vous un songe
Qui n'aura plus ces couleurs de mensonge
Qu'aux yeux de chair l'onde et l'or font ici?
Chanterez-vous quand serez vaporeuse?
Allez! Tout fuit! Ma présence est poreuse,
La sainte impatience meurt aussi!

Maigre immortalité noire et dorée,
Consolatrice affreusement laurée,
Qui de la mort fais un sein maternel,
Le beau mesonge et la pieuse ruse!
Qui ne connaît, et qui ne les refuse,
Ce crâne vide et ce rire éternel!

Pères profonds, têtes inhabitées,
Qui sous le poids de tant de pelletées,
Êtes la terre et confondez nos pas,
La vrai rongeur, le ver irréfutable
N'est point pour vous qui dormez sous la table,
Il vit de vie, il ne me quitte pas!

Amour, peut-être, ou de moi-même haine?
Sa dent secrète est de moi si prochaine
Que tous les noms lui peuvent convenir!
Qu'importe! Il voit, il veut, il songe, il touche!
Ma chair lui plaît, et jusque sur ma couche,
A ce vivant je vis d'appartenir!

Zénon! Cruel Zénon! Zénon d'Élée!
M'as-tu percé de cette flèche ailée
Qui vibre, vole, et qui ne vole pas!
Le son m'enfante et la flèche me tue!
Oh! le soleil . . . Quelle ombre de tortue
Pour l'âme, Achille immobile à grands pas!

Non, non! . . . Debout! Dans l'ère successive!
Brisez, mon corps, cette forme pensive!
Buvez, mon sein, la naissance du vent!
Une fraîcheur, de la mer exhalée,
Me rend mon âme . . . O puissance salée!
Courons à l'onde en rejaillir vivant!

Oui! Grande mer de délires douée,
Peau de panthère et chlamyde trouée
De mille et mille idoles du soleil,
Hydre absolue, ivre de ta chair bleue,
Qui te remords l'étincelante queue
Dans un tumulte au silence pareil,

Le vent se lève! . . . il faut tenter de vivre!
L'air immense ouvre et referme mon livre,
La vague en poudre ose jaillir des rocs!
Envolez-vous, pages tout éblouies!
Rompez, vagues! Rompe d'eaux réjouies
Ce toit tranquille où picoraient des focs!


## CANTIQUE DES COLONNES

*à Léon-Paul Fargue*

Douces colonnes, aux
Chapeaux garnis de jour
Ornés de vrais oiseaux
Qui marchent sur le tour,

Douces colonnes, ô
L'orchestre de fuseaux!
Chacun immole son
Silence à l'unisson.

—Que portez-vous si haut,
Égales radieuses?
—Au désir sans défaut
Nos grâces studieuses!

Nous chantons à la fois
Que nous portons les cieux!
O soule et sage voix
Qui chantes pour les yeux!

Vois quels hymnes candides!
Quelle sonorité
Nos éléments limpides
Tirent de la clarté!

Si froides et dorées
Nous fûmes de nos lits
Par le ciseau tirées,
Pour devenir ces lys!

De nos lits de cristal
Nous fûmes éveillées
Des griffes de métal
Nous ont appareillées.

Pour affronter la lune,
La lune et le soleil,
On nous polit chacune
Comme ongle de l'orteil!

Servantes sans genoux,
Souirires sans figures,
La belle devant nous
Se sent les jambes pures,

Pieusement pareilles,
Le nez sous le bandeau
Et nos riches oreilles
Sourdes au blanc fardeau,

Un temple sur les yeux
Noirs pour l'éternité,
Nous allons sans les dieux
A la divinité!

Nos antiques jeunesses,
Chair mate et belles ombres,
Sont fières des finesses
Qui naissent par les nombres!

Filles des nombres d'or,
Fortes des lois du ciel,
Sur nous tombe et s'endort
Un dieu couleur de miel.

Il dort content, le Jour,
Que chaque jour offrons
Sur la table d'amour
Étale sur nos fronts.

Incorruptibles sœurs,
Mi-brûlantes, mi-fraîches,
Nous prîmes pour danseurs
Brises et feuilles sèches,

Et les siècles par dix,
Et les peuples passés,
C'est un profond jadis,
Jadis jamais assez!

Sous nos mêmes amours
Plus lourdes que le monde
Nous traversons les jours
Comme une pierre l'onde!

Nous marchons dans le temps
Et nos corps éclatants
Ont des pas ineffables
Qui marquent dans les fables . . .


## L'INSINUANT

O Courbes, méandre,
Secrets du menteur,
Est-il art plus tendre
Que cette lenteur?

Je sais où je vais,
Je t'y veux conduire,
Mon dessein mauvais
N'est pas de te nuire . . .

(Quoique souriante
En plein fierté,
Tant de liberté
La désoriente!)

O Courbes, méandre,
Secrets du menteur,
Je veux faire attendre
Le mot le plus tendre.

## LA FAUSSE MORTE

Humblement, tendrement, sur le tombeau charmant,
    Sur l'insensible monument,
Que d'ombres, d'abandons, et d'amour prodiguée!
    Forme ta grâce fatiguée,
Je meurs, je meurs sur toi, je tombe et je m'abats,

Mais à peine abattu sur le sépulcre bas,
Dont la close étendue aux cendres me convie,
Cette morte apparente, en qui revient la vie,
Frémit, rouvre les yeux, m'illumine et me mord,
Et m'arrache toujours une nouvelle mort
    Plus précieuse que la vie.


## LES GRENADES

Dures grenades entr'ouvertes
Cédant à l'excès de vos grains,
Je crois voir des fronts souverains
Éclatés de leurs découvertes!

Si les soleils par vous subis,
O grenades entre-bâillées,
Vous ont fait d'orgueil travaillées
Craquer les cloisons de rubis,

Et que si l'or sec de l'écorce
A la demande d'une force
Crève en gemmes rouges de jus,

Cette lumineuse rupture
Fait rêver une âme que j'eus
De sa secrète architecture.


## LE VIN PERDU

J'ai, quelque jour, dans l'Océan,
(Mais je ne sais plus sous quels cieux)
Jeté, comme offrande au néant,
Tout un peu de vin précieux . . .

Qui voulut ta perte, ô liqueur?
J'obéis peut-être au devin?
Peut-être au souci de mon cœur,
Songeant au sang, versant le vin?

Sa transparence accoutumée
Après une rose fumée
Reprit aussi pure la mer . . .

Perdu ce vin, ivres les ondes! . . .
J'ai vu bondir dans l'air amer
Les figures les plus profondes . . .


## INTÉRIEUR

Une esclave aux longs yeux chargés de molles chaînes
Change l'eau de mes fleurs, plonge aux glaces prochaines,
Au lit mystérieux prodigue ses doigts purs;
Elle met une femme au milieu de ces murs
Qui, dans ma rêverie errant avec décence,
Passe entre mes regards sans briser leur absence,
Comme passe le verre au travers du soleil,
Et de la raison pure épargne l'appareil.


## PALME

*à Jeannie*

De sa grâce redoutable
Voilant à peine l'éclat,
Un ange met sur ma table
Le pain tendre, le lait plat;
Il me fait de la paupière
Le signe d'une prière
Qui parle à ma vision:
—Calme, calme, reste calme!
Connais le poids d'une palme
Portant sa profusion!

Pour autant qu'elle se plie
A l'abondance des biens,
Sa figure est accomplie,
Ses fruits lourds sont ses liens.
Admire comme elle vibre,
Et comme une lente fibre
Qui divise le moment,
Départage sans mystère
L'attirance de la terre
Et le poids du firmament!


Ce bel arbitre mobile
Entre l'ombre et le soleil,
Simule d'une sibylle
La sagesse et le sommeil,
Autour d'une même place
L'ample palme ne se lasse
Des appels ni des adieux . . .
Qu'elle est noble, qu'elle est tendre!
Qu'elle est digne de s'attendre
À la seule main des dieux!


L'or léger qu'elle murmure
Sonne au simple doigt de l'air,
Et d'une soyeuse armure
Charge l'âme du désert.
Une voix impérissable
Qu'elle rend au vent de sable
Qui l'arrose de ses grains,
À soi-même sert d'oracle,
Et se flatte du miracle
Que se chantent les chagrins.


Cependant qu'elle s'ignore
Entre le sable et le ciel,
Chaque jour qui luit encore
Lui compose un peu de miel.
Sa douceur est mesurée
Par la divine durée
Qui ne compte pas les jours,
Mais bien qui les dissimule
Dans un suc où s'accumule
Tout l'arôme des amours.

Parfois si l'on désespère,
Si l'adorable rigueur
Malgré tes larmes n'opère
Que sous ombre de langueur,
N'accuse pas d'être avare
Une Sage qui prépare
Tant d'or et d'autorité:
Par la sève solennelle
Une espérance éternelle
Monte à la maturité!

Ces jours qui te semblent vides
Et perdus pour l'univers
Ont des racines avides
Qui travaillent les déserts.
La substance chevelue
Par les ténèbres élue
Ne peut s'arrêter jamais
Jusqu'aux entrailles du monde,
De poursuivre l'eau profonde
Que demandent les sommets.

Patience, patience,
Patience dans l'azur!
Chaque atome de silence
Est la chance d'un fruit mûr!
Viendra l'heureuse surprise:
Une colombe, la brise,
L'ébranlement le plus doux,
Une femme qui s'appuie,
Feront tomber cette pluie
Où l'on se jette à genoux!

Qu'un peuple à présent s'écroule,
Palme! . . . irrésistiblement!
Dans la poudre qu'il se roule
Sur les fruits du firmament!
Tu n'as pas perdu ces heures
Si légère tu demeures
Après ces beaux abandons;
Pareille à celui qui pense
Et dont l'âme se dépense
A s'accroître de ses dons!

## CHANSON À PART

Que fais-tu? De tout.
Que vaux-tu? Ne sais,
Présages, essais,
Puissance et dégoût . . .
Que vaux-tu? Ne sais . . .
Que veux-tu? Rien, mais tout.

Que sais-tu? L'ennui.
Que peux-tu? Songer.
Songer pour changer
Chaque jour en nuit.
Que sais-tu? Songer
Pour changer d'ennui.

Que veux-tu? Mon bien.
Que dois-tu? Savoir,
Prévoir et pouvoir
Qui ne sert de rien.
Que crains-tu? Vouloir.
Qui es-tu? Mais rien!

Où vas-tu? A mort.
Qu'y faire? Finir,
Ne plus revenir
Au coquin de sort.
Où vas-tu? Finir.
Que faire? Le mort.

# Bibliography

## GENERAL

Balakian, A.: *Literary Origins of Surrealism*. New York and London, 1947.

Bayley, J.: *The Romantic Survival*. London, 1957.

Bowra, C. M.: *The Heritage of Symbolism*. London and New York, 1943 and 1951; *The Romantic Imagination*. Cambridge (Mass.), 1949.

Brereton, G.: *An Introduction to the French Poets: Villon to the Present Day*. London and Fair Lawn (N.J.), 1956.

Chiari, J.: *Symbolisme from Poe to Mallarmé*. London, 1956; New York, 1957.

Chisholm, A. R.: *Towards Hérodiade, a literary genealogy*. Melbourne, 1934.

Cornell, K.: *The Symbolist Movement*. New Haven, 1951.

George, A. J.: *The Development of French Romanticism: the Impact of the Industrial Revolution on Literature*. Syracuse (N.Y.), 1955.

Jones, P. M.: *The Background of Modern French Poetry*. Cambridge (England), 1951.

Lehmann, A. G.: *The Symbolist Aesthetic in France*. Oxford, 1950.

Lemaitre, G.: *From Cubism to Surrealism in French Literature*. London and Cambridge (Mass.), 1947, rev. ed.

Lucas, F. L.: *The Decline and Fall of the Romantic Ideal*. New York and Cambridge (England), 1936.

Olson, E.: "A Dialogue on Symbolism," in *Critics and Criticism*, ed. by R. S. Crane. Chicago, 1952, pp. 567–94.

Praz, M.: *The Romantic Agony*. London, 1933; New York, 1956.

Quennell, P.: *Baudelaire and the Symbolists*. London, 1954, rev. ed.

Raymond, M.: *From Baudelaire to Surrealism*. New York, 1950.

Rhodes, S. A.: "Candles for Isis." *Sewanee Review*, April–June 1933, pp. 212–24; July–September 1933, pp. 286–300.

Smith, J. M.: "The Sphinx, the Chimera and the Pursuit of Novelty in Post-Romantic French Literature." *Symposium*, Vol. 8 (1955), pp. 289–308.

Starkie, E.: *Petrus Borel, the Lycanthrope*. London and New York, 1954; "Eccentrics of Eighteen-Thirty." *Horizon*, May 1944, pp. 309–23; June 1944, pp. 402–23.

Symons, A.: *The Symbolist Movement in Literature*. London, 1899.

Temple, R. Z.: *The Critics' Alchemy*. New York, 1953.

Tindall, W. Y.: *The Literary Symbol*. New York, 1955.

Van Rooesbroeck, G. L.: *The Legend of the Decadents*. New York, 1927.

Wilson, E.: *Axel's Castle*. New York, 1931.

Winters, Y.: *Primitivism and Decadence*. New York, 1937.


NERVAL

BEST EDITION: *Oeuvres*, ed. by A. Béguin and Jean Richer. Paris: Bibliothèque de la Pléiade: 1952.

Engstrom, A. G.: "The 'Horus' of Gérard de Nerval." *Philological Quarterly*, 33 (1954), pp. 78–80.

Leventhal, A. J.: "Gérard de Nerval: Poet and Schizophrenic." *Dublin Magazine*, October–December 1941, pp. 48–55.

Rhodes, S. A.: "Poetical Affiliations of Gérard de Nerval." *PMLA*, 1938, 53, pp. 1157–71; *Gérard de Nerval, 1808–1855, Poet, Traveller, Dreamer*. New York, 1951.

Rudwin, M. J.: "Gérard's Germanic Fantasies," in *Todd Memorial Volumes*, ed. by J. D. Fitz-Gerald and P. Taylor. New York, 1930, Vol. 2, pp. 127–38.

Smith, J. M.: "Gérard de Nerval." *Emory University Quarterly*, 3 (1953), pp. 157–66.

Whitridge, A.: *Critical Ventures in Modern French Literature*. New York, 1924.

## BAUDELAIRE

BEST EDITIONS: *Oeuvres Complètes,* ed. by Y.-G. Le Dantec. Paris: Bibliothèque de la Pléiade: 1954. *Oeuvres Complètes,* ed. by J. Crepet. Paris: Conard: 1922–53, 19 vols.

Auerbach, E.: "The Aesthetic Dignity of the *Fleurs du Mal.*" *Hopkins Review,* Autumn 1950, pp. 28–45.

Bennett, J. D.: *Baudelaire.* Princeton, 1946, 2nd. ed.

Bondy, L. J.: "The Legacy of Baudelaire." *University of Toronto Quarterly,* July 1945, pp. 414–30.

Cantor, J.: *The Literary Reputation of Baudelaire in England and America.* Harvard Univ. dissertation, 1940.

Chisholm, A. R.: "The Duality of the *Fleurs du Mal.*" *French Quarterly,* December 1932, pp. 148–52.

Clapton, G. T.: *Baudelaire the Tragic Sophist.* Edinburgh, 1934.

Du Bos, C.: "Reflections on the Life of Baudelaire." *Hound and Horn* (New York), Summer 1931, pp. 461–96.

Eliot, T. S.: "Poet and Saint." *Dial,* May 1927, pp. 425–31; *For Lancelot Andrewes,* London, 1928, New York, 1929; Introduction to Baudelaire's *Intimate Journals,* London and New York, 1930; *Essays Ancient and Modern,* London and New York, 1936; *From Poe to Valéry. The Hudson Review,* Autumn 1949, pp. 327–42; *Complete Essays.* London and New York, 1953.

Ellis, H.: *The Philosophy of Conflict.* London and New York, 1919; *Impressions and Comments,* 3rd Series. Boston and London, 1924; *Selected Essays.* London, 1936.

Galand, R.: "T. S. Eliot and the Impact of Baudelaire." *Yale French Studies,* 1950, 6, pp. 27–34.

Hassan, I. H.: "Baudelaire's Correspondence. The Dialectic of a Poetic Affinity." *French Review,* 27 (1954), pp. 437–45.

Hubert, J. D.: "Symbolism, Correspondence and Memory." *Yale French Studies,* #9, pp. 46–55; "Baudelaire's Revolutionary Poetics." *Romanic Review,* October 1955, pp. 164–77.

Hyslop, L. B. and F. E. (eds.): *Baudelaire: A Self Portrait.* New York, 1957.

Jones, P. M.: *Baudelaire*. Cambridge (England) and New Haven, 1952.

Laforgue, R.: *The Defeat of Baudelaire*. London, 1932.

Manheim, E. and L.: "Baudelaire's 'L'Irremediable.'" *Explicator*, XII, viii, item 52.

Morgan, E.: *Flower of Evil: a Life of Baudelaire*. New York, 1943.

Porche, F.: *Charles Baudelaire*. New York and London, 1928.

Rhodes, S. A.: *The Cult of Beauty in Charles Baudelaire*. London and New York, 1929, 2 vols.

Sartre, J. P.: *Baudelaire*. London, 1949; New York, 1950.

Shanks, L. P.: *Baudelaire, Flesh and Spirit*. Boston, 1930; London, 1931.

Starkie, E.: *Baudelaire*. London, 1957, new ed.

Symons, A.: *Charles Baudelaire*. London, 1920.

Turnell, M.: *Baudelaire*. London and New York, 1953.

Turquet-Milnes, G.: *The Influence of Baudelaire in France and England*. London, 1913.

Valéry, P.: *Variety*. 2nd Series. New York, 1938.

Weaver, W. M.: "Baudelaire's 'Spleen.'" *Explicator*, XII, iii, item 19.

## CORBIÈRE

BEST EDITION: *Les Amours Jaunes*, ed. by Y.-.G Le Dantec. Paris: Gallimard: 1953.

Jarrell, R.: *Poetry and the Age*. New York, 1953, pp. 149–78.

Laforgue, J.: *Selected Writings*. New York, 1956, pp. 217–24.

Legge, J. G.: *Chanticleer, a study of the French Muse*. London, 1935.

Shanahan, C. M.: "Irony in Laforgue, Corbière and Eliot." *Modern Philology*, November 1955, pp. 117–28.

Turnell, G. M.: "Introduction to the Study of Tristan Corbière." *Criterion*, April 1936, pp. 393–417.

## VERLAINE

**BEST EDITIONS:** *Oeuvres Poétiques Complètes*, ed. by Y.-G. Le Dantec. Paris: Bibliothèque de la Pléiade: 1949.
*Oeuvres Complètes*, ed. by Y.-G. Le Dantec. Paris: 1947–49, 4 vols.

Applegate, B.: *Paul Verlaine*. New York, 1916.

Blunt, H. F.: *Great Penitents*. London and New York, 1921, pp. 194–223.

Colum, M.: *From These Roots*. New York, 1937, pp. 312–60.

Coulon, M.: *Poet under Saturn: the Tragedy of Verlaine*. London, 1921.

Ellis, H.: *From Rousseau to Proust*. Boston, 1935, pp. 268–83.

Grierson, F.: *Parisian Portraits*. London, 1913.

Hare, H.: *Sketch for a Portrait of Rimbaud*. London, 1937.

Huneker, J. G.: *The Pathos of Distance*. New York, 1913.

Lepelletier, E.: *Paul Verlaine: His Life, His Work*. London, 1913.

Nicolson, H.: *Paul Verlaine*. London, 1921.

Roberts, C. E. B.: *Paul Verlaine*. London, 1937.

Rothenstein, W.: *Paul Verlaine*. London, 1898.

Thorley, W.: *Paul Verlaine*. London and Boston, 1914.

Valéry, P.: *Variety*, 2nd. Series, New York, 1938, pp. 3–32.

Zweig, S.: *Paul Verlaine*. Dublin, London and New York, 1913.

## RIMBAUD

**BEST EDITION:** *Oeuvres Complètes*, ed. by R de Renéville and J. Mouquet. Paris: Bibliothèque de la Pléiade: 1946.

Bercovici, K.: *Savage Prodigal*. New York, 1948.

Capetanakis, D.: *The Shores of Darkness*. New York, 1949, pp. 53–71.

Carré, J. M.: *A Season in Hell: The Life of Arthur Rimbaud*. New York, 1931.

Chisholm, A. R.: *The Art of Arthur Rimbaud*. Melbourne, 1930.

Clarke, M.: *Rimbaud and Quinet.* Sydney, 1946.

Connolly, C.: *The Condemned Playground.* New York, 1946, pp. 68–75.

Fowlie, W.: *Rimbaud.* New York, 1946; London, 1947; *Rimbaud's Illuminations.* London and New York, 1953; *The Clown's Grail,* London, 1948.

Frohock, W. M.: "Rimbaud Poetics: Hallucination and Epiphany." *Romanic Review,* October 1955, pp. 192–202.

Hare, H.: *Sketch for a Portrait of Rimbaud.* London, 1937.

Mackworth, C.: "Arthur Rimbaud." *Horizon,* March 1944, pp. 180–92.

Meyerstein, E. H. W.: "The Latinity of Rimbaud." *Durham University Journal,* March 1940, pp. 102–21; "Baudelaire and *Les Illuminations,*" *Mandrake* (London), #3.

Miller, H.: *The Time of the Assassins.* New York, 1956, rev. ed.

Moore, G.: *Impressions and Opinions.* London, 1891.

Rhodes, S. A.: "Rimbaud Today." *Romanic Review,* October–December 1932, pp. 341–47.

Rickword, E.: *Rimbaud, the Boy and the Poet.* London and New York, 1924.

Roditi, E.: "A French Poet and his English Critics." *Sewanee Review,* Winter 1944, pp. 102–17.

Sackville-West, E.: *The Apology of Arthur Rimbaud.* London, 1927.

Starkie, E.: *Arthur Rimbaud.* London and New York, 1947, rev. ed.; "New Light on a Poem of Rimbaud," *Life and Letters,* March 1944, pp. 156–61.

Weinberg, B.: "*Le Bateau Ivre,* or the Limits of Symbolism." *PMLA,* March 1957, pp. 165–93.

Zabel, M. D.: "Rimbaud, Life and Legend." *Partisan Review,* July–August 1940, pp. 268–82.

## MALLARMÉ

BEST EDITION: *Oeuvres Complètes,* ed. by H. Mondor & G. Jean-Aubry. Paris: Bibliothèque de la Pléiade: 1945.

Chiari, J.: *Symbolisme from Poe to Mallarmé.* London, 1956; New York, 1957.

Chisholm, A. R.: *Towards Hérodiade*. Melbourne, 1934.

Cohn, R. G.: *Mallarmé's "Un Coup de Dés": an exegesis*. New Haven, 1949.

Cooperman, H.: *The Aesthetics of Stéphane Mallarmé*. New York, 1933.

Davies, G.: "Stéphane Mallarmé: Fifty Years of Research." *French Studies* (Oxford), January 1947; "The Devil of Analogy," *French Studies*, July and October 1955.

Fowlie, W.: *Mallarmé as Hamlet: A Study of* Igitur. Yonkers, 1949; *Mallarmé*. Chicago, 1953.

Gill, A.: "Mallarmé's Debt to Chateaubriand." *Modern Language Review*, October 1955.

Grierson, F.: *Parisian Portraits*. London, 1913.

Mauron, C.: "Commentaries on the Poems of Mallarmé," in Stéphane Mallarmé: *Poems*. New York, 1951.

Miller, R. R.: "Mallarmé's 'Le vierge, le vivace . . .'" *Explicator*, XII, i, item 6.

Ramsey, W.: "View of Mallarmé's Poetics." *Romanic Review*, October 1955, pp. 178–91.

Simons, H. Wallace Stevens. *Modern Philology*, May 1946, pp. 235–59.

Smith, M. M.: "Mallarmé and the *Chimères*." *Yale French Studies*, #11 (1953), pp. 59–72.

Valéry, P.: *Selected Writings*. New York, 1950, pp. 213–21.

## LAFORGUE

BEST EDITIONS: *Poésies Complètes*, ed. by M. G. Jean-Aubry. Paris: Editions de Cluny: 1943, 2 vols.
*Oeuvres Complètes*, ed. by M. G. Jean-Aubry. Paris: Mercure de France: 1922–30, 6 vols.

Bolgar, R. R.: "Jules Laforgue." *French Studies* (Oxford), July 1950, pp. 193–207.

Carrière, J. M.: "Jules Laforgue and Leopardi." *Romanic Review*, February 1943, pp. 50–53.

Champigny, R.: "Situation of Jules Laforgue." *Yale French Studies*, #9, pp. 63–73.

Fowlie, W.: "Jules Laforgue." *Poetry*, July 1951, pp. 216–22; "A Note on Jules Laforgue." *Newberry Library Bulletin*, 3 (1954), pp. 94–100.

Golffing, F.: "Jules Laforgue." *Quarterly Review of Literature*, Summer 1946, pp. 55–67.

Huneker, J.: *Ivory, Apes and Peacocks*. New York, 1915.

Moore, G.: *Impressions and Comments*. London, 1891.

Pound, E.: "Irony, Laforgue and some Satire," *Poetry*, November 1917, pp. 93–98; *Literary Essays*. New York, 1954, pp. 280–84.

Ramsey, W.: *Jules Laforgue and the Ironic Inheritance*. New York, 1953.

Shanahan, C. M.: "Irony in Laforgue, Corbière and Eliot." *Modern Philology*, November 1955, pp. 117–28.

Turnell, G. M.: "The Poetry of Jules Laforgue." *Scrutiny*, September 1936, pp. 128–49; "Jules Laforgue," *Cornhill Magazine*, Winter 1947–48, pp. 74–90.

## APOLLINAIRE

BEST EDITION: *Oeuvres Poétiques*, ed. by M. Adéma and M. Décaudin. Paris: Bibliothèque de la Pléiade: 1956.

Adéma, M.: *Apollinaire*. New York and London, 1955.

Balakian, A.: "Apollinaire and the Modern Mind." *Yale French Studies*, Vol. 2, #2, pp. 79–90.

Bowra, C. M.: *The Creative Experiment*. London and New York, 1949, pp. 61–93.

Breunig, L. C.: "The Chronology of Apollinaire's *Alcools*." *PMLA*, 67, pp. 907–23; "Apollinaire since 1950." *Romanic Review*, February 1955, pp. 35–40.

Drake, William: *Contemporary European Writers*. New York, 1928, pp. 124–29.

Fowlie, W.: *Age of Surrealism*. New York, 1950, pp. 83–101.

Good, T.: "Enter Apollinaire." *New Road* (London), 1945, pp. 162–75.

Hamburger, M.: "Apollinaire." *Poetry Quarterly* (London), Autumn 1950, pp. 171–75.

Mackworth, C.: "Je suis Guillaume Apollinaire." *Horizon*, February 1945, pp. 90–103.

Rosenfeld, P.: *Men Seen*. New York, 1925.

## VALÉRY

BEST EDITIONS: *Poésies*. Paris: Gallimard: 1942;
Oeuvres Complètes. Paris: Gallimard:
1931–52, 12 vols.

Bishop, J. P.: *Collected Essays*. New York, 1948, pp.
14–22.

Bosanquet, T.: *Paul Valéry*. London, 1933.

Chiari, J.: *Contemporary French Poetry*, New York, 1952,
pp. 13–43.

Chisholm, A.: *An Approach to Mr. Valéry's "La Jeune
Parque."* Melbourne and London, 1938.

Eliot, T. S.: *From Poe to Valéry*. New York, 1948.

Fisher, H. A. L.: *Paul Valéry*. London, 1927.

Geoffrey, W.: "Paul Valéry, Hero of the Mind." *South At-
lantic Quarterly*, 45 (1940), pp. 489–503.

Guenther, C.: "Poetry and Abstract Thought." *Kenyon Re-
view*, 1954, 16, pp. 208–33.

Hartman, G. H.: *The Unmediated Vision*, New Haven,
1954.

Mathews, J.: "Poïetics of Paul Valéry." *Romanic Review*,
October 1955, pp. 203–17.

Moore, T. S.: "A Poet and His Technique." *New Criterion*
(London), 1926, 4, pp. 421–35.

Rice, P. B.: "Paul Valéry." *Symposium* (New York), 1930,
1, pp. 206–20.

Roditi, E.: "Paul Valéry: Poetics as Exact Science." *Kenyon
Review*, Summer 1944, pp. 398–408.

Scarfe, F.: *The Art of Paul Valéry*. London, 1954.

Sewell, E.: *Paul Valéry: The Mind in the Mirror*. Cam-
bridge (England) and New Haven, 1952.

Suckling, N.: *Paul Valéry and the Civilized Mind*. London
and New York, 1954.

Turquet-Milnes, G. R.: *Paul Valéry*. London, 1934.

Weinberg, B.: "An Interpretation of Valéry's *Le Cimetière
Marin*." *Romanic Review*, April 1947, pp. 133–58.

Whiting, C.: "Femininity in Valéry's Early Poetry." *Yale
French Studies*, #9, pp. 74–83.

# ACKNOWLEDGMENTS

The editor wishes to thank for kind and expert assistance: Jason Epstein, Andrew Chiappe, and Jacqueline Chalaire, of Anchor Books; Bert M-P. Leefmans, Columbia University; Barney Rosset, of Grove Press; and Joseph Brewer, Robert Colby, Kenneth Freyer, and Elizabeth Brenner, of the Paul Klapper Library of Queens College.

Acknowledgments are due the following publishers and translators:

Anthony Bower for his translation of *Fantaisie* by Gérard de Nerval from *A Little Treasury of World Poetry*, ed. by Hubert Creekmore (New York: Charles Scribner's Sons, 1952).

Vernon Watkins for his translations of *Écoutez la chanson bien douce* . . . and *Et f'ait revu l'enfant unique* by Verlaine from *A Little Treasury of World Poetry*, ed. by Hubert Creekmore (New York: Charles Scribner's Sons, 1952); for his translation of *Le Crapaud* by Corbière and of *Cantique des colonnes* by Valéry from *A Mirror for French Poetry*, ed. by Cecily Mackworth (London: Routledge and Kegan Paul).

Grove Press for William Jay Smith's translations of the following poems by Laforgue from *Selected Writings of Jules Laforgue*, ed. by William Jay Smith (New York: Grove Press, 1956; © 1956 by William Jay Smith): *La Première nuit, L'Impossible, Complainte du Roi de Thulé, Complainte de l'oubli des morts, J'entends battre mon Sacre-Cœur, Romance, Solo de lune, Paysage d'été, Soir de printemps sur les boulevards, Crépuscule de mi-juillet, huit heures, Après-dîner torride et stagnante, Coup de foudre, Crépuscule.*

Harcourt, Brace and Company for Richard Wilbur's translation of *L'Invitation au voyage* by Baudelaire from *Things of This World* by Richard Wilbur (New York: Harcourt, Brace and Company, 1956; © 1956 by Richard Wilbur).

The Hudson Review for Frederick Morgan's translation of *L'Après-midi d'un faune* by Mallarmé from *The Hudson Review*, VI, No. 3 (Autumn 1953; Copyright 1953 by The Hudson Review, Inc.); and for Richmond Latti-

more's translations of *El Desdichado* and *Delfica* by Nerval from *The Hudson Review*, IV, No. 1 (Spring 1951; Copyright 1951 by The Hudson Review, Inc.).

The Johns Hopkins Press for Bradford Cook's translation of *Le Nénuphar blanc* by Mallarmé from *Mallarmé: Selected Prose Poems, Essays and Letters*, trans. and with an intro. by Bradford Cook (Baltimore: The Johns Hopkins Press, 1956; © 1956, The Johns Hopkins Press, Baltimore 18, Md.).

Librairie Gallimard for the selections from Apollinaire and Valéry included herein.

Tiber Press for Daisy Aldan's translation of *Un Coup de dés* by Mallarmé.

*Wake* Magazine for Barbara Howes' translations of *Le Vin perdu* and *Intérieur* by Valéry; for Hubert Creekmore's translation of *Las de l'amer repos . . .* by Mallarmé; and for Daisy Aldan's translations of *Rhénane d'Automne* and *J'ai eu le courage* by Apollinaire.